Lutherans and the
Longest War

Lutherans and the Longest War

Adrift on a Sea of Doubt about the Cold and Vietnam Wars, 1964–1975

David E. Settje

LEXINGTON BOOKS

A division of
ROWMAN & LITTLEFIELD PUBLISHERS, INC.
Lanham • Boulder • New York • Toronto • Plymouth, UK

LEXINGTON BOOKS
A division of Rowman & Littlefield Publishers, Inc.
A wholly owned subsidiary of The Rowman & Littlefield Publishing Group, Inc.
4501 Forbes Boulevard, Suite 200, Lanham, MD 20706

Estover Road, Plymouth PL6 7PY, United Kingdom

British Library Cataloguing in Publication Information Available

Library of Congress Cataloging-in-Publication Data

Settje, David E., 1970–
    Lutherans and the longest war : adrift on a sea of doubt about the Cold and Vietnam
Wars, 1964–1975 / David E. Settje.
       p. cm.
    Includes bibliographical references and index.
    ISBN-13: 978-0-7391-1531-2 (cloth : alk. paper)
    ISBN-10: 0-7391-1531-6 (cloth : alk. paper)
    ISBN-13: 978-0-7391-1532-9 (pbk. : alk. paper)
    ISBN-10: 0-7391-1532-4 (pbk. : alk. paper)
    1. Christianity and politics—Lutheran Church—History—20th century. 2. Lutheran
Church—Doctrines—History—20th century. 3. Lutheran Church—History—20th
century. 4. Lutheran Church—United States. I. Title.
BR115.P7S393 2007
261.8'70882841—dc22

                                                                            2006026503

Printed in the United States of America

⊗™ The paper used in this publication meets the minimum requirements of American
National Standard for Information Sciences—Permanence of Paper for Printed Library
Materials, ANSI/NISO Z39.48-1992.

To my parents,
for everything

To Mary Todd,
for mentorship

Contents

0913437

Acknowledgments

The list of people to whom I owe a debt of gratitude for this project is immense. It seems inadequate to simply list them below, yet words would ring just as hallow, considering that each of them in one way or another touched me and the now ten-year journey of writing this book. I dread and know that I have forgotten someone and plead for their forgiveness in advance. For financial support, I wish to thank Kent State University for assistance during my graduate career and Concordia University Chicago for summer research grants, and my colleagues at each university. The Institute for the Study of American Evangelicals also provided a research grant. For gracious access to their archives, thanks to Concordia Historical Institute, Evangelical Lutheran Church in America Archives, Billy Graham Center and Library, Lutheran Laymen's League, Swarthmore College Peace Collection Archives, Trinity Lutheran Seminary Library, Wisconsin Evangelical Lutheran Church Archives, and Wittenberg University Library. Thank you to the staff at Lexington Books, especially MacDuff Stewart and Anna Schwartz. Professionally, I would like to thank the Lutheran Historical Conference, Kim Butler, Karen Coffing, Brigitte Conkling, Tim Dane, Larry Eskridge, Jennifer Farmer, Linda Fry, Jill Gill, Jay Green, Hope Lutheran Church in Cleveland Heights, Ohio, and its members, Marvin Huggins, John Jameson, David Kyvig, Leslie Leidel, David Lindbergh, Donna Martsolf, Earl Matson, Elaine McCoy, Janyce H. Mosgowitz, David Odell-Scott, Kristina Gray Perez, Kurt Stadtwald, Ellen Swain, Shirley Wajda, Jonathan Wakelyn, Elisabeth Wittman, Christine D. Worobec, and Clarence E. Wunderlin, Jr. I want to add a special line to Ann Heiss, for guiding me through the doctoral process and getting my professional career underway. Numerous friends and family contributed, too, both intellectually and spiritually: Robin Bowden, Dave

Dauberman, Jule Nyhuis, Julie Rahn, Virginia Serbu, Becky Settje, Mark Settje, Don Wilson, Melody Wilson, and Paul Wilson. Finally, to Mary Todd for guiding me through the maize of becoming a professional historian with patience, nurturing, and care; and, most of all, to Mary and Allen Settje, my loving parents to whom I owe more than I can ever repay.

Chapter One

Lutherans and the Cold and Vietnam Wars, 1964–1975: An Introduction

This study examines the dialogue between American Lutherans about foreign policy issues during the contentious decade from 1964 to 1975. Doing so contributes two insights to the historiography of America during the Vietnam War era. First, it outlines how this diverse group of Christians in America understood foreign policy and the churches' relationship to it. Lutherans offer a broad spectrum of religious, political, and diplomatic points of view because they have never been either a homogenous or unified group in U.S. history. This very diversity creates a rich way to look at their reactions to foreign policy. Second, this investigation simultaneously offers the perspective of one cross-section of Americans who often remain hidden from historic memory: "the silent majority" as so labeled during the Richard M. Nixon administration. While studies have scrutinized the far-left/antiwar movement and the far-right/conservative resurgence of the 1960s, few have delved into Americans whose ideological bent lay somewhere between these extremes. Indeed, this investigation demonstrates that "the silent majority" hardly remained quiet and that they were not completely of one mind regarding foreign policy concerns. Lutherans contribute such a study in their own unique way.

Lutherans, whether at national conventions, through their myriad of periodicals, or in writing to one another, both among the laity and leadership, had a lot to say about foreign policy matters throughout this decade. They often spoke with virtually one voice against the Union of Soviet Socialist Republics (USSR) and People's Republic of China (PRC) as atheist states that oppressed their own citizens and wanted to purge the world of religion. Yet this Cold War harmony disappeared when Lutherans discussed other foreign policy matters, such as the domestic threat of Communist infiltration or the Vietnam War. Here, a wide variety of opinions existed. Some Lutherans maintained a fear that Communists were attempting to undermine American

1

democracy by subtly planting socialist ideas in the minds of Americans. Others insisted that a more overt attempt to control America was underway with Communists who had infiltrated U.S. institutions to undermine democracy. A variety of Lutherans combined such sentiments with a firm belief in containment and the domino theory regarding U.S. foreign policy. They believed that a monolithic Communist force existed, that the United States had to stand up against it, and that the Vietnam War was therefore a necessary evil. But other Lutherans challenged these perceptions and argued against any fear that Communists directly threatened U.S. society and saw the Vietnam War as a civil war, unrelated to the Cold War against the Soviet Union and Red China. These debates and the wide array of viewpoints also concerned domestic issues that stemmed from the Vietnam War, such as the draft, conscientious objection, and amnesty for draft resisters.

Lutheran Americans debated foreign policy in a number of ways. Often, this included a summary of how their religious convictions related to their arguments. But at other times, both lay individuals and Lutheran leaders stated firm opinions about foreign policy without placing it in a theological context. In other words, their theological beliefs sometimes affected their thinking but at other times remained curiously hidden, given the fact that their viewpoints appeared in religious writings, journals, and at denominational conventions. Lutherans and Americans in general must grapple with how the interplay between religion, foreign policy, and American citizens' views of both played out during a time of war. Without such deliberations, historians and Americans in general cannot hope to understand completely this decade and the legacy that it has left both within Lutheranism and U.S. society as a whole.

HISTORICAL BACKGROUND

A brief overview of the diplomatic, political, and religious landscape of this decade will provide needed context for the Lutheran contributions to it. When this study refers to the "1960s," it generally begins after John F. Kennedy's assassination in 1963 and concludes with Richard M. Nixon's resignation in 1974. Diplomatically, the decade starts with Cold War tensions, the escalation of war in Vietnam under Lyndon B. Johnson in 1964, détente with the Soviet Union and Red China under Nixon, the withdrawal of U.S. troops from Southeast Asia in January 1973, and North Vietnam's triumph over South Vietnam in 1975. Domestically, it includes Johnson's Great Society initiative, social unrest, generational conflict, protesting, Nixon's election and reelection, and Watergate.

The Cold War context actually began following World War II and the development of an arms race between the United States and Soviet Union. Because of their dissimilar forms of government and opposing economic systems, leaders of these two nations harbored mistrust and dislike for one another that led to the contentious and often dangerous standoff. Each nation ultimately manufactured nuclear arms and fought this "war" by threatening the other with total annihilation. Specifically for the United States, the Cold War created a firm belief in the domino theory and containment, which held that the United States had to contain communism where it already existed and therefore stem the tide of its alleged expansionist aims. By the 1960s, this diplomatic ideology had firmly entrenched itself in the minds of American leaders and civilians alike.

Part of this foreign policy ideology concerned irrational fears of the Soviet Union, while other aspects of it relied on the knowledge of Soviet persecution of its own people. During the 1950s, Americans became so worried about Communist expansion that they feared it was attempting to infiltrate U.S. institutions, including the government, school systems, and even churches. While this later proved false and led to harmful accusations against innocent people, the Soviet regime was oppressive, imprisoned many within its borders who dared question it, and especially went after Christian churches because of its atheist policies. By the 1960s, Americans had a difficult time articulating how they understood this Communist enemy. Some Americans, both civilian and government leaders alike, continued to fear that Communist spies had infiltrated many aspects of U.S. life. These Americans persisted with harsh condemnations of any Communist government throughout the world. But others cautioned that communism was not a force within the United States and developed a more complex understanding of the world situation that assessed each nation and individual separately.[1]

In other words, throughout the 1950s, Americans had believed almost universally that communism represented one, worldwide monolithic force attacking capitalism and democracy with the hope of instituting a Communist system around the globe. But foreign policy realities softened this black and white approach by the 1960s. Some Americans continued to live in a world that denounced all communism and insisted that it was a unified force to combat. Others viewed the situation in more complex terms. For example, the People's Republic of China had grown strong enough to consider itself a Communist leader, much like the Soviet Union. This fact led to tension between the two Communist giants over their leadership of world communism and shared border disputes. In addition, smaller Communist countries played the two giants off of one another to gain economic and military aid from each. The monolith therefore proved illusory, and some Americans recognized this infighting. This recognition even came from the conservative Nixon administration, which took advantage of the conflict to further split the USSR and the PRC by establishing relationships with both nations, including historic visits by Nixon to Moscow and Beijing.[2]

Yet if a cooling between the United States and Communist giants signaled reduced tension, Southeast Asia kept antagonisms high, and U.S. policy demonstrated a continued reliance on containment theory. Following the French pull-out from Vietnam in 1954, the United States took over imperial protectorship of that nation in order to prevent it from becoming a completely Communist state. Nonetheless, Ho Chi Minh became the leader of North Vietnam and established a Communist nation that allied with the Soviet Union and Red China. In contrast, the United States, between 1954 and the fall of Saigon to North Vietnam in 1975, backed a series of corrupt regimes and dictators in South Vietnam simply because they opposed communism and because U.S. leaders did not think that a viable alternative outside of a Communist government presented itself. By 1964, South Vietnam and its war with southern insurgents and the North Vietnamese became unstable enough that Lyndon B. Johnson convinced Congress to pass the Gulf of Tonkin Resolution that gave him war powers in Southeast Asia. U.S. involvement in the Vietnamese civil war escalated slowly thereafter, through Johnson's administration and into Richard M. Nixon's term in office. Both Johnson and Nixon argued that America had to protect the South Vietnamese from falling into Communist hands based on the domino theory, even during Nixon's efforts toward détente with the USSR and PRC. Officials within the State and Defense Departments, however, were not of one mind regarding this war. Unlike previous Cold War harmony that advocated containment and firmly believed in the domino theory, during Vietnam a vibrant debate took place over the legitimacy of these theories as applied to Southeast Asia. Where some officials, including the presidents, saw a dangerous Communist enemy, others depicted a civil war that had nothing to do with U.S. national security. Though this opposition group failed to win the governmental debate, their voice affected policy and had support from outside Washington, D.C.[3]

From the very beginning, various groups of Americans questioned U.S. involvement in Vietnam on the grounds that this "civil war" hardly endangered the United States and because they saw little justification for America to place itself on the side of dictatorial powers in South Vietnam. Continuing a long legacy of pacifist advocacy in American history, an intellectual movement from the 1950s that had opposed the Cold War arms race began the Vietnam antiwar movement, followed quickly by college-age students who agreed with this earlier movement and had the added incentive of being subject to the draft. Throughout the Vietnam War, this antiwar advocacy grew steadily to the point that, by the early 1970s, more and more Americans outside of the vocal demonstrators agreed with their cause and sent politicians to Congress to vote on their behalf. Those who condemned the war had a variety of reasons for doing so. Some felt that the United States had no business fighting in this war, while others felt that a war the United States showed no sign of winning had simply gone on for too long. They therefore wanted to end the bloodshed and loss of life as soon as possible. Those Americans who opposed the Vietnam War agreed with the government officials who had come to question containment theory.[4]

But the complexity of this period makes it impossible to place Americans into one ideological category, especially as related to the war. While many came to protest it either publicly or privately, the neo-conservative movement that emerged after World War II—advocating a strong state and especially championing Cold War antagonisms—remained vibrant throughout the 1960s and supported the Vietnam War. This presence helps explain the election of Richard M. Nixon in 1968 on a law and order platform in the midst of antiwar protests and, even more so, his reelection in 1972 despite the persistence of a war he had promised to end. These Americans continued to fear communism, including a belief that this monolith still worked to infiltrate the United States and had to be stopped in Southeast Asia. The common perception of a decade rife with rights movements, student unrest, and antiwar protests misses the reality of America at that time. While these things happened, other Americans challenged them and maintained a faith in the government and trust in containment theory.[5]

Religious institutions played an important role in all of the above foreign policy debates. Christians in particular participated in Cold War antagonisms throughout the 1950s and continued to do so into the 1960s. They disdained the atheist mantra of the Soviet Union and Red China and felt duty bound to assist Christians trapped inside the Iron Curtain. Furthermore, a number of religious leaders intensified McCarthy-era paranoia, none more famously so than Billy Graham, who took advantage of Cold War fears during his crusades to warn of an imminent Communist victory that would signal the end times. Whether part of the milieu of the time or genuinely concerned about Communist threats, Christians added a religious fervor to the Cold War during the first two decades of the standoff. But, as with the rest of the nation, the 1960s debate about foreign policy factionalized Christianity. Two of the primary ways of viewing diplomatic concerns that emerged were a persistent Cold War fear that backed the Vietnam War as necessary and a belief that the war was unjust and the domino theory outdated. While this split specifically concerned Vietnam, it relates to significant theological arguments within American Christianity at that time. Quite often, the conservatives who supported the Vietnam

War also espoused a fundamentalist view of the world, or at least a very conservative theology, that denounced modernism and interfaith dialogues between Christians who disagreed theologically, between Jews and Christians, between Christians and Muslims, and especially any conversations between religious believers and atheist Communists.[6] Other Christians, in contrast, advocated global cooperation. Discussions with a diversity of religions and people gave them a much different view of the war. Instead of viewing politics or theology as black and white issues, they saw variances that separated people religiously and politically but that did not necessarily mandate contention. The Christians who advocated a modernist understanding of the world (one that allowed for other faiths and scientific thinking) also felt that the United States could coexist with Communist nations peacefully. Those on this side of the debate spent much of the 1950s and 1960s promoting dialogue between Christian denominations, espousing religious cooperation, and working through organizations such as the National Council of Churches of Christ to foster unity. While the above represents but two of the Christian modes of analysis regarding foreign policy, these examples demonstrate the amount of attention that religions gave to diplomacy during this decade.[7]

In addition, this Christian dialogue included musings on the justness of the Vietnam conflict. History has firmly established the seven just war criteria that began with Augustine and have been refined through the ages: 1) the cause of the war must be just; 2) war must be waged by a legitimate authority; 3) the war must be formally declared; 4) it must be fought with the right intention of instituting a just peace; 5) there must be a reasonable chance for success; 6) war must be a last resort; and 7) the means of waging it must be proportional to the ends. The prowar side felt that the war met these criteria while antiwar advocates insisted that it did not. In other words, religious exegesis provided no more concrete answers to the debate over Vietnam than did the secular political/diplomatic debate.[8]

Finally, beginning in 1973 and certainly by the time that North Vietnam took control of the South in April 1975, this vibrant debate over foreign policy had all but disappeared. The nation had become weary of the constant fighting, breathed a sigh of relief when Nixon withdrew American troops from Southeast Asia in January 1973, and tried to ignore the collapse of South Vietnam in 1975. The war had gone on for too long for a nation with a history of having a short attention span. Student unrest disappeared, questioning of U.S. foreign policy faded, and discussions about the Vietnam War ceased to exist in a public way. Even religious institutions put behind them much of the tension that had characterized this decade. And throughout this era, Lutherans had taken part in this discussion and represented the points of view outlined above. Turning attention to Lutheran Americans will explain why they make an interesting case study for religion, Americans, and foreign policy in the 1960s.

LUTHERAN HISTORICAL BACKGROUND

American Lutherans represent a broad spectrum of political, religious, and social ideologies that influenced perceptions of communism and war between 1964 and 1975. Indeed, Lutherans provide a sampling of Christian viewpoints on a variety of issues. Most studies suggest that Lutherans from every denomination primarily belong to a middle-class group of predominately white Americans. The examples in this study include Lutherans from every region of the United States, though a majority of Lutherans resided in the Midwest. And, despite a collective claim of belonging to a similar Lutheran tradition, Lutherans represented the entire spectrum of political opinions, from evangelical/fundamentalist conservative thinking, through mainline Protestant thought, to liberal ideals. Furthermore, Lutheran denominations had a fairly high level of lay participation. While the clergy held most leadership positions, laypeople had strong voices through the various denominational conventions, through control of their local congregations, and in economically supporting their church bodies. In other words, Lutherans left a record of how both the clergy and laity felt about foreign policy and religious issues during this decade. In the end, Lutherans represent at least one microcosm of average Americans and the contention that swept the nation during this period.[9]

With exceptions on the left and the right, a majority of Lutherans historically belonged to a group of moderate to conservative middle-class Americans who seldom pronounced their views in loud and demonstrative ways despite having strong convictions about politics and foreign policy. Indeed, most of the laypeople, clergy, and national leadership examined in this study were not individuals likely to declare their position on these issues in a large public forum or in a bellicose manner. They participated in such debates through traditional means that affected political leaders with petitions, letters, and voting. They openly deliberated in their periodicals, with letters to the editor and to church leaders, at churchwide assemblies, and in official and private correspondence. But seldom did their discourses appear in secular newspapers or on television. Lutherans therefore functioned as part of the silent majority; they affected foreign policy and perceptions of communism but did so without leaving the sort of prominent record that most histories of the 1960s employ. In other words, the Lutherans here, who otherwise left little evidence of their positions on the Cold War, internal communism, and the Vietnam War, did leave a paper trail in their church records because they were comfortable discoursing about these contentious issues in a conventional manner. A brief survey of Lutheranism in the 1960s will help establish this reality.[10]

The Lutheran Church in America (LCA) was the largest Lutheran denomination and generally espoused a mainline Protestant viewpoint that advocated moderate to liberal positions on theology, foreign policy, and domestic political issues. Its membership ranged from 3.2 million people throughout the 1960s to 3 million in the early 1970s. Four Lutheran denominations had merged in 1962 to form the LCA, including the United Lutheran Church in America, which traced its history to the pre-revolutionary period and included the first quasi-national Lutheran body, the General Synod, formed in 1820. This long history Americanized the LCA more than the other Lutheran churches; it also meant that the LCA more closely reflected a "typical" mainline Protestant viewpoint because it and its predecessor denominations had joined in alliances with other Protestants. For example, this was the only Lutheran church that belonged to the National Council of Churches of Christ (NCC), an interdenominational body that lobbied on behalf of shared beliefs around the nation and orchestrated national and global relief efforts to more effectively utilize the resources offered by a variety of denominations. The LCA presidents during this period, Dr. Franklin Clark Fry (1962–1968) and Dr. Robert J. Marshall (1968–1978), embodied mainline ideologies. Regarding communism, both denounced the contention that a Communist world monolith wanted to infiltrate U.S. institutions but regularly condemned Soviet and Chinese Communists. They opposed U.S. involvement in Vietnam but sought to effect change through traditional political channels, such as urging the laity to speak out when voting; neither supported radical demonstrations or burning draft cards. Despite general agreement with the opinions of their presidents among the LCA leadership and many lay members, a number of LCA members took more conservative stances. This, too, mirrors other mainline Protestant denominations in that the clerical leadership often took more liberal positions regarding theology and politics than did the laity. Some members, for example, complained about the denomination's support of amnesty for draft resisters and felt that the LCA's membership in the NCC affiliated it with an organization that supported Communist causes. The same spectrum held true for LCA theological beliefs. Its seminaries trained pastors in biblical criticism, and it regularly dialogued with other Lutherans, Protestants, and Catholics to seek common interests and reduce previous hostilities between Christian groups. The largest Lutheran denomination personified a predominately moderate position and gave these average Americans an outlet to voice their opinions without vocally protesting or publicly demonstrating for various causes.[11]

Closely related to the LCA was the American Lutheran Church (ALC). Four Lutheran denominations of ethnic makeup (primarily German, Norwegian, and Danish) had merged in 1960 to form the ALC. From 1964 to 1975, the ALC fluctuated between 2.4 and 2.5 million members and constituted the third-largest Lutheran body in the United States. The ALC membership shared the LCA's moderate opinions on foreign policy, domestic politics, communism, and most theological issues. The ALC presidents, Dr. Frederick A. Schiotz (1960–1971), Dr. Kent S. Knutsen (1971–1973), and Dr. David W. Preus (1973–1988), mirrored their LCA colleagues' sentiments regarding foreign policy and domestic political issues. Yet ALC leaders avoided taking public positions and tried to remain neutral in secular debates that they felt divided their church. These leaders' opinions reflected the ALC membership, albeit with exceptions on the left and the right. But, here again, the clerical leadership tended toward more liberal policies than did the laity. And a conservative faction fought the ALC's moderate political stances and called for a strict interpretation of the Bible as the inerrant word of God. This small but vocal contingent eventually broke away from the main church to form Lutherans-Alert National, which provides an example of far-right theological and political thinking. The ALC represents another mainline church that primarily espoused a moderate political and theological position.[12]

The Lutheran Church–Missouri Synod (LCMS) followed a much different ideological path than that of the other two large Lutheran denominations by espousing politically and theologically conservative points of view. Its membership grew from 2.6 million in 1964 to 2.8 million in 1974, making it slightly larger than the ALC. Established in 1847, the LCMS had a staunchly German background and, unlike the other two major Lutheran bodies, experienced no significant mergers to seriously alter its tradition. By the early 1970s, the LCMS advocated biblical inerrancy by disputing historical criticism. Significantly for the LCMS during this period, this position caused a major rift within the denomination because some people fought this conservative viewpoint. A faction broke away from the LCMS in the mid-1970s because of a dispute over teaching biblical criticism at Concordia Lutheran Seminary in St. Louis. Presidents Oliver R. Harms (1962–1969) and Jacob Aall Ottesen Preus (1969–1981) epitomized LCMS conservative thought regarding the above controversy and when considering political topics. Both despised all forms of communism and supported governmental policy regarding the Vietnam War. Preus visited Nixon in the White House and aided government efforts to free U.S. prisoners of war. LCMS members reflected their leadership's convictions even more strongly than LCA and ALC constituents did. In this regard, the LCMS defies the notion that mainline denominational leaders held more liberal points of view than their constituencies; if anything, the LCMS inverted this trend because its leaders reflected conservative lay opinions but had moderate to liberal members who disagreed with them. In addition to LCMS periodicals and letters that reveal the denomination's beliefs, the LCMS provides an important example of using mass media because of its affiliation with the Lutheran Laymen's League, which broadcast a weekly radio program titled "The Lutheran Hour." And, despite the uniformity of a majority of the LCMS members and leaders, the LCMS also had a radical right movement within its ranks that held to even more conservative judgments. The LCMS was an insular denomination that harbored suspicions against anyone who participated in interfaith dialogues and even condemned those who prayed with non-LCMS Lutherans. It therefore offers an example of conservative political thought and quasi-fundamentalist leanings in some of its theology, demonstrates how Protestants used mass media formats, and includes a radical right element. And although the LCMS did not "Americanize" in the way of the LCA and ALC, evidence suggests that it did Americanize along the lines of conservative fundamentalism and conservative Protestants and Catholics who throughout the century campaigned against the "negative" influences of modernism.[13]

In addition to issuing individual opinions and working on church-related matters, the three largest churches combined to form the Lutheran Council in the U.S.A. (LCUSA) in 1965. LCUSA coordinated projects upon which the three Lutheran bodies could agree, thereby streamlining their budgets through such cooperative ventures. For example, LCUSA organized some foreign mission efforts, served as a publicity bureau, and handled most of the churches' relations with the government. Furthermore, it contained a Division to Military Service Personnel that recruited Lutheran military chaplains, published a newsletter for Lutheran soldiers, and aided returning veterans. Despite this collaboration, theological disagreements often led the LCMS to refuse to participate in some LCUSA enterprises, particularly in regard to practices involving religious services. Though the LCMS worked with the LCUSA military service division, it also maintained a separate LCMS Armed Forces Board that organized religious services for its soldiers because LCMS doctrine forbade members from taking communion from non-LCMS clergy. Additionally, the LCMS declined participation in the Lutheran World Federation (LWF), an international body of Lutheran churches that cooperated on various worldwide issues, and in Lutheran World Relief (LWR), an organization that provided food, shelter, clothing, and support to war refugees and victims of natural disasters. No LCUSA issue, however, rankled the LCMS more than its study of the ordination of women. In 1970, the LCA and ALC began ordaining women, in part based on an LCUSA report that concluded that no biblical mandate either prohibited or called for the ordination of women. The

LCMS lambasted their decision to ordain women as heretical. Indeed, despite LCUSA being a cooperative venture and symbol of unity during this decade, these signs of discord revealed a growing movement within the LCMS to distance itself from the LCA and ALC, which it slowly did throughout the 1970s. Nonetheless, LCUSA regularly issued Lutheran statements regarding political issues on behalf of each of the three major Lutheran denominations. Its staff came from each of the churches and reached compromises on how to approach subjects ranging from prisoners of war to Communist refugees.

Outside of the Lutheran bodies outlined above, some smaller churches and organizations existed, all but one of which adhered to even more conservative points of view than did the LCMS. The Wisconsin Evangelical Lutheran Synod (WELS) was the largest of these. With a membership of 350,000 to 380,000, it outnumbered any other smaller Lutheran denomination; the other synod memberships ranged from a high of 20,000 to a low of 3,000. The WELS held a firm view that religion and politics should never mix and therefore seldom issued pronouncements about political topics and held strongly to a literal interpretation of the Lutheran confessions. The same attitude held true for most of the other small denominations. Despite admonitions to stay out of politics, however, members in these churches freely discussed the Communist "menace" and cautioned that it could doom Christianity and the United States. They also viewed civil unrest and student movements as threats to the established order. Members and clergy in the WELS and the smaller Lutheran bodies contribute an important voice to a study of the Cold War, fears of internal communism, and the Vietnam War because they represent very conservative people who claimed to disdain political dialogue within the church while still seeing communism as a dangerous foe. In addition, they implored people to trust government policy and thereby tacitly supported the domino theory and even the Vietnam War. In addition to these conservative groups, one significant liberal Lutheran organization represents another voice. The Lutheran Peace Fellowship took a traditional antiwar stance and fought unsuccessfully to move Lutherans toward pacifism. Lutheran diversity, further showcased in these smaller bodies, contributes to a fuller understanding of how some Americans remained publicly quiet about communism and the Vietnam War but still swayed policy by voting.[14]

In the context of this Lutheran diversity and disagreement about theology, politics, and Americanization, Lutheran Americans provide a broad spectrum of political and theological viewpoints regarding foreign policy issues. This variety of convictions appears within each Lutheran denomination, between the various denominations, among the Lutheran churches' leadership, and within each denomination's laity. Some Lutherans maintained a conservative viewpoint that supported presidential policy and efforts to block communism's growth while others leaned toward a moderate to liberal outlook that questioned the use of scare tactics in the United States and the war in Southeast Asia. Still other smaller factions existed within Lutheranism. A far left group upheld a pacifist doctrine while opponents of these voices balanced this leftist rhetoric with a fundamentalist credo that called for churches to stay out of politics and maintain a strict separation of church and state. All of the denominations discussed in this study claimed the title Lutheran, but the individuals within them often had little else in common with fellow Lutherans outside of their own church body.

To grapple with Lutheran responses to foreign policy during this decade, especially because of the diversity outlined above, a note about terminology/categorization is necessary. While categorizations about Lutherans and foreign policy are necessary, Lutheran political and diplomatic opinions defy cut-and-dried classification. Nonetheless, the next paragraph details the following groups: liberals, moderates, conservatives, and ultra-conservatives, groupings that refer primarily to the person's interpretation of the Cold and Vietnam Wars with attention to how theology often played a role in shaping it. While it would be desirable to know how economic, ethnic, denominational, regional, or other historic factors contributed to an individual Lutheran's outlook, the sources are unfortunately silent. An example demonstrates this dilemma: this study uses both published and unpublished letters to the editors of various Lutheran periodicals to portray an aspect of how Lutherans discussed these matters; but these letters seldom give information about economic status or ethnic heritage, and they almost never reveal a person's political party affiliation. It would be guessing at best, therefore, to make such determinations. In addition, Lutherans crossed over many lines typically used by historians to demark the political and diplomatic landscape. For example, some Lutherans may have espoused conservative theological opinions but denounced Vietnam as unjust, thereby standing with many theologically moderate to liberal Lutherans on this secular issue. To create a category that indicated theological convictions and how they led to an antiwar attitude would therefore necessitate either an inaccurate oversimplification or so many categorizations as to overwhelm the reader. It is important to note that the designations used herein apply only to the specific example or topic outlined in the text, unless examining a major figure, such as the leaders within the various denominations who left more records. Regarding foreign policy from 1964 to 1975, Lutherans reveal a continuum of positions, both politically and theologically, as they related to the Cold and Vietnam Wars. They backed the Cold War against the USSR and PRC, critiqued the U.S. government, and defended their patriotism regardless of how they felt about the Vietnam War, all in nuanced categories that many times defy standard characterizations by political party and theological identification.

Despite the difficulties noted above, the following designations provide an accurate depiction of Lutheran viewpoints regarding communism, the Cold War, and the Vietnam War. A small faction appeared on the left of Lutheranism, both politically and theologically. Most of these individuals hailed from the LCA and ALC, vehemently protested the Vietnam War, and advocated an inclusive theology that valued unity and understanding over insularity and protection of a "true faith." This study refers to them as liberals. A larger group, but still a minority, adhered to a radically conservative theological and political outlook. They denounced all supposedly socialist policies, including Johnson's Great Society programs, equated all views that competed with their opinions with communism, and strictly interpreted the Bible and Lutheran confessions. This study labels them the far-right or ultra-conservatives. A larger group of Lutherans were middle-of-the-road politically and theologically. They vacillated between moderate/liberal viewpoints and moderate/conservative opinions based on the issue at hand and how it affected their religious sensibilities. This study refers to them as moderates. While most of them belonged to the LCA and ALC, a significant number came from the LCMS but began leaving for other Lutheran denominations after the conservatives gained control of that synod in the late-1960s. The other large group of Lutherans in this study leaned toward a moderately conservative to conservative viewpoint and are therefore labeled as conservatives. They supported the government in Cold War policies, including the Vietnam War, and tended to view the Bible as inerrant. Conservatives are found in the LCA and ALC, though a majority of them come from the LCMS, WELS, and the smaller confessional bodies. Taken together, the Lutheran continuum represents a cross-section of the so-called silent majority. Lutheran Americans included the extreme left and right, but the majority of them were either politically and religiously moderate or conservative. Both moderates and conservatives supported efforts against the Soviet Union and People's Republic of China, but diverged over the threat of internal communism and the Vietnam War, leading to a split between those who clung to long-standing Communist fears and those who shunned arch anti-Communist dogmas.

To this end, Lutherans sometimes molded their political beliefs to reflect their theological doctrines, while at other times their political ideology shaped their theology. Religious historians often grapple with whether the church shapes society or society shapes the church. This study argues that both ideas worked within American Lutheranism during the Vietnam War era. The Lutheran churches by and large reflected U.S. society and therefore appear to be primarily molded by it. Yet Lutherans contributed a theological voice that added unique opinions to the subject matter. In the case of Lutheran perceptions of the Vietnam and Cold Wars, it becomes impossible to separate the two concepts and choose one side over the other. Indeed, Lutheran theology offers a unique perspective and underscores the fact that Lutherans both represented a group of average Americans and provided a distinctive theology because of Lutheran paradox. Lutheran theology holds to justification by faith alone and yet adheres to biblical law at the same time. Lutheran two kingdoms theology is one example of this thinking. Lutherans believe in participating in the world but not being of the world; they obey secular law as a gift from God to order society but allow for dissent if these laws conflict with theology or harm innocent people. And, while they believe in the Lutheran confessions, not all agree on the meaning of these documents that condemn legalism within Christianity. During the 1960s and 1970s in America, this theological approach led to the diversity of opinions outlined above, and each group could use part of this theology to justify their religious and political convictions. In other words, no one group could claim to represent true Lutheranism because, at the same time, all of these groups represented Lutheranism.[15]

Finally, Lutherans are a good subject of study because of the part they played in both mirroring and molding the history of U.S. society during the Vietnam era. Prior to 1964, a majority of laypeople, clergy, and officials promoted the Cold War, still feared communism's influence on Americans, and cautiously supported U.S. participation in other countries' conflicts. Despite this former consensus, Lutherans disagreed with one another by 1964. Some denounced the Vietnam War and questioned the domino theory; these people also doubted that Communist forces had infiltrated U.S. institutions. But their Lutheran counterparts clung to traditional anti-Communist doctrines. Lutherans continued to reflect U.S. society when interest and coverage of the Vietnam War tapered off by the early 1970s. By the mid-1970s, Lutherans debated whether or not to stay in Vietnam, the degree to which people should support governmental policies in Southeast Asia, and how to fight the Cold War.

CONCLUSION

Lutherans voiced a myriad of points of view about foreign policy from 1964 to 1975. They did so through their theological convictions and with mere secular opinions, despite all of this appearing in religious conversations. But they concluded the decade without either resolving the conflict or even agreeing to disagree. They just moved forward. Americans continue to grapple with the meaning of the "1960s" in a number of ways, including the wartime issues that so factionalized it. Lutherans played a role in this endeavor. Yet seldom do scholars point their attention away from the left and right extremes to see what other Americans thought and how they contributed to this dialogue, and no Lutheran historian has spent time articulating the Lutheran reaction to the Cold and Vietnam Wars. But Lutherans and Americans in general today live in a world profoundly affected by this legacy. In particular, the push to "move on" after the Vietnam War ended left unresolved many of the arguments that had raged. Lutherans sought reconciliation at a time when the rest of America also longed for a truce. This tranquility happened at the expense of learning lessons about how everyone, including Lutheran Americans, affected the history of that era. In the midst of a new American battle against an insurgent movement in a foreign land, returing to the 1960s can assist us in understanding how people react today, in both positive and negative ways, as American citizens, Christians, and Lutherans.

NOTES

1. For the best source on Soviet persecution of the churches, see volumes one and two of Dimitry Pospielovsky's *The Russian Church under the Soviet Regime, 1917–1982*, 2 vols. (Crestwood, NY: St. Vladimir's Seminary Press, 1984); Owen Chadwick, *The Christian Church in the Cold War* (New York: Penguin Books, 1992); Stephane Courtois et al., *The Black Book of Communism: Crimes, Terror, Repression* (Cambridge, MA: Harvard University Press, 1999); Dianne Kirby, ed., *Religion and the Cold War* (New York: Palgrave Macmillan, 2003); Elliott Abrams, ed., *The Influence of Faith: Religious Groups and U.S. Foreign Policy* (Lanham, MD: Rowman and Littlefield Publishers, 2001).

2. Gordon H. Chang, *Friends and Enemies: The United States, China, and the Soviet Union, 1948–1972* (Stanford: Stanford University Press, 1990).

3. Gary R. Hess, "The Unending Debate: Historians and the Vietnam War," in Michael J. Hogan, ed., *America in the World: The Historiography of American Foreign Relations since 1941* (Cambridge: Cambridge University Press, 1995), 358–94; Robert Buzzanco, *Masters of War: Military Dissent and Politics in the Vietnam Era* (Cambridge: Cambridge University Press, 1996); Allen J. Matusow, *The Unraveling of America: A History of Liberalism in the 1960s* (New York: Harper and Row, 1984); Robert S. McNamara, *In Retrospect: The Tragedy and Lessons of Vietnam* (New York: Random House Books, 1995).

4. Charles DeBenedetti and Charles Chatfield, *An American Ordeal: The Antiwar Movement of the Vietnam Era* (Syracuse, NY: Syracuse University Press, 1990); Mitchell K. Hall, *Because of Their Faith: CALCAV and Religious Opposition to the Vietnam War* (New York: Columbia University Press, 1990); Melvin Small, *Johnson, Nixon, and the Doves* (New Brunswick, NJ: Rutgers University Press, 1988); William J. Duiker, *Sacred War: Nationalism and Revolution in a Divided Vietnam* (New York: McGraw Hill, 1995).

5. For excellent scholarship on the rise of the new right, see Lisa McGirr, *Suburban Warriors: The Origins of the New American Right* (Princeton, NJ: Princeton University Press, 2001); Jonathan M. Schoenwald, *A Time for Choosing: The Rise of Modern American Conservatism* (New York: Oxford University Press, 2001); Mary C. Brennan, *Turning Right in the Sixties: The Conservative Capture of the GOP* (Chapel Hill: University of North Carolina Press, 1995); Dan T. Carter, *The Politics of Rage: George Wallace, the Origins of the New Conservatism, and the Transformation of American Politics* (Baton Rouge: Louisiana State University Press, 2000); John A. Andrew III, *The Other Side of the Sixties: Young Americans for Freedom*

and the Rise of Conservative Politics (New Brunswick, NJ: Rutgers University Press, 1997). For the religious context, see Patrick Allitt, *Religion in America since 1945: A History* (New York: Columbia University Press, 2003); Paul Boyer, *By the Bomb's Early Light: American Thought and Culture at the Dawn of the Atomic Age* (Chapel Hill: University of North Carolina Press, 1985).

6. This study employs a broad meaning for the terms fundamentalism and evangelicalism. In the case of fundamentalism, it includes a theological understanding of people who interpreted the Bible as the inerrant word of God. Some evangelicals believed this as well, though not as universally. Fundamentalists traced their tradition back to the modernist controversy of the late nineteenth and early twentieth centuries. Evangelical history goes back farther in U.S. history to the First Great Awakening. Defining the words in their political context becomes more complex. Some fundamentalists clung to the theory that religion and politics should never intermingle and so claimed to stay out of secular discussions. However, by the early 1970s, evangelicals began efforts to influence political topics with conservative Christian thinking. But even these theorists insisted that they wanted a strict separation of church and state. Thus, although various evangelicals and fundamentalists differed in their actual practice of separating religion and politics, they all maintained that the two should not fraternize because religion represented God's will while secular topics were impure. The terms evangelicalism and fundamentalism, then, indicate people who held to strict interpretations of the Bible. It is also important to note that not everyone who adhered to these conservative religious principles also practiced conservative politics; it was possible to maintain liberal democratic ideals in conjunction with evangelical religious notions. The best discussion of early fundamentalism is George M. Marsden, *Fundamentalism and American Culture: The Shaping of Twentieth-Century Evangelicalism, 1870–1925* (New York: Oxford University Press, 1980). For a more extensive discussion of the terms fundamentalism and evangelicalism, see Peter W. Williams, *America's Religions: Traditions and Cultures* (New York: Macmillan Publishing Company, 1990), 322, 351–54, and Martin E. Marty, *Pilgrims in Their Own Land: 500 Years of Religion in America* (New York: Penguin Books, 1984), 470–71.

7. Allitt, *Religion in America since 1945*; Martin E. Marty, *Modern American Religion*, vol. 3, *Under God, Indivisible, 1941–1960* (Chicago: University of Chicago Press, 1996); James Hudnut-Beumler, *Looking for God in the Suburbs: The Religion of the American Dream and Its Critics, 1945–1965* (New Brunswick, NJ: Rutgers University Press, 1994); Mark David Hulsether, *Building a Protestant Left: Christianity and Crisis Magazine, 1941–1993* (Knoxville: University of Tennessee Press, 1999); Seth Jacobs, "'Our System Demands the Supreme Being': The U.S. Religious Revival and the 'Diem Experiment,' 1954–55," *Diplomatic History* 25 (Fall 2001): 589–624; Gerald L. Sittser, *A Cautious Patriotism: The American Churches and the Second World War* (Chapel Hill: University of North Carolina Press, 1997); Stephen J. Whitfield, *The Culture of the Cold War* (Baltimore: Johns Hopkins University Press, 1991).

8. Richard B. Miller, *Interpretations of Conflict: Ethics, Pacifism, and the Just-War Tradition* (Chicago: University of Chicago Press, 1991); Michael Walzer, *Just and Unjust Wars: A Moral Argument with Historical Illustrations* (New York: Basic Books, 1977); Jean Bethke Elshtain, ed., *Just War Theory* (New York: New York University Press, 1992).

9. Williams, *America's Religions*, and Marty, *Pilgrims in Their Own Land*. Williams gives the most succinct definition of mainline Protestantism: it refers to a group of Christians encompassing white, middle- and upper-class Protestant churches, including Baptists, Congregationalists, Disciples of Christ, Episcopalians, Lutherans, Methodists, and Presbyterians (323–28). Politically, most mainline Protestants espoused moderate views on domestic and international issues; these stances ranged from moderately liberal to semi-conservative. Another good source for understanding "mainline" denominations is Wade Clark Roof and William

McKinney, *American Mainline Religion: Its Changing Shape and Future* (New Brunswick, NJ: Rutgers University Press, 1987).

10. The largest survey of American Lutheran history traces the mergers of various Lutheran denominations throughout U.S. history and explores how different immigration patterns changed the churches or created new factions: E. Clifford Nelson, ed., *The Lutherans in North America* (Philadelphia: Fortress Press, 1975). A good articulation of the wide variances in faith beliefs among the clergy and laity and between the various Lutheran denominations is Lawrence L. Kersten, *The Lutheran Ethic: The Impact of Religion on Laymen and Clergy* (Detroit: Wayne State University Press, 1970). For a guide to Lutheran church bodies in the United States, see Robert C. Wiederaenders, ed., *Historical Guide to Lutheran Church Bodies of North America*, 2nd ed. (St. Louis: Lutheran Historical Conference, 1998). L. DeAne Lagerquist, *The Lutherans* (Westport, CT: Greenwood Press, 1999); Richard Cimino, ed., *Lutherans Today: American Lutheran Identity in the 21st Century* (Grand Rapids, MI: William B. Eerdmans, 2003).

11. W. Kent Gilbert's *Commitment to Unity: A History of the Lutheran Church in America* (Philadelphia: Fortress Press, 1988) provides a solid overview of the LCA's activities during its existence from 1962 to 1988. See also Christa R. Klein, *Politics and Policy: The Genesis and Theology of Social Statements in the Lutheran Church in America* (Minneapolis: Fortress Press, 1989). Benson Y. Landis, ed., *Yearbook of American Churches: Information on all Faiths in the U.S.A.* (New York: National Council of Churches of Christ, 1965), 61; Constant H. Jacquet, Jr., ed., *Yearbook of American Churches: Information on All Faiths in the U.S.A.* (New York: National Council of Churches of Christ, 1970), 50; Jacquet, ed., *Yearbook of American and Canadian Churches, 1974* (Nashville: Abingdon Press, 1974), 234.

12. Charles P. Lutz, ed., *Church Roots: Stories of Nine Immigrant Groups that Became the American Lutheran Church* (Minneapolis: Augsburg Publishing House, 1985); L. DeAne Lagerquist, *From Our Mothers' Arms: A History of Women in the American Lutheran Church* (Minneapolis: Augsburg Publishing House, 1987); Landis, *Yearbook,* 60; Jacquet, *Yearbook* (1970), 16; Jacquet, *Yearbook* (1974), 230.

13. Landis, *Yearbook,* 58, Jaquet, *Yearbook* (1974), 234. The best history of the LCMS is Mary Todd's *Authority Vested: A Story of Identity and Change in the Lutheran Church–Missouri Synod* (Grand Rapids, MI: William B. Eerdmans, 2000). For another overview of the Lutheran Church–Missouri Synod during this period, see August R. Suelflow, *Heritage in Motion: Readings in the History of the Lutheran Church–Missouri Synod, 1962–1995* (St. Louis: Concordia Publishing House, 1998). For a history of the LCMS laity, see Alan Graebner, *Uncertain Saints: The Laity in the Lutheran Church–Missouri Synod, 1900–1970* (Westport, CT: Greenwood Press, 1975). Fred and Edith Pankow, *75 Years of Blessings and the Best is Yet to Come! A History of the International Lutheran Laymen's League* (St. Louis: International Lutheran Laymen's League, 1992).

14. Steven Schroeder, *A Community and a Perspective: Lutheran Peace Fellowship and the Edge of the Church, 1941–1991* (Lanham, MD: University Press of America, 1993). Joseph H. Levang, *The Church of the Lutheran Brethren, 1900–1975: A Believers' Fellowship—A Lutheran Alternative* (Fargus Falls, MN: Lutheran Brethren Publishing Company, 1980). Landis, *Yearbook,* 257–58; Jacquet, *Yearbook* (1974), 230–37.

15. James M. Kittelson, *Luther the Reformer: The Story of the Man and His Career* (Minneapolis: Augsburg Publishing House, 1986); Lisa Sowle Cahill, *Love Your Enemies: Discipleship, Pacifism, and Just War Theory* (Minneapolis: Fortress Press, 1994); Eric W. Gritsch and Robert W. Jenson, *Lutheranism: The Theological Movement and Its Confessional Writings* (Philadelphia: Fortress Press, 1976).

Chapter Two

Tortured for Christ:
Lutheran Assessments of
Global Communism, 1964–1975

By the mid-1960s, the United States had for two decades been fighting a global Cold War against what its leaders characterized as an atheistic, anti-democratic, Communist demon that threatened to take over the world. Cold War hostilities started after World War II between the United States and Union of Soviet Socialist Republics (USSR), prompting Americans to intensify a suspicion and hatred for this Communist power that had begun with Vladimir Lenin's takeover of Russia at the end of World War I. The arms race, cultural warfare, and division of the rest of the world into spheres of influence throughout the 1950s had led to a persistent tension between the two nations by the 1960s. U.S. citizens had long criticized this totalitarian regime because of its oppressive tactics, purges of dissidents, and antagonistic rhetoric against capitalism. Furthermore, the Soviet Union adhered to the Marxist principle that labeled religion, and especially Christianity, a tool that the upper and middle classes used to subjugate the working class. Despite a lull in religious suppression following Josef Stalin's death in 1953, by the late 1950s and throughout the 1960s, Soviet Premiers Nikita Khrushchev and Leonid Brezhnev persisted with bureaucratic efforts to confiscate Christian-owned lands, to prohibit the establishment of new churches, and to persecute priests for anti-Soviet activity. They also forbade religious education for young Soviet citizens, whether in churches or in private home gatherings. This religious oppression especially worried Christians in the United States. U.S. religious institutions during the Cold War regularly spoke out against the Soviet Union and participated in propaganda efforts throughout the world to undermine Communist authority and buttress western defenses against it. By the mid-1960s, more and more proof slipped out of the Soviet Union that verified the Communist attempt to close churches and eliminate religion. Like their Christian counterparts around the world, Lutherans therefore sustained their

Cold War posturing against the Soviet Union from 1964 to 1975 and worried about the fate of Christians inside its borders.

But this concern about communism did not stop with the USSR because by 1964 the People's Republic of China (PRC) had become a world Communist power as well. Chinese Communists came to power during the Chinese Revolution that began in the midst of World War II. Led by Mao Zedong, Communists endeared people to their cause by promising land reform, economic changes, and, perhaps most importantly, an end to foreign influences in China. Once Mao's government took control, China moved quickly throughout the 1950s to establish itself as a global Communist leader, especially by supporting rhetorically, economically, and at times militarily, various nationalist movements in Asia. Indeed, this posturing and assistance fostered an alliance throughout Asia between revolutionary movements and the PRC, a growing influence that concerned the United States. Similar to perceptions of the Soviet Union, American citizens quickly came to dislike the Chinese Communists and saw them as every bit the threat posed by the Soviet Union. And, just as the case with the USSR, proof of Communist oppression of those who disagreed with it and especially the denunciations of religion angered churches throughout America. The Chinese actually exacerbated this antagonism when they came to power by expelling almost all Christian missionaries and greatly curtailing the authority of the Catholic Church, including the demand that the PRC appoint Catholic bishops, in place of the Vatican. Lutherans were not immune to this problem. Various Lutheran denominations and a number of people within them had participated in missionary work to China and experienced the removal from the mainland in the late 1940s. Thus, by the 1960s, Lutherans had developed a firm stance against the PRC and its irreligion.

A study of Lutherans therefore demonstrates that these Christian Americans maintained Cold War antagonisms toward the USSR and PRC from 1964 to 1975 with a largely unanimous voice. Lutherans distrusted the Soviet Union and Red China because of religious persecution and reminded one another that the United States had to combat this evil. To this end, the Lutheran churches' leadership ensured that constituents remembered the Communist peril and insisted that young people must "know the demonic possibilities in the communist menace." Laypeople agreed with their leaders. As one Lutheran Church in America (LCA) member pleaded, "Let us pray for our brothers suppressed under the rule of Communism and look for the freedom which God breathes into every man to eventually overthrow this Godless ideology." Immigrants from Communist nations also reminded people that the fight continued. A Lutheran pastor from Romania frequently spoke about the abuse he received from Communist governments and beseeched those with whom he talked to assist their fellow Christians.[1]

Yet some differences separated conservative Lutherans, both among the clergy and laity, from moderate to liberal Lutherans, primarily from the leadership ranks of the American Lutheran Church (ALC) and Lutheran Church in America. Conservatives were especially vocal in constantly condemning the large Communist nations as "demonic" forces, while moderate and liberal Lutherans cautioned that condemnatory rhetoric might hinder future chances for Christian growth inside Communist borders and hamper efforts to ease Cold War tensions. This divergence especially came to light during the Richard Nixon administration's efforts toward détente. Nixon decreased tension with the Soviet Union by emphasizing arms limitation agreements and by selling food to Russia after drought seriously threatened many of its citizens with starvation. He also opened relations with China, in part to exacerbate border disagreements and feuds about the future of global communism that the PRC had with the USSR. Nixon's most historic move came with 1972 visits to both Moscow and Beijing, trips that affected American perceptions of the Cold War. While almost no one ceased their suspicion of the Communist giants, some Americans, such as ALC and LCA officials, hoped that détente could reduce world tension and the threat of nuclear war, as well as allow more Christians to visit fellow believers inside Communist nations. Conservatives, on the other hand, distrusted the Communists and thought little could come from talking to them. Furthermore, despite this more open stance toward diplomatic contacts and cooperation with the churches inside the Communist bloc, moderate to liberal thinkers still distrusted communism and supported U.S. Cold War policies. And Lutherans agreed that this in part was a war of Christianity versus Communist atheism; while they never called the Cold War a holy war, failed to place their views in the context of Lutheran theology, and almost never applied the just war criteria to it, Lutheran discussions about the Cold War reminded Americans that communism threatened the church and its people with a godless ideology.

LUTHERAN DEMONIZING OF THE USSR

This Cold War hostility toward the Soviet Union led American Lutherans from 1964 to 1975 to blast the Soviet government on a regular basis, to decry the persecution of religious believers inside Soviet borders, and to lament that young people in the Soviet Union seldom heard the Christian message. However, although Lutherans agreed on the above ideals, they differed over how the U.S. government and the churches should respond. Conservative thinkers insisted that the United States and Christians resist any contact with the Soviet Union because it was evil. Other Lutherans cautioned that this alienated true believers in the USSR and threatened to lead to a global war; they argued instead for limited cooperation. But all Lutherans in some way battled the Soviet Union in order to protect Christianity.[2]

Throughout the Cold War, Christians, including Lutherans, had demonized the Soviet Union because of its firm stance against organized religion. Proof of this Soviet oppression especially bothered them. For example, the Lutheran Church in America and American Lutheran Church participated in the Lutheran World Federation (LWF), an international organization that focused on coordinating Lutheran relief efforts around the world and in dialoging about differences within the broad category of "Lutheranism." This focus meant that LWF could and did provide alarming reports from inside the Iron Curtain about the closure of churches and harassing of Lutheran believers. Lutherans of every political persuasion and religious conviction therefore used religious imagery to depict the Soviet Union; they saw it as a demonic force on earth because the Cold War included a theological battle versus Satan as represented by atheistic communism. A 1964 issue of the Lutheran periodical *Evangelize* quoted Zechariah 14:2, "I will gather all nations against Jerusalem to battle." The editor insisted that "students of prophecy know that Russian armies will one day invade Palestine in an all-out effort to take over the Middle East" and thus fulfill the biblical prediction of an ominous country becoming the devil's agent. Rhetoric from Lutheran leaders echoed this sentiment of a diabolic Soviet Union. J. A. O. Preus, a political and theological conservative who was elected president of the Lutheran Church–Missouri Synod (LCMS) in 1969, stated that "communism is the most terrible evil that the world has ever known." He later portrayed the USSR's fight against religion as "wicked." Lay constituents in the LCA concurred with this assessment in 1971, when they called the Soviet Union "a monstrous dictatorial empire." Lutherans of all stripes persisted with Cold War depictions of the Soviet Union as an evil influence and thereby continued the United States' intense fear of Soviet communism into the 1960s and 1970s on the grounds that this conflict was in part a religious war.[3]

This Lutheran conviction that the Soviet Union was an evil force led them to wrongly blame only it for the arms race. In truth, the United States and the Soviet Union shared equal guilt for this drastic buildup in armaments because both sides feared that the other side would attack if their side appeared weak. But in the midst of the 1960s Cold War, anti-Soviet passions blinded most Americans to this reality. They thought that only a "demonic" nation would create destructive atomic weapons and therefore assigned no culpability in the struggle to the United States, which they thought had merely reacted to the Soviet buildup. Lutherans shared this opinion. For example, the 1968 convention of the American Lutheran Church adopted a resolution that called for

the U.S. president to try to work with the Soviet Union for a "verifiable re-
duction in armaments." But the resolution clearly blamed the Soviets for "en-
courag[ing]" the United States to "challenge" them in the arms race. Laypeople also voiced this sentiment independently. A Lutheran Church in America
layperson claimed that the USSR's leadership ignored the plight of its citizens
in favor of funding weapons construction: "The main reason the living standards of the people in the Soviet Union are so low is that the Soviet Union
spends so much on the build-up of armament."[4]

Knowledge that the Soviet Union oppressed Christianity by controlling the
Russian Orthodox Church unified Lutheran Americans even more. Leaders of
the Russian Orthodox Church played a dangerous political game throughout
the Cold War by balancing their faith life and responsibility to the church with
the constant surveillance of the Soviet government, which threatened to arrest
anyone who contradicted the official state policy that denounced organized
religion. Christians around the world grappled with the meaning of this reality, including Lutherans, who shared stories about this suppression of religious belief. In 1964, one laywoman stated that "there are no true churches in
Russia except in Siberia where the prisons are, as most of the churches are
state run." Her statement demonstrates a typical Lutheran concern about the
Soviet micromanagement of Russian institutions, which led them to believe
that the government also controlled the Russian Orthodox Church. It led her
and others to the erroneous conclusion that the Russian Orthodox Church was
therefore not a "true church" because atheists in the government monitored
its polity. Russian Christians, both among the clergy and laity, maintained
their faith throughout the Cold War despite these oppressive conditions. Yet
she and other Lutherans jumped to the questionable conclusion that the Russian Orthodox Church no longer devoted itself to true Christianity. The president of a small conservative Lutheran denomination, the Synod of Evangelical Lutheran Churches, suggested that the Soviet state used "fierce floods of
violently opposed propaganda and opinions" to turn people against religion.
Even into the 1970s, Lutherans alerted one another to the danger posed by the
Soviet Union's dominion over its largest church body. As Soviet authorities
persisted with undermining the church and promoting atheism, one minister
reminded his flock that the Soviet government silenced dissent by supervis-
ing leaders of the Russian Orthodox Church. He lamented their acquiescence
to Communist dictates because "silence can be the worst possible betrayal of
our Lord."[5]

The Lutheran Church in America had even better first-hand evidence of
what the Soviet Union did to religious believers. In cooperation with the
United Presbyterian Church, the Protestant Episcopal Church, and the
American Baptist Church, the LCA had created the Protestant Church in

Moscow. It primarily functioned as a place for American Christians to attend while stationed in or visiting the Soviet Union. But its existence provided the LCA with concrete evidence about the Soviet control over religion. James L. Barkenquast served as its pastor from 1964 to September 1967 and reported back to LCA officials. He asserted that the Soviets distrusted him because he was an American and because he held religious meetings. This forced him to take precautionary measures because his "flat is observed constantly by a Soviet police official. It is assumed that it is wired to pick up conversation." Barkenquast also reported that the Soviet government watched him closely to prevent him from "unauthorized contact" with Soviet citizens. Because their participation in efforts to provide a Protestant ministry to Americans in Moscow furnished actual proof that the Soviet state oppressed religious belief, such evidence further hardened Lutheran opinions against communism and strengthened the notion that the Cold War was in part a religious war.[6]

Americans who toured the USSR during the Cold War often reported that the Soviet government orchestrated their visit to hide poverty and the lack of freedom, religious and otherwise. Indeed, the Soviet Union maintained a vast propaganda machine that attempted to hide how poor the average Russian was and to conceal Soviet tactics in putting down dissent. Despite these efforts, Lutheran accounts revealed the truth that the Soviets especially enjoyed fooling tourists by manipulating visits to their country so that "gullible Americans who visit" saw a utopian Soviet Union without its many blemishes. One Lutheran tourist suspected the motives of a Russian tour guide who asked about religion; after seeing little evidence of a religious life in the Soviet Union during her visit, she wondered whether this guide sincerely appreciated what the Americans had to say or if her "interest in my church women [was] a carefully calculated question to make a U.S. tourist feel things are 'open' in the USSR."[7]

In addition, a tourist in Russia took pictures of former Lutheran church buildings, published them in the *Lutheran Scholar*, and lamented that the closed churches "are the skeletal remains of what once was a large, vibrant institutional church." Another visitor pointed out that Kiev, a "city of nearly 2,000,000 people," had only "SEVEN functioning churches." Another report explained that "for 1,400,000 Soviet citizens of German Lutheran origin there are only 10 . . . churches" to attend and "none of the congregations has an ordained pastor." Lutherans also asserted that the Soviet Union forced various denominations to merge into one institution and placed "Communist party puppets" at their head. These actual cases of Soviet controls on religious expression fueled passionate denunciations by Lutherans when they commented on the Communist superpower. Lutheran support for U.S. Cold War policy therefore was partially motivated by the religious conviction that the Soviet Union wanted to eliminate the Christian faith inside its borders.[8]

More proof of how badly the Soviet government treated Christianity came from Lutherans who attempted to smuggle Bibles into Russia. During the Cold War, a variety of Christians sought ways to reach inside Soviet borders to support Christian believers who could not otherwise hear the Christian message or obtain Christian information. This included persistent attempts to get Bibles inside the Soviet Union, which forbade its publication and distribution. *Faith and Fellowship*, the official periodical of the Church of the Lutheran Brethren, reported, "The mere act of receiving a Bible from a tourist is grounds for imprisonment. Bible studies inside or outside of churches are also illegal." This pronouncement from a Biblical literalist Lutheran body that generally avoided commentary about politics underscores an important point. When the Soviet state oppressed religion, conservatives were spurred to respond because they then saw the issue as a moral one the church had to address. Trying to stop people from obtaining Bibles kept them from salvation; thus, even conservative Lutherans who claimed to separate politics and religion had to comment. The Soviet government's antagonistic reaction to Bible distribution also manifested itself when Representative Earl F. Landgrebe, a Republican Lutheran from Indiana, tried to sneak three hundred Russian-language Bibles into the Soviet Union during an official trip to study Soviet education. The Soviets promptly expelled him after two hours of questioning, even though, as Landgrebe noted, "Russians wept and kissed the Bibles as I gave them to people." In short, the Soviet policy of disallowing Bibles heightened Lutheran Americans' disdain for Communist policies. Though not violent, the repartee over Bibles was part of the Cold War religious battle.[9]

Lutherans also protested the Soviet government's prohibition of teaching younger people about religion. Indeed, Christians throughout the world used these Soviet laws as proof about the plight of religious believers in the Soviet Union. Lutherans were no exception in lamenting what this did to Soviet young people, some of whom felt spiritually lost and some of whom sought religion despite these restrictions. A visitor to the Soviet Union declared that Soviet teens were "in religious turmoil." She further asserted that "while many still see religion as the root of darkness and ignorance, others enthusiastically absorb the Gospel" despite their government's opposition. Another tourist sensed the same confusion among Soviet youth: "It is not a conscious search for God, so much as a yearning for something deeper than what one young Russian bluntly called, 'the vulgar materialisms of the Party.'" By the mid-1970s, Lutherans received reports that the Communists had stepped up their efforts to keep religion away from Soviet youth. They noticed that "young people in Russia are not being taught to believe in the God of heaven and earth, but in the Russian system." Lutherans therefore lamented together the sad future of Russian children and teenagers who grew up in a world where they were sure godless Marxism had replaced Christianity at the behest of an oppressive state.[10]

Soviet suppression of religion finally led American Lutherans to call for helping fellow Christians in need. Indeed, Christians throughout the Cold War had known about Soviet anti-religious policies, had evidence that the government oppressed Christian advocates, and therefore concluded that the Cold War was in part a religious war. Believing this to be the case, Lutherans called for action. One LCA layperson stated that "the Christians in the Western world must not ignore their brethren in the Communist countries. One thing we must do is call the attention of the world to their plight and not lightly brush it aside." Others sought broader global action against the entire Communist bloc of nations by asking, "Why don't we support all the *Lutherans* held captive in Russian-occupied Germany and the rest of Europe . . . not only *morally* but *financially*." In more graphic language, the 1975 LCMS convention passed a resolution of "solidarity with the suffering, bleeding, yet confessing church under oppression" and urged prayer "for the conversion of their tormentors." After outlining valid reasons for despising the demonic Other as manifested in the Soviet government, Lutherans from every denomination urged people to act on their behalf as part of the religious Cold War struggle.[11]

Lutherans also wanted to come to the aid of those oppressed inside the Soviet Union because they knew that some Soviet citizens maintained their Christian faith. Throughout the Cold War, Christians in every country sought and received information about the plight of religious believers inside the Soviet Union and shared it with one another. For example, Vatican radio reported in 1965 the discovery of a secret religious publishing operation in Moscow that the Soviet government promptly destroyed. They shared this information with Christians throughout the world to show that the Soviet Union could not vanquish religion despite its efforts. Thus, despite the negative outcome, the fact that Soviet citizens risked their lives to print God's Word inspired American Lutherans. Reports about the survival of Soviet *Lutherans* especially excited their U.S. colleagues. A minister who had recently served for several years in Siberia informed an international gathering of Lutheran leaders that Lutherans in the Soviet Union continued to lead active religious lives even after they lost their organized church structure and suffered government persecution. While constantly grieving for their subjected brethren, American Lutherans gladly reported that even Soviet authorities could not destroy all religious faith.[12]

Because some Soviet citizens maintained their faith, and because American Lutherans wished to act on their behalf, Lutheran organizations raised money to broadcast radio programs into the Soviet Union. In such an endeavor, Lutherans joined a host of Christian organizations from around the globe that broadcast into the Soviet Union in order to reach Christians. For example, Eugene R. Bertermann, a prominent LCMS pastor, worked for the non-denominational Far East Broadcasting Company (FEBC). This cooperative venture ensured that people heard the Christian message in areas reached by no other religious propaganda. A narrated film used to solicit donations for the FEBC explained that these broadcasts formed "the lifelines for the spiritual life of the people" in the Soviet Union, China, and Tibet. In addition, the LCMS-sponsored "Lutheran Hour" broadcast into Communist nations. Begun in the 1930s and most famous for broadcasting a weekly radio program in the United States, the "Lutheran Hour" had expanded by the 1960s into an international institution. This included efforts to reach inside the Soviet Union. As an LCMS magazine reported in 1965, "Lutheran Hour programs in Europe are transmitted over two of the world's most powerful stations, Radio Luxembourg and Radio Europe. From these two stations the Word of reconciliation penetrates countries behind the Iron Curtain."[13]

Despite general Lutheran opposition to the Soviet Union that mirrored American hostility as a whole, certain variances existed between conservative Lutherans and their liberal and moderate counterparts. Conservative Lutherans never swayed from impassioned pronunciations against the Soviet empire and constantly warned people that it could ultimately threaten U.S. security. They also maintained this posture with little change throughout the 1964 to 1975 decade, regardless of détente or arms limitation agreements. In contrast, less ardent Lutheran Cold Warriors wondered whether cooperation between the United States and the Soviet Union might benefit Christianity by easing Cold War tensions.

Two ultra-conservative Lutheran periodicals demonstrate the vehemence of conservative denunciations. The *Christian News*, whose editor left the LCMS because he believed its leadership was too liberal after Concordia Seminary professors refused to ordain him, and *Jesus to the Communist World*, an independent journal solely dedicated to convincing Americans about Communist evils, portrayed the USSR as a demon waiting to pounce upon innocent victims. Neither periodical was affiliated officially with a denomination, yet they found enough of an audience among rightist Lutherans to continue publishing their ideas. Each maintained conservative theological and political points of view, regardless of the topic; thus, their denunciations of the Soviet Union fit a pattern of extreme patriotism and criticizing anything that appeared "liberal" to them. For the *Christian News*, this especially meant a hostility toward biblical criticism and antiwar activities. Regarding Communist Russia, *Christian News* warned readers that Soviet officials falsely advertised that they had stopped persecuting religious believers; it insisted that responsible Americans knew differently. In 1967, the periodical stated that Russian authorities still "ruthlessly crushed" all attempts at self-determination. In 1968, the Soviet Union provided more evidence to the journal of its true intent when it and eastern bloc allies invaded Czechoslovakia because the Czech government had begun to question hard-line communism and implemented certain steps toward more freedoms for its citizens. For example, the Czech government loosened restrictions on religious publishing and services. When the Soviet military cracked down on these initiatives, the *Christian News* called the invasion a "rape." *Jesus to the Communist World* was even more adamant throughout the decade in its stance against the Soviet Union. It claimed that the leader of the Russian Orthodox Church instructed his bishops to "follow in all church-matters exactly the demands of the Atheistic government" and that Russians who persisted with their belief in Jesus Christ found themselves placed in insane asylums. The journal also outlined the horrors of military raids without documenting the reports' validity: "A Christian lady . . . *was raped by the Communists, mistreated and thrown down in the end from an attic. . . .* At a raid on the monastery of Pochaev, *girls were raped*, money taken away, and people beaten." Finally, the periodical advised Christians not to buy lumber exported from the Soviet Union because "pieces of wood from Siberia have been found on which prisoners had written with their own blood, 'Don't buy this. It has been prepared for export through the sacrifice of our lives.'" Using such accusations, these ultra-conservative Lutheran journals declared that any leniency toward the Soviet Union ignored the plight of innocent Christians.[14]

But accusations against the Soviet Union during the Cold War were not exclusive to ultra-conservatives, even well into the 1960s. Almost universally, Americans and their Christian institutions decried Soviet oppression and called for a campaign to promote religious freedom in that country. A group of conservative members from the Lutheran Church in America, the mainline denomination within Lutheranism at the time, also passionately rebuked the Soviet Union. The LCA demonstrates the fact that many mainline denominations were led by pastors much more liberal than their constituencies. For example, G. Elson Ruff, the editor of the LCA's *Lutheran* magazine, consistently took more moderate stances on theological issues, such as biblical criticism and the ordination of women, and political matters, such as presidential elections, than the average LCA member. This dichotomy extended to foreign policy when Ruff wanted the United States to soften its harsh criticism of the Soviet Union in 1968. This outraged some conservative LCA members. Unfortunately for Ruff, the issue arrived in most people's homes the day after Soviet troops invaded Czechoslovakia. Conservative LCA people replied that the latest Soviet actions proved that the Communists maintained their sinister goals and demanded that church leaders and the U.S. government continue to fight the "diabolical" USSR. The same attitude persisted for conservative LCA members well into the 1970s, when they accused people who had relaxed their stance against the USSR of wearing "blinders of immense proportion." Another reader questioned *Lutheran* editors about Soviet intentions by asking, "Queer, isn't it, how the USSR is depriving its citizens of consumer goods and well deserved comforts in order to outdo the USA in nuclear headed missiles and other sophisticated weapons?"[15]

The ALC and LCMS leaderships and laity also disagreed over how much to advocate U.S. cooperation with the Soviet Union, even though they both deplored its religious oppression. The ALC, which was more theologically conservative than the LCA but elected moderate to liberal leaders, debated the issue in similar ways to its mainline counterpart. The LCMS maintained a more consistently conservative point of view among its leadership and laity, which was reflected in their Cold War opinions. Yet both denominations housed individuals who denounced the Soviet Union throughout the decade. As late as 1974, an ALC constituent wrote to President David W. Preus to explain the truth behind Soviet intentions: "It requires only a rudimental knowledge of recent Soviet history to recognize that such persecutions continue as a staple of Soviet domestic policy." LCMS leaders agreed. As tension between the United States and Soviet Union eased in the late 1960s, one LCMS pastor lamented the opening of more cooperative relations, stating that "since the Russian premier received the welcome-mat for his visit to the United States some years ago, the Moscow murder machine has pretty well been forgotten." Despite these conservative opinions, leaders within the ALC disagreed and hoped that better relations with the Soviet Union could ease world tensions. As ALC President Frederik A. Schiotz explained in 1970, "I'm afraid . . . that we have not always dealt with Communists as people." Schiotz generally held moderate foreign policy opinions and recognized the dictatorial posturing of the Soviet Union; yet this statement demonstrates a realistic approach to the USSR. The pastor and ALC president wondered if a continued hard-line stance against communism really aided the United States or simply exacerbated tensions.[16]

But such moderate stances regarding the Soviet Union stemmed more from concern about the continued arms race and international political tension than from sympathy for the Russian government. Examples from the editors of the *Lutheran* suggest that these moderate LCA leaders sought to ease tensions with the Soviet Union based on the actions of its government and the possibility of reaching more people with the Christian message. G. Elson Ruff stated as early as 1965 that "the Russians now have what you might call 'matured communism,' which is more concerned with keeping what it has" than with expanding. He continued by saying that "I am convinced that we can't settle the Communist problem by military measures alone." His successor, Albert P. Stauderman, asserted in 1974 that "there has been an opening in the Iron Curtain" that he hoped would eventually prove "extremely valuable in strengthening Christian witness in an Atheistic country." Although both men continued to suspect the Soviet government and remained steadfast in their opposition to communism, they also realized the possible advantages of an open dialogue with Russian leaders that might lead toward peace and further ease Cold War posturing that often threatened a global war.[17]

In addition, ALC and LCA leaders believed that cooperating with the Soviet government protected Christians inside Soviet borders. These church officials regularly received confidential reports from credible sources within the Lutheran World Federation and World Council of Churches about the plight of Christians inside the Soviet Union. Rather than intensifying their Cold War passions, however, these leaders hoped that good relations between the Cold War rival governments would open the door toward helping these victimized people. They especially held this opinion after Richard Nixon's famous trip to the Soviet Union, which had fostered better relations between the nations. ALC President Preus explained in 1974 that "heavy criticism of Soviet governmental practices only leads to further problems for our Christian brothers and sisters in those nations" because it alienates them from the outside world. *Lutheran* editor Albert P. Stauderman admonished a reader in 1975 who complained after Soviet church officials visited the United States without denouncing the Communist government. These Russian church leaders came at the request of the National Council of Churches, which toured them throughout the country in order to better educate Americans about the truth of continued religious belief within the Soviet Union. Stauderman asserted that "these visitors are Christians who are confessing their faith under extremely adverse circumstances and who require our support and our prayers." As LCA President Robert J. Marshall later rationalized, "If I become aligned with that cause [extreme anti-Soviet rhetoric] I stand in danger of weakening my influence for greater freedom for Lutherans in the Soviet Union." These men cautioned that further angering the Soviet Union only injured innocent people trapped within its borders; they advocated allying with the Communists but still portrayed the USSR as an oppressive state.[18]

Because even moderate oratory about Soviet communism understood how it oppressed Christians and other citizens, Lutherans disagreed only slightly in their views of the USSR between 1964 and 1975. They unanimously decried the government's oppressive tactics, lamented the persecution of Christians, praised any sign of continued religious faith, and characterized the Soviet Union as a harmful nation that Christians had to combat. The only signs of discord occurred when they speculated on the degree of good that came from the easing of U.S.-Soviet relations. Some church officials began to see potential in an alliance while many of their colleagues, and most of the Lutheran laity, disagreed.

LUTHERANS ON SOVIET SATELLITE NATIONS

U.S. citizens became even more vocal against the Soviet Union when they discussed the satellite nations that it held in its orbit, generally against the will of the citizens of those nations. And, as Christians had with the Soviet Union, they took special umbrage at the closing of churches in these lands and the arrest of church officials. American Lutherans were almost totally united in seeing these countries as proof that Soviet communism was an evil force enveloping the world. Although subtle differences over how to address relations with the Soviet Union also crept into Lutheran views of the Communist governments' control over these nations, they occurred much less frequently. This also strengthened the Lutheran argument that this was more than a political or economic battle: it was also a war to protect Christianity.

Some members of the Lutheran Church in America maintained a hard-line stance against anything Communist when they wrote letters to the editor of the *Lutheran* regarding the Soviet Union's world sphere of influence. The following examples outline the general argument against the Soviet Union that conservatives made from 1964 to 1975. They reminded people that the Soviets still sought to eliminate religion regardless of "whether it is in East Germany or Viet Nam, Russia or China" and asserted that "a look at a map of the world and events since World War II are sufficient evidence" to prove "Lenin's plan for communist encirclement of the world." The number of Communist nations demonstrated to them that communism was slowly spreading across the globe and threatening freedom. The revelation "that Communism has conquered more people in the last 25 years than we, as Christians, have converted since Christ was among us on earth" further supported their cause and transformed the Cold War into a religious crusade.[19]

The Lutheran Church–Missouri Synod, a theologically and politically conservative denomination even before the controversy over biblical criticism that split it apart by the mid 1970s, concurred with fears about Soviet expansionism. For example, many constituents pleaded with the LCMS to do more to help Christians behind the Iron Curtain who were being tortured. LCMS leaders joined this conservative chorus when President J. A. O. Preus, elected when conservative theological members took control of the denomination in 1969, stated, "We certainly do believe that there are tortured Christians in Communist countries. I certainly also share your concerns that Communism does not spread throughout the world." LCMS officials and members alike discussed the fate of the satellite nations by assailing the Soviet Union as wicked and calling for aid to Christians trapped behind enemy lines.[20]

Liberal to moderate Lutherans from other denominations disagreed with these pronouncements only in intensity. G. Elson Ruff maintained "that the situation in eastern Europe under communism is extremely difficult and dangerous." But he also stated that on some level "conditions in [Communist nations] are much better now than 10 years ago." Ruff joined his conservative colleagues in condemning Communist domination but saw some hope for change. And at the 1966 American Lutheran Church convention, delegates voted to censure Soviet expansion when they resolved that the United States needed to remember its "special role" in world politics because "it appears to us that the communistic governments of Russia and China prefer captive or satellite nations dependent on them rather than genuinely independent nations."[21]

Lutherans of all stripes took the same stance when they deliberated about Czechoslovakia, especially after it provided them a clear example of Soviet tyranny in the 1968 invasion. One LCA member asserted in 1964 that "*the only peace they [Communists] know is*, *piece* of Poland, *piece* of Czechoslovakia. . . . Why are we *not concerned about the freedom* of these people in slavery of Communist Russia?" A Lutheran immigrant from a satellite nation chastised Communist governments and Americans who sought cooperation with them by saying, "I guess it is hard for someone who has lived all his life in a democracy to understand communist tactics. I have lived under communist rule and still have relatives who must live there and I know how little freedom they have." Similar sentiments came from a man whose 1972 confrontation with the Communist police in Czechoslovakia during a visit there shaped his hard-line opinion. Although they took nothing from him and released him unharmed, he stated that the Bibles he harbored in his bags enraged them and led them to threaten him. Sounding the familiar refrain of an evil might encircling the globe, Lutherans used Czechoslovakia as a prime example of communism's immoral aims.[22]

If the general plight of Czechoslovakia worried Lutherans, the 1968 Soviet and eastern bloc invasion infuriated them. G. Elson Ruff's *Lutheran* editorial about softening U.S. views of communism sparked an anti-Communist outrage. "Regarding the updating of opinions of Communists," one man asked, "Since Czechoslovakia, have *you* updated yours?" Another reader asked whether Ruff could reconcile his statements with "the events of the last few hours." She concluded, "Poor, poor Czechoslovakia."[23] The lines between conservative and moderate/liberal Lutherans and denominational disagreements continued to blur throughout the Czechoslovakian invasion. The only difference surfaced because liberal and moderate Lutherans wanted to protect Christians inside Communist borders from harassment. They feared that if they openly condemned communism the Communists would intensify anti-Christian subjugation: "For security reasons, we can never be careful enough in protecting our friends behind the Iron Curtain." An American representative to the Lutheran World Federation worried about the safety of Christians inside Czechoslovakia after the Soviet Union took control. Czech pastors had written a letter of protest about Soviet domination of their country to the World Council of Churches. The LWF official suggested, "The less we applaud what's happening over there, the better it will be for our friends!" He meant that publicly applauding the resistance efforts might bring more wrath from Communist officials than would silently praying for their success. Importantly, moderates' resistance to hard-line denunciations of the Communists in Czechoslovakia did not mean they were less worried about Communist tyranny: "The aggressions of the Communists in Cuba, Czechoslovakia, China and elsewhere clearly indicate that although world communism is not as monolithic as it once was, it seems still striving for world domination through the use of armed forces such as intercontinental rockets armed by atomic bombs." Lutherans were clearly unified on despising the Communist invasion of Czechoslovakia. But, although moderate leaders disdained Soviet aggression, they did so quietly in order to avoid a Communist crackdown on their lines of communication with Christians inside this satellite nation; though they varied in what tactics to support, they recognized the religious wars taking place within the larger Cold War.[24]

This same kind of opposition was evident throughout American Lutheranism in rhetoric about the Baltic nations of Estonia, Latvia, and Lithuania. The USSR had taken advantage of the turmoil wrought by the German invasion during World War II to invade and take control of these nations against their will. It did so in order to protect its western border from future attacks and because it feared that the United States and its allies would seek to control these nations to weaken the Communist government. Regardless of motive, Americans understood that the citizens of these nations were captives of a dictatorial government in which they had no standing. Lutherans had special knowledge from inside these countries because of previously thriving Lutheran churches that had slowly lost membership and almost died because of Communist policies against religion. By the period 1964 to 1975, U.S. Lutherans derided the Soviet government's presence in these regions, which they knew had resulted in a severe decline in the number of Lutheran worshippers and in the closing of many

Lutheran churches. For example, *Lutheran Forum*, which was not affiliated with any denomination and otherwise held moderate political points of view, questioned the 1968 resignation of the Estonian Lutheran archbishop, Jaan Kiivit, respected by Lutheran World Federation leaders for his service to the church. After the Soviets suddenly announced that he was sick, Lutherans speculated that the Soviets really created this story in order to install someone they could better manipulate. Even more suspicion surrounded the 1970s burning of churches in Latvia. The Latvian Lutheran Church Archbishop, Janis Matulis, privately reported at an LWF assembly that arsonists had destroyed a few churches in Latvia. Authorities never apprehended the culprits, which led LWF leaders to wonder what role Soviet officials had played in this catastrophe. They suspected that anti-Christian sentiment either inspired the arsonists or, even worse, that Soviet agents set the fires to reduce the number of churches in the region. Lutherans clearly banded together in mourning Soviet communism's negative effect on Lutheranism in the Baltic nations.[25]

Despite this lamenting, American Lutherans mocked the Soviet failure to entirely eliminate Baltic Lutheranism even as they simultaneously described the difficulties facing the Lutheran church. After Estonian Archbishop Kiivit's resignation, reports about his successor's installation in the six-hundred-year-old Tallin Cathedral proved that Lutheranism survived and needed leadership. Although Lutheran leaders from around the world were suspicious that Soviet officials had forced Kiivit's resignation, they applauded the new archbishop, Alfred Tooming, for supporting Christianity by accepting the strenuous position of leading a Christian church inside Soviet borders. After meeting Tooming they apparently concluded that he had the church's best interest in mind and was not a Soviet puppet. By 1971, Tooming happily reported that 22 percent of the Estonian population still belonged to the three hundred thousand member Lutheran church despite the fact that the Soviets only allowed parents to teach youth about God at home. A 1972 report indicated that "the churches in the former Baltic lands where Lutheranism is still a major religious force are faring a little better, but are suffering from attrition and regulation." In short, Lutherans applauded people such as "the pastors of [the Estonian Lutheran Church], most of whom have had to spend some time in concentration camps in Siberia, particularly in the Stalinist period," because they "continue day in and day out to try to keep the Gospel alive among the people."[26]

Yet not all Lutherans adopted the same tone. As on other issues, ultra-conservatives used harsher language when they discussed the Baltic situation. An examination of *Christian News* and *Jesus to the Communist World* again demonstrates this point. *Christian News* outlined the oppression suffered by Latvian Lutherans, reporting on a Latvian family whose "three children were placed in a boarding school because the parents were said to be 'spoiling the children's souls by indoctrinating them with religious superstitions.'" Into the 1970s, *Christian News* warned that "religious life in Latvia is gravely imperiled by an atheistic communist regime." *Jesus to the Communist World* also responded to reports on the fate of religion in the Baltic region: "Christianity in Lithuania and in other parts of the Communist camp has survived and will triumph. As *to murderous and poisonous Communism, we say, by our authority as ministers of God, 'PERISH' and perish it will*, as Nazism has perished."[27]

But not only far-right Lutherans believed in condemning the treatment of Lutherans in the Baltic states. In response to a Lithuanian refugee's 1970 tale of fleeing the Communists, LCMS President J. A. O. Preus responded, "I share your dismay and horror at what has happened to your family as a result of Communist invasion of your native land." The man had written to Preus about his 1939 experience when "the red devil took over my country, Lithuania, and in a few days killed, arrested and sent to Siberia eighty thousand people"; they also murdered his father, mother, and oldest sister. He next quoted a recent letter from his cousin: "Red devil made us slaves and dumb." One LCA member concurred with this assessment when he asked the *Lutheran* editor, "If you really want . . . a Lutheran cause, why don't you explore the slavery of thousands of Lutherans in East Germany, Estonia, and the occupied areas of Finland?"[28]

Despite being more liberally inclined regarding theology, politics, and foreign policy, even the leadership of the Lutheran World Federation and Lutheran Church in America seldom differed from their conservative counterparts regarding the Baltic states; examples of Soviet restrictions proved to them the Soviet efforts against Christianity. For example, the Soviets blocked a 1969 Lutheran World Federation delegation from visiting Lutherans in Baltic regions, where they had attended the installation of the new Lutheran archbishop. The USSR claimed that Lithuanian "congregations are in an area not open to visitors" and blocked their going to Estonia because Archbishop Tooming had a "serious illness." This gave the generally left-leaning LWF members reason to question the Soviet government's true reasons for forbidding their visit. A 1971 article by a Lithuanian reiterated this point when it lamented that "LWF representatives haven't up to now paid a visit to [the Lithuanian Lutheran] Church" because Soviet officials prohibited them from traveling in Lithuania. The same circumstances prevailed in 1974, when LCA President Robert J. Marshall visited the Soviet Union. Marshall enjoyed meeting Archbishop Tooming and appreciated his positive attitude in the face of adversity but also detailed the difficulty of educating future pastors inside the USSR because the government refused to allow the operation of seminaries.

These instances in which moderate Lutheran leaders confronted Soviet suppression of religion intensified their dislike for the Communist government, aligned them with conservatives, and solidified the notion that the Cold War was a battle to preserve Christianity.[29]

Nonetheless, these moderate to liberal leaders of national and international Lutheran bodies at times were less resolute in their condemnations due to their desire not to expose associates in the Baltic countries to Communist persecution. As one official warned LCA President Franklin Clark Fry in 1964, "Any sign of an *organized* support to the pastors may prove very hazardous to them." They thus operated a pastors' relief program "without any publicity and no public campaign." Ten years later "the Lutheran World Federation continue[d] in this concern, on the basis of well thought out and sober judgements, through carefully negotiated and delicately maintained channels of communication, and with deep love and concern for those who are less than free." These examples demonstrate why liberal to moderate Lutherans remained silent at times despite their dislike of the Soviet Union and made clear that only differences in tactics separated them from conservatives regarding Baltic Christians' persecution.[30]

Although a small gap existed between conservative and liberal/moderate Lutherans when they discussed the Soviet satellite nations, this distinction proves illusory when compared to the actual emotions that drove each side. Lutherans, regardless of education, leadership position, denomination, or political affiliation, deplored the plight of Christians inside Soviet-dominated regions. This paralleled their disgust with Soviet communism in general. Between 1964 and 1975, Lutherans maintained Cold War rhetoric when they looked at the Soviet Union's empire; but the other Communist giant received similar wrath, and so the repugnance Lutherans displayed toward Soviet Communists provided an example of how to treat any Communist nation attempting to vanquish Christianity.

LUTHERAN ALARM TOWARD RED CHINA

From 1964 to 1975, Lutherans viewed Red China the same way that they did the Soviet Union. The churches in America had maintained hostility toward the PRC ever since the expulsion of their missionaries in 1949 and the persistent news coming out of China about the suppression of religious belief and condemnation of Chinese Christians. Lutherans agreed with the U.S. Christian community about this anti-PRC rhetoric. Although differences once again existed between conservative, moderate, and liberal opinions, Lutheran leaders and the laity ultimately united in condemning Chinese communism as a force no less dangerous than its Soviet counterpart. And the confrontation with China was also political *and* religious in nature. Further paralleling the Soviet situation, proof that the Chinese Communists sought to eliminate organized religion intensified Lutheran misgivings about its government. From the beginning, the Communist government had made a concerted effort to eradicate Christian belief; the PRC first expelled all foreign missionaries and then forced Protestant denominations to merge and took control of selecting Catholic bishops. This Chinese policy of harassing religious institutions and championing atheistic principles persisted from 1964 to 1975 even though few openly Christian people remained inside Red China because of threats to their freedom and even their lives.[31]

To that end, Lutherans protested that China's Communist government oppressed its citizens. Even the Wisconsin Evangelical Lutheran Synod (WELS), a theologically conservative Lutheran body of just over 350,000 people that generally avoided making political or diplomatic statements as a church body, commented on the plight of Christians in China. In 1965, a WELS convention resolution described how Chinese refugees sent "thousands of food packages everyday back to Red China to save their relatives from starvation" because the Communist economy so badly failed to even feed people. They got this information from WELS missionaries serving in Hong Kong and Taiwan who knew the people who sent this food back. That same year, a moderate counterpart from the LCA, *Lutheran* editor G. Elson Ruff, warned against trusting Red China because "it is still in its violently aggressive stage." And two years later, another Lutheran official blasted the "bellicosity of the Red regime." The LCA, ALC, and LCMS all supported in various forms missionary and relief efforts for Chinese refugees in Hong Kong and Taiwan, which will be described later in a separate section. However, these endeavors relate to Red China because American Lutherans came into contact with refugees who had fled the Chinese mainland because of Communist tyranny. To that end, Lutherans across the political spectrum accused the Chinese government of terrorizing humanity when those who fled from the mainland relayed how "they had seen fellow villagers killed trying to escape." A converted Lutheran who fled from China also described to LCMS missionaries Red China's cruelty. After this minister stole away from his Chinese captors, he declared that "the Communists persecuted me running to Taiwan."[32]

In another parallel to their depiction of the Soviet empire, Lutherans particularly decried the Chinese oppression of Christianity. In 1965, *World Encounter*, the publication of the LCA's Board for World Mission, bemoaned, "Many [Chinese] Christians no longer participate in public worship nor have any connection with the churches" because of state prohibitions. A small conservative Lutheran journal from the Evangelical Lutheran Synod continued this thinking a couple of years later. The *Lutheran Sentinel* reported the statement of a Christian refugee who escaped from China in 1971 by swimming to Hong Kong: "If they [Communist officials] had found a Bible, it would have been destroyed and we would have been punished." As with the Soviet Union, evidence from tourists to China confirmed these dire observations. A delegation from the Lutheran Church in America reported that during "four weeks in China they met no Christians" and "saw no functioning churches." Even after President Nixon opened diplomatic relations with Red China in the early 1970s, which included his historic 1972 visit to Beijing, Lutherans derided the Chinese government for hindering religious practices: "The Spiritual vacuum created by communism in China was not reported by the press during the president's eight-day stay, but it was apparent to anyone who watched the TV coverage of life in China's communes. Not only was it apparent, it was tragic." Red China's demolition of Christian missions led Lutherans to a unified denunciation of its atheistic goals and solidified the notion that the Cold War was in part a religious crusade.[33]

The 1960s Cultural Revolution also fueled Lutheran accusations that Red China sought to destroy Christianity. Inspired by Mao Zedong and primarily implemented by Chinese young adults who organized a "Red Guard," the Cultural Revolution was a crusade against intellectuals, religious believers, and anyone else who questioned strict Communist doctrines as expressed by Mao. In response to criticism of the poor economy and because of Mao's waning influence, Mao and his supporters used this Cultural Revolution to divert attention from the problems they created and to vanquish their opposition. Characterized by a violence against institutions and people whom these young individuals confronted, the movement imprisoned religious leaders, burned Bibles, and forcibly closed the few churches that remained in China. Lutherans across the board portrayed the Red Guard's treatment of Christians as tyrannical: "Christians in China are being humiliated by the Red Guards and in some instances have had their heads shaved, and have been compelled to sit in city street gutters." Furthermore, the "storm troopers" ravished church buildings, and "Catholic and Protestant churches, desecrated by the Marauding Red Guard, were closed." Even articles that attempted to depict China objectively portrayed the nation and its youth as militaristic during the Cultural Revolution. For example, *World Encounter* explained that "a visible, functioning church does not exist in China today."[34]

Yet in the midst of the admonishment of the Communist government, American Lutherans, as they did with the Soviet Union, celebrated proof that Christianity survived inside Red China. *Faith and Fellowship*, the periodical for the small, conservative Church of the Lutheran Brethren, described a story of faith in the midst of misery. It reported how one family "celebrated

Christmas by covering windows with winter underwear to deaden the noise, climbing into a bed and covering themselves and their radio with blankets in order to sing along with Christmas carols broadcast from Hong Kong." Lutheran World Federation circulated material that also illustrated Christianity's survival. In 1973, LWF interviewed Chinese who had fled Red China and reported that, despite the potential for punishment, a high number of Chinese citizens listened to illegal radio broadcasts beamed into China by various religious groups. They further noted that most of the interviewees "believed that the Christians in China still practiced some kind of worship within the family circle" even though they "never do it in front of friends and neighbors."[35]

Further paralleling their treatment of the Soviet Union, Lutherans focused their efforts to assist oppressed Christians by broadcasting religious material into China. LCMS Pastor Eugene R. Bertermann's work with the Far East Broadcasting Company provided one outlet for such missions. By March 1968, FEBC had already received twenty-five letters that year from Chinese people who listened to its broadcasts, applied biblical tales to their lives, and wanted "to get out of Egypt" or hoped "to cross the Red Sea." Lutheran broadcasting also responded to the calls for radio programming to China. An LWF report explained that, because China's one-fourth of the world's population had "an almost frightening potential for good or evil," the Radio Voice of the Gospel had to try to convert it to Christianity. The WELS also broadcast into China even though "only God today knows how many people living in Red China have been strengthened to remain loyal in the face of persecution." Because Lutheran broadcasters received letters and met refugees that testified to the effectiveness of these transmissions in converting people, Lutherans fought hard to maintain radio traffic into Mainland China. They saw this as one way to wage war against the PRC.[36]

Yet condemnations of the People's Republic of China came from laypeople, too. Non-published letters to the editor of the *Lutheran* demonstrate how deeply they despised Communist China. One reader explained to G. Elson Ruff that "both Russia and China have a common denominator—Communism," and to forget this would be "disastrous." Another LCA member stated that "Russian and Chinese Communism differ only in the tactics of propagation; sociological versus bellicose means." She concluded with a theological argument that reminded Ruff that "this is a war of Christian against evil in all respects." These Lutheran Americans insisted that Mao Zedong's brand of communism represented a force just as evil as that of the Soviet Union and warned against any cooperation with it. While they seldom applied just war language to their condemnation of the PRC, they clearly articulated religious and political reasons for combating this Communist state.[37]

ALC laypeople also attacked Red China by writing to their church president about the Beijing government. ALC President Frederik A. Schiotz and other Lutheran officials had called beginning in the 1960s for the admittance of the People's Republic of China into the United Nations. The PRC had been kept out of the UN by the United States since the Communist takeover on the specious grounds that it was not a legitimate government. Instead, China was represented by the Chinese Nationalists from Taiwan who the United States had unsuccessfully supported during the Chinese Revolution. After two decades of this charade, and despite misgivings about the Communists, Schiotz and other Lutheran officials felt that it did more harm than good to exclude the world's largest country from the UN. This did not sit well, however, with some ALC constituents. For example, Schiotz received a letter that simply asked, "How can we as Christians give support to countries who are against Christ?" Another constituent disliked a *Teen Ways* article about China that said nothing about the "inhumane atrocities committed against the people by the Communists." She stated that "this article would lead one to believe that life in China is ideal and that the people are very happy about it."[38]

LCA President Robert J. Marshall received mail from constituents that sounded the same refrain because he took similar positions as Schiotz toward China. These Lutherans claimed that the Chinese could not defend themselves from Mao Zedong's tyrannical government and asserted that "this so called 'Government' is not by any stretch of the imagination a legal government of these 700,000,000 people, but is just a group of criminals which has seized power over these unfortunate people."[39]

Yet these characterizations of Red China paled in comparison to the rhetoric used by the far-right Lutheran journals. Similar to their depiction of the Soviet Union, they viewed Chinese Communists as sadistically cruel; more than any other Lutherans, they combined politics and theology in their argument against the PRC. The *Christian News* declared that the "only remaining witnesses to Christianity in China are believed to be the 'handful' of Chinese clergy and laymen still languishing in Red prisons" because the Communists allegedly incarcerated *all* Christians. *Jesus to the Communist World* accused the PRC of fiendish methods of torture: "*Christians are put to stand at attention for two hours before the picture of Mao Zedong, having three bricks on each shoulder. Every twenty minutes a brick is added. In the end they have to carry 18 bricks. If their knees bend for a moment, the torture begins again. Other Christians have their heads shaved. On the bald head hot ashes are put, while the victim stands at attention before the idol Mao.*" The periodical went to great lengths to illustrate the fierceness of Chinese communism. For example, an article described how "the Communists force young women to take off their clothes and beat their breasts with horse tails." These conservative journals further emphasized Chinese Communist tortures as extremely demented; to them, the Cold War was not merely a battle of ideologies but an ethical obligation to protect innocent people.[40]

In contrast, moderate Lutheran officials from the ALC, LCA, and LCMS avoided such volatile descriptions because they believed that the potential for mission efforts outweighed the Communist capacity for evil if Lutherans relaxed their criticisms. The Lutheran Council U.S.A. (LCUSA) secretary for the Far East provides such an example. The LCA, ALC, and LCMS belonged to LCUSA, an agency designed to coordinate Lutheran relief and lobbying efforts upon which the three bodies could agree. LCUSA's combined voice gave then greater leverage in publicity and politics because of better economic cooperation and greater numbers of constituents. The Far East Secretary explained about China that he agreed with many reproofs against China but also wanted to be "alert to any and every opportunity which the Lord provides to share the love of God in Christ Jesus with those living in that great land." Others recognized that "the Red Chinese government has been anything but 'nice,'" and yet wondered, "What is our obligation as Christians to the 700 million people living under this government?" Thus, these Lutheran leaders decided that "all we can do now for the church in Red China is to pray, to preach through radio broadcasts, and to believe that God will not forsake the 700,000,000 people in China." Yet they still hoped they could implement steps to convert the Chinese to Christianity and prepared "for that day" by training "those [Chinese Lutherans] who have held to their faith in Christ during these many trying years."[41] Furthermore, these Lutheran pastors and administrators wondered if this potential to work with the Chinese might lead the Communist government to act less sternly. In 1964, one person simply felt that "everything depends on what China will achieve in world affairs within the next decade, and what can be done to determine whether this role will be for peace or war." By 1968, many believed that the United States could negotiate with the Chinese to ease Cold War hostilities. For example, the New England Synod urged the LCA leadership to lobby the U.S. government to seek ways to get the PRC into test ban treaty negotiations. Further proof of this possibility rested with Nixon's visit to China. Albert P. Stauderman "considered Mr. Nixon's willingness to take a courageous step by visiting China a hopeful sign."[42]

The three largest denominations' periodicals also suspected the PRC but desired an easing of Cold War tensions by the late 1960s and early 1970s. In the LCA's *Lutheran*, a former missionary explained his excitement about seeing Christian believers during a 1971 visit to China and noted that he "never heard anyone in China attack Christianity." The writer concluded that this "was a . . . glimmer of hope." In the pages of the ALC's *Lutheran Standard*,

President Kent S. Knutson approved of Nixon's announcement in 1971 that he planned to visit China in 1972 because the clergyman felt that it offered the hope for peace. Knutson liked the possibility of again working with Chinese Christians when he said, "We are anxious to come in contact again with the Christian people in mainland China and want them to know that we have prayed for them during these years of separation and now are encouraged by the possibility of being together again." As Sino-American tensions eased further throughout the early 1970s, the editors noted that Christians in China needed support. The LCMS's *Lutheran Witness* editor called the Lutheran World Federation's Radio Voice of the Gospel that beamed into China a "leap forward" and reported that "the Chinese do listen to the broadcasts." The persistent faith of some Chinese led these moderate periodicals to soften their stance against Red China even while they continued to lament its form of government. It is crucial to note that theology guided their thinking just as much as it did conservative opinions; but where conservative theology called for protecting Christians with force, liberal to moderate theology asked for peaceful solutions that would lead to further mission opportunities.[43]

China represented another Communist country with which to contend between 1964 and 1975, and Lutherans viewed it much as they did the Soviet Union. They generally mistrusted its government and despised its treatment of Christianity. Differences existed but did not weaken their overall agreement that Communist China threatened the future of religion. Conservatives said that the barbarity of Chinese communism endangered Christians. In contrast, liberal/moderate rhetoric included the hope that the United States could persuade the Chinese away from expansionist style communism and rigid atheism. Regardless of these differences, Lutherans displayed a unanimous wariness about the People's Republic of China and warned against its Communist government.

CHINA'S COMMUNIST REACH

American Lutherans' views on Chinese communism again paralleled their discussion about the Soviet Union when they looked at how the People's Republic of China influenced other nations. Although China had fewer direct satellite nations than the Soviet Union, it did seek to control those around it and threatened their security with its military might. After the Communist takeover in 1949, the People's Republic of China had supported revolutionary activity throughout Asia as a means of ending western imperialism and expanding its influence over global communism. By the 1960s, the PRC added African and Latin American countries to its list of hoped-for Communist allies and revolutionaries. Hong Kong provides the best example for how the Lutheran churches viewed this situation. A number of Lutheran denominations had established missions on the island and thereby received reliable information from people who witnessed China's empirical aims. Although China did not control Hong Kong, which was a British protectorate throughout this period, the Communist mainland still affected the island because it coveted Hong Kong's economic power. China therefore worked covertly to promote communism in Hong Kong while the British resisted such efforts. The threat of an invasion hung in the air constantly, and thousands of refugees fled China for Hong Kong's safety, which led to deplorable living conditions due to overpopulation and extreme poverty. This poverty erupted into rioting in 1967 when pro-Communist factions tried to take control of the island. After a few tense months, Great Britain regained its firm hold. Nonetheless, the threat of war over Hong Kong remained. This tension and the massive population migration goaded Lutheran anti-Communist sentiments with more proof of how Communist governments treated Christians and their citizens in general; Hong Kong, too, was both a political and religious concern for Lutherans during the Cold War.[44]

From 1964 to 1975, Lutherans feared the danger China posed to their Hong Kong missions because it might invade the island. As delegates to the 1965 Wisconsin Evangelical Lutheran Synod convention warned, "You cannot be aware of the very real pressures of Communism" over Asian areas. *Lutheran Women*, the LCA women's journal, printed an excellent example of this fear:

> "At 1 o'clock one morning last spring," a missionary [from Hong Kong] told me, "I was awakened by a faint hup—2, 3, 4. 'The Communists have come,' I thought. 'They are here. It has happened.' I jumped out of bed and peered out of our apartment window. On the street, eight floors down, about 120 black-booted, steel-helmeted police were going through maneuvers in formation.
>
> "I turned on the radio immediately. The men were not Communist soldiers. They were policemen preparing to quell a riot several blocks away.
>
> "Until that night I had not realized how much the fear of a Communist take-over permeates the atmosphere. Until that night, I did not even know that I was afraid."

An LCMS mission later sounded similar fears, saying that "the one thing which unites it [Hong Kong] is the feeling of urgency—the necessity to outrun the shadow of the hovering Red Dragon." Indeed, by 1974 feelings had changed little because Lutherans feared that "with the snap of his fingers, the leader of the People's Republic of China could seize Hong Kong with no difficulty." Lutherans with one voice viewed Red China as a constant menace to Hong Kong and portrayed the PRC as a tiger waiting to pounce. And this diplomatic concern was fused with religious worry because it threatened the vibrant Lutheran mission efforts on the island.[45]

Lutherans thought that these fears had come to fruition in May 1967 when rioting broke out in Hong Kong over its deplorable economic and living conditions, especially for the thousands of refugees who had fled the mainland, and when the tensions between China and Great Britain threatened to erupt into warfare. Lutherans agonized that Red China would conquer Hong Kong even as the State Department assured Americans that "the Communist element in Hong Kong has been quite effectively isolated by the firm handling of the situation by the British Government." The apprehensions had eased by July, when the Lutheran Council U.S.A. Far East secretary reported that "rioting in Hong Kong during the last few days is on a smaller scale" than the initial outbreaks. But in 1968, Lutherans still worried that the riots had destabilized Hong Kong's economy. People suffered from unemployment "either from losing their jobs because their places of work had to close or for fear of incurring the wrath of the Communists who threatened people in certain occupations." Finally, the WELS inter-convention report stated that the "Communist-inspired uprising" revealed how "the devil uses many tricks and stratagems in his satanic effort to foil the saving purpose of the Gospel and to undermine the Kingdom of God." The WELS statement further proves that this diplomatic/political topic was fused with theological concerns. Not only was China despotic and a threat to Lutheran missions, but they also claimed that it was inspired by "the devil" himself.[46]

Lutherans' constant contact with fearful Chinese refugees in Hong Kong perpetuated their insistence that Red China represented a diabolical force. The sheer number of defectors indicated a problem with the PRC because "the never ending influx of refugees from the mainland of China has swamped clinics and hospitals" in Hong Kong. The American Lutheran Church's 1968 World Missions report explained that Chinese fugitives "knew at firsthand the fate of all religions under the Maoist regime." Other Lutherans described the letters they received from Chinese mainlanders who sought clothes and medical supplies because the government failed to provide them. Lutherans used their experiences in Hong Kong to further demonstrate Red China's oppression of its citizens.[47]

Examples from the Lutheran Church–Missouri Synod delineate how this unified view of Hong Kong spurred further abhorrence of Red China. The LCMS had a vibrant mission to Hong Kong, which included the founding of the now renowned Hong Kong International School in 1966. Thus, LCMS leaders and laypeople alike had first-hand evidence of PRC tactics when *Lutheran Women's Quarterly* called communism "the tyrant that spelled the finish of our work in China." But the article continued that China's tyranny "was indirectly responsible for the Lutheran Church's new ministries in Hong Kong." China's despotism offered the LCMS a sign of hope: although the people fled China in fear, they arrived in Hong Kong needing help and were therefore receptive to the Christian message. Hong Kong represented a center of both Communist and anti-Communist influences in which the "situation in this colony makes it difficult for us to know when or how the freedom to evangelize may be stopped." In short, such images and language demonstrate that Lutherans, too, saw themselves as fighting the Cold War through their religious efforts in Hong Kong, once again blurring the lines between theology and politics.[48]

China's hovering presence in Hong Kong unified Lutherans who otherwise had slight differences regarding Chinese communism. The Lutheran belief that Communist China might take over Hong Kong proved to them that Communists wanted to expand their global influence. Furthermore, news from inside Hong Kong and the Chinese refugee stories confirmed what Lutherans had felt for years: communism impoverished people physically and spiritually. Most importantly for the churches, Hong Kong provided ample evidence that Christianity was threatened by PRC policies. Hong Kong allied Lutherans in their condemnation of the People's Republic of China and made them feel that a demonic monster really did control Chinese communism.

CONCLUSION

Lutheran views of the two Communist giants between 1964 and 1975 illustrate how they supported Cold War antagonisms against the USSR and the PRC. Lutherans unanimously castigated the Soviet Union and China for their dictatorial governments and oppression of religious belief. They felt that U.S. efforts to fight the effects of communism on these countries warranted support. Although differences existed, they failed to weaken the combined Lutheran wish for the Communist nations' collapse. Communism especially proved hazardous for nations and areas that lay near Communist borders, as the Soviet satellite countries and Hong Kong proved to Lutherans all too well. In many instances, Lutheran fears of the Soviet Union and China were justified by the gathered evidence of torture and suppression. To most, the Cold War was not simply an economic or political battle but a religious war. Lutherans seldom articulated a theological justification for this position because it seemed obvious to them: innocent people needed their help and Christians could not openly worship. The Communist campaign to eradicate religion within these countries presented more than a mere ideological or political battle to American Lutherans because it threatened Christianity, including

Lutheran churches and missionary efforts. This concern for religion prompted Lutherans to use the language of religious warfare and sent them on a Cold War crusade against communism. American Lutherans, who had a long history of religious and political disagreements, banded together during this decade in their concern for religion and people trapped inside Communist borders. And this anti-Communist philosophy persisted throughout the 1964 to 1975 period even as other circumstances accentuated differences within Lutheranism and pitted Lutheran against Lutheran.

NOTES

1. David Brown to Theodore B. Hax, 12 November 1964, Evangelical Lutheran Church in America Archives, Chicago, Illinois (hereafter ELCA), Frederik A. Schiotz Papers, box 25, "Youth Activity-David Brown"; Daniel C. Ost to G. Elson Ruff, 30 August 1968, ELCA, G. Elson Ruff Papers, box 21, "O"; Richard Wurmbrand, *Tortured for Christ* (Bartlesville, OK: Living Sacrifice Book Company, 1998).

2. Although American Christian hatred of the Soviet Union went to extremes, subsequent scholarship justifies some of this fear by revealing that the Soviet Union hindered Christian practices well into the 1960s and 1970s. This historical record mirrors the findings of American Lutherans in the 1960s, who stated that Soviet persecutions continued but that Russian citizens resisted. Dimitry Pospielovsky, *The Russian Church under the Soviet Regime, 1917–1982*, 2 vols. (Crestwood, NY: St. Vladimer's Seminary Press, 1984); Owen Chadwick, *The Christian Church in the Cold War* (New York: Penguin Books, 1992); Nathaniel Davis, *A Long Walk to Church: A Contemporary History of Russian Orthodoxy* (Boulder, CO: Westview Press, 1995); Dianne Kirby, ed., *Religion and the Cold War* (New York: Palgrave Macmillan, 2003).

3. Martin E. Marty, *Modern American Religion*, vol. 3, *Under God, Indivisible, 1941–1960* (Chicago: University of Chicago Press, 1996); Patrick Allitt, *Religion in America since 1945: A History* (New York: Columbia University Press, 2003). Theodore B. Hax, "Signs of the Times," *Evangelize* 20 (September 1964): 12–13; J. A. O. Preus to Betty Ann Haase, 14 October 1969, Concordia Historical Institute, St. Louis, Missouri (hereafter CHI), Executive Office, box 10, "Communism, 1962–1972"; J. A. O. Preus to Kathy Kruger, 23 June 1970, CHI, Executive Office, UPN box 82, "Wurmbrand, Reverend Richard"; Martin A. Karolis to Albert P. Stauderman, 22 October 1971, ELCA, Stauderman Papers, box 87, "K."

4. American Lutheran Church, 1968 Convention Minutes, 40, ELCA; Juhan Kangur to Albert P. Stauderman, 17 October 1971, ELCA, Stauderman Papers, box 87, "K."

5. Pospielovsky, *The Russian Church*; Chadwick, *The Christian Church in the Cold War*. Mrs. H. Winquist to G. Elson Ruff, September 1964, ELCA, G. Elson Ruff Papers, box 16, "Win"; John Daniel, "Address and Report of President," *Lutheran Beacon* 22 (October 1964): 147–49, 154; "Rocking the Boat," *Affirm* 2 (August 1972): 8.

6. Lutheran Church in America, 1966 Convention Minutes, 416, ELCA; James L. Barkenquast to R. H. Edwin Espy, 31 October 1964, ELCA, Franklin Clark Fry Papers, box 64; Lutheran Church in America, 1968 Convention Minutes, 404–6, ELCA.

7. Edward J. Amend to G. Elson Ruff, 29 October 1971, ELCA, Stauderman Papers, box 86, "A"; Evelyn Streng, "In the Shadow of the Kremlin," *Scope* 14 (October 1974): 24–26, 28.

8. Douglas C. Stange, "Church and People in Russian Lutheranism," *Lutheran Scholar* 27 (July 1970): 2–7; Ida M. Simon to Frank D. Starr, 26 June 1975, CHI, *Lutheran Witness* Letters,

box 3, "Se-Su"; "Plight of German Lutherans in USSR cited in Report," 21 July 1975, ELCA, LCUSA 16/6/6, Office of Communication and Interpretation, News Bureau, Country Topical Files, box 17, "USSR"; P. B. Prange, "'God in the Soviet Union Is Far from Dead,'" *Sola Scriptura* 3 (July/August 1972): 29–30.

9. Paul Peterson, "Russian Christian Press," *Faith and Fellowship* 37 (5 October 1970): 7–8; "Bibles Get Lutheran Solon into Trouble in Moscow," 20 January 1972, ELCA, LCUSA 16/6/6, Office of Communication and Interpretation, News Bureau, Country Topical Files, box 17, "USSR."

10. Ethel E. Wallis, "The Truth About Russia?" *Lutheran Women's Quarterly* 30 (Summer 1972): 13–15; Kenneth Bagnell, "Conversations with Soviet Youth," *Arena* 73 (March 1965): 18–21; Harold E. Wicke, "Briefs by the Editor," *Northwestern Lutheran* 60 (20 May 1973): 150.

11. Steve Myntti to Albert P. Stauderman, 27 October 1971, ELCA, Stauderman Papers, box 87, "M"; G. Smith to Albert P. Stauderman, 23 July 1972, ELCA, Stauderman Papers, box 90, "Sj-Sz, 1972" (emphasis in original); Lutheran Church–Missouri Synod, 1975 Convention Minutes, 164, CHI.

12. "Secret Religious Printing Plant Uncovered in Moscow," *Lutheran Laymen* 36 (September 1965): 8; "Soviet Lutherans Maintain Religion Despite Persecution," 1 March 1974, ELCA, LCUSA 16/6/6, Office of Communication and Interpretation, News Bureau, Country Topical Files, box 17, "USSR."

13. Far East Broadcasting Company, Board of Directors Minutes, 20 November 1965, Billy Graham Center Archives, Chicago, Illinois (hereafter BGCA), Bertermann Papers, FEBC, box 1, "File 5"; Delmor J. Glock, "How the Lutheran Hour Works," *Advance* 13 (December 1966): 4–5.

14. "Church under Communist Persecution," *Lutheran News* 4 (27 June 1966): 6; "Day of Mourning for Victims of Communism," *Lutheran News* 5 (11 December 1967): 10; "'U.S. Girl Held in Moscow!!!'" *Christian News* 2 (20 January 1969): 4; James D. Bales, "Persecution of Religion in the USSR," *Christian News* 5 (18 September 1972): 5; Richard Wurmbrand, "Our Beloved Ones," *Jesus to the Communist World* (July 1968): 1–4; Wurmbrand, "Clergy Blesses Murderers," *Jesus to the Communist World* (November 1970): 1–4; "Raping of Christian Women," *Jesus to the Communist World* (December 1969): 1 (emphasis in original); Wurmbrand, "Unheard-of Tortures in Communist Prisons," *Jesus to the Communist World* (February 1972): 1–4.

15. Roberta A. Rupp to G. Elson Ruff, 22 August 1968, ELCA, G. Elson Ruff Papers, box 21, "Rig-Rz"; Charles Lindgren to Albert P. Stauderman, 28 October 1971, ELCA, Albert P. Stauderman Papers, box 87, "K"; Ruth H. Pool to Albert P. Stauderman, n.d., ELCA, Albert P. Stauderman Papers, box 95, "P 1974"; C. Bruce Wenger to Albert P. Stauderman, 3 February 1972, ELCA, Albert P. Stauderman Papers, box 90, "W, X, Y, Z 1972."

16. Charles F. Wente to David W. Preus, 5 December 1974, ELCA, David W. Preus Papers, box 24, "?"; H. C. Wendler, "Pastor Urges Prayers for Nation in Fight against Communist Aggression," *Lutheran Laymen* 39 (March 1968): 9; "Ministry to Communists Seen Hindered by Fears," 9 February 1970, ELCA, LCUSA 16/6/2, Office of Communication and Interpretation, News Bureau, General Topics Files, box 17, "?".

17. G. Elson Ruff to Clarence H. Hall, 30 June 1965, ELCA, G. Elson Ruff Papers, box 6, "Hal-Han"; Albert P. Stauderman to Ernestine James, 20 August 1974, ELCA, Stauderman Papers, box 94, "I-J 1974."

18. David W. Preus to Duane C. Nelson, 4 December 1974, ELCA, David W. Preus Papers, box 24–25, "?"; Albert P. Stauderman to June M. Porter, 20 February 1975, ELCA, Stauderman Papers, box 97, "N, O, P 1975"; Robert J. Marshall to John F. Steinbruck, 22 December 1976, ELCA, Robert J. Marshall Papers, box 1, "Assorted Correspondence."

19. Mrs. Glenn Miller to G. Elson Ruff, 7 May 1968, ELCA, G. Elson Ruff Papers, box 20, "Mi-Mz"; Harry S. Riley to Ruff, 20 January 1965, ELCA, G. Elson Ruff Papers, box 82, "Extremists 1965"; Clarence G. Nowak to Ruff, 6 January 1965, ELCA, G. Elson Ruff Papers, box 82, "Extremists 1965"; Ernest Clay to Ruff, January 1965, ELCA, G. Elson Ruff Papers, box 82, "Extremists 1965."

20. Ronald P. Wiederaenders to Philip Schmidt, 12 November 1969, CHI, Executive Office, UPN box 82, "Wurmbrand, Rev. Richard"; Judy Hasbargan to J. A. O. Preus, 4 September 1971, CHI, Executive Office, UPN box 62, "President-JAOP-Correspondence-1972"; J. A. O. Preus to Judy Hasbargan, 15 September 1971, CHI, Executive Office, box UPN 62, "President-JAOP-Correspondence-1972."

21. G. Elson Ruff to Mrs. William L. Berner, 22 March 1965, ELCA, G. Elson Ruff Papers, box 1, "Beo-Bet"; American Lutheran Church, 1966 Convention Minutes, 35, ELCA.

22. Mrs. J. J. Klik to G. Elson Ruff, December 1964, ELCA, G. Elson Ruff Papers, box 8, "Kl" (emphasis in original); Vera Kriisa to Albert P. Stauderman, 16 September 1968, ELCA, G. Elson Ruff Papers, box 9, "Kr"; Steve Meyer, "An Encounter with Communism," *Evangelize* 28 (August/September 1972): 6.

23. Donald H. Glass to G. Elson Ruff, 7 September 1968, ELCA, G. Elson Ruff Papers, box 5, "Gi"; Mary C. Erickson to G. Elson Ruff, 21 August 1968, ELCA, G. Elson Ruff Papers, box 18, "E."

24. Blahoslav Hruby, Confidential Report, 26 October 1966, ELCA, Franklin Clark Fry Papers, box 95, "?"; Paul C. Empie to Members of USA National Committee of LWF, 26 July 1968, ELCA, LWM 3/4, Lutheran World Ministries, General Secretary, Country Files, box 7, "Czechoslovakia, 1967–1970"; Frank P. Zeidler, "The Lord's Angry with All Nations," July 1971, ELCA, Division of Ministry to North America-Department to Church in Society, box 402.

25. "And in the USSR," *Lutheran Forum* 2 (January 1968): 13; All 1974 letters, ELCA, Lutheran World Ministries, LWM 3/4, General Secretary, Country Files, box 34, "Latvia, 1948–1977."

26. Picture, 25 June 1968, ELCA, National Lutheran Council, NLC 3/1/3, box 6, "Estonia, General"; "Worship Service Is Center of Estonian Religious Life," 2 September 1971, ELCA, LCUSA 16/6/6, Office of Communication and Interpretation, News Bureau, Country Topical Files, box 6, "Estonia"; Albert P. Stauderman to R. T. Davies, 31 January 1972, ELCA, Albert P. Stauderman Papers, box 88, "C-D 1972"; Carl H. Mau, Jr., to S. Eduard Lind, 17 September 1974, ELCA, Lutheran World Ministries, LWM 3/4, General Secretary, Country Files, box 14, "Estonia 1949–1978."

27. "Struggle against Religion in Latvia," *Christian News* 1 (12 August 1968): 5; "The Church in Latvia Today," *Christian News* 5 (18 December 1972): 5; "Persecution in Lithuania," *Jesus to the Communist World* (March 1970): 2 (emphasis in original).

28. J. A. O. Preus to Joseph Vaich, 15 December 1970, CHI, Executive Office, UPN box 62, "President—JAOP—Correspondence 1972"; Vaich to Preus, n.d., CHI, Executive Office, UPN box 62, "President—JAOP—Correspondence 1972."

29. "Two from LWF Assist in Latvian Ceremony," 29 September 1969, ELCA, LCUSA 16/6/6, Office of Communication and Interpretation, News Bureau, Country Topical Files, box 14, "Latvia"; James Kalvanas, "Lithuanian Lutherans' Apostolic Existence," *Lutheran Forum* 5 (November 1971): 8–9; Robert J. Marshall to Archbishop Konrad Veem, 10 October 1974, Robert J. Marshall Papers, box 1, "Misc."

30. Alfred J. Anderson to Franklin Clark Fry, 29 October 1964, ELCA, Franklin Clark Fry Papers, box 64, "?"; Rollin G. Shaffer to Uno A. Plank, 21 February 1966, ELCA, Lutheran World Ministries, LWM 3/4, General Secretary, Country Files, box 14, "Estonia 1949–1978";

Morris A. Sorenson, Jr., to Glen Saban, 18 March 1974, ELCA, American Lutheran Church, Division of World Missions, box 10, "Voice of the Martyrs."

31. John McManners, ed., *The Oxford History of Christianity* (New York: Oxford University Press, 1993), 532; Luo Zhufeng, ed., *Religion under Socialism in China* (Armonk, NY: M. E. Sharpe, 1991); John K. Fairbank and Edwin O. Reischauer, *China: Tradition and Transformation*, Revised ed. (Boston: Houghton Mifflin, 1989); Jasper Becker, *Hungry Ghosts: Mao's Secret Famine* (New York: Free Press, 1996); Janice Kerper Brauer, ed., *One Cup of Water: Five True Stories of Missionary Women in China* (St. Louis: International Lutheran Women's Missionary League, 1997); Charles Horner, "China's Christian Connections," in Elliott Abrams, ed., *The Influence of Faith: Religious Groups and U.S. Foreign Policy* (Lanham, MD: Rowman and Littlefield Publishers, 2001).

32. Wisconsin Evangelical Lutheran Synod, Convention Minutes, August 1965, 218, Wisconsin Evangelical Lutheran Synod Archives, Mequon, WI (hereafter WELS); G. Elson Ruff to Clarence H. Hall, 30 June 1965, ELCA, G. Elson Ruff Papers, box 6, "Hal-Hon"; Notes on Lutheran World Relief/Christian World Mission Related Meetings, 17 and 18 April 1967, CHI, Board for Missions, Supplement 18, box 3, "?"; "Escapees from China Mainland Receive Aid," 28 October 1968, ELCA, LCUSA 16/6/6, Office of Communication and Interpretation, News Bureau, Country Topical Files, box 11, "Hong Kong"; Titus Lui to Edgar Fritz, 30 March 1972, CHI, Board for World Mission, Supplement 13, box 5, "Lui, Rev. Titus—Taiwan."

33. Richard C. Bush, "What Has Happened to the Church in Communist China?" *World Encounter* 2 (April 1965): 11–13; Peter Chang, "Christianity and Communist China," *Lutheran Sentinel* 54 (11 March 1971): 70–71; Donald E. MacInnis to David L. Angersbach, 13 August 1971, ELCA, LCA—East Asia, UPN box, "Tourists-East Asia"; "'The New China,'" *Northwestern Lutheran* 59 (23 April 1972): 145.

34. Henry C. Nitz, "Christians Humiliated in China," *Northwestern Lutheran* 54 (14 May 1967): 159; "Churches Closed Christmas Day in China Capital," *Lutheran Witness Reporter* 2 (15 January 1967): 3; Wallace C. Merwin, "Did We Learn Anything in China?" *World Encounter* 5 (June 1968): 5–13. McManners, *Oxford History*; Fairbank and Reischauer, *China*; Jasper, *Hungry*; Brauer, *One*.

35. "Chinese Swallow Marx," *Faith and Fellowship* 40 (20 February 1973): 8–9; William B. Dingler, LWF Broadcast Service Hong Kong Office Director, "China Interview Summary," June 1973, CHI, Board for Missions, Supplement 25, box 12, "China."

36. Far East Broadcasting Company Board Minutes, March 1968, BGCA, Eugene R. Bertermann Papers, FEBC, box 1, "File 8"; Fifth Lutheran World Assembly, July 1970, *The Lutheran World Federation Broadcasting Service Report, 1963–1969*, BGCA, International Christian Broadcasting, box 24, "File 22"; "Christianity and Communism," *Northwestern Lutheran* 58 (25 April 1971): 143.

37. Richard C. Beck to G. Elson Ruff, 10 April 1968, ELCA, G. Elson Ruff Papers, box 17, "B"; Joao Muller Carioba to G. Elson Ruff, 22 April 1968, ELCA, G. Elson Ruff Papers, box 17, "Ca-Co."

38. Harvey Warren to Frederik A. Schiotz, 13 February 1968, ELCA, Frederik A. Schiotz Papers, box 58, "Possible ALC Membership, NCC"; Mrs. W. R. Leininger to Frederik A. Schiotz, 1 May 1969, ELCA, Frederik A. Schiotz Papers, box 47, "WCC Reactions to 1968 Assembly I."

39. Arnold J. Nelson to Robert J. Marshall, 19 May 1970, ELCA, Robert J. Marshall Papers, box 105, "?".

40. "Christians in Red China—Are There Any Left?" *Christian News* 3 (14 December 1970): 1; "Ted Kennedy's Fun with Red China," *Jesus to the Communist World* (September

1969): 3 (emphasis in original); Richard Wurmbrand, "Atrocities in Red China," *Jesus to the Communist World* (November 1972): 1.

41. Paul H. Strege to Donald E. MacInnis, 8 December 1966, CHI, Board for Missions, Supplement 10, box 1, "China Committee"; Gau Ma-li, "Shouldn't Christians Ask: What About China?" *This Day* 18 (January 1967): 4–7, 46–47; Wu Ming Chieh, "In China, Taiwan, Hong Kong, Korea," in Andrew S. Burgess, ed., *Lutheran Churches in the Third World* (Minneapolis: Augsburg Publishing House, 1970); Paul H. Strege to William Lehmann, Jr., 9 May 1973, CHI, Board for Missions, Supplement 25, "China."

42. G. Elson Ruff to L. Warren Strickler II, 26 July 1966, ELCA, G. Elson Ruff Papers, box 14, "Sti"; Lutheran Church in America, Convention Minutes, June 1968, 358, ELCA; Albert P. Stauderman to Elsie M. Stone, 7 October 1971, ELCA, Albert P. Stauderman Papers, box 88, "Sj-Sz 1971."

43. Edgar R. Trexler, "Christians in Red China?" *Lutheran* 9 (18 August 1971): 6–11; "Peking Trip Hailed," *Lutheran Standard* 11 (3 August 1971): 19; Martin W. Mueller, "Leap Forward," *Lutheran Witness* 91 (24 September 1972): 364.

44. Peter Weseley-Smith, *Unequal Treaty, 1897–1997: China, Great Britain, and Hong Kong's New Territories* (New York: Oxford University Press, 1983); Judith M. Brown and Rosemary Foot, eds., *Hong Kong's Transitions, 1842–1997* (New York: St. Martin's Press, 1997).

45. Wisconsin Evangelical Lutheran Synod, Convention Minutes, August 1965, 217, WELS; John M. Mangum, "Courage and Loneliness," *Lutheran Women* 5 (April 1967): 18–21; Mildred Moller, "Hong Kong: City of Two Faces," *Lutheran Women's Quarterly* 28 (Fall 1970): 8–9; Lester F. Heins, "Businessman in Hong Kong," *World Encounter* 12 (October 1974): 1–3.

46. Paul H. Strege to W. F. Wolbrecht, 31 May 1967, CHI, Board for Missions, Supplement 10, box 2, "Hong Kong 1967 Situation"; Paul H. Strege, Report on the Hong Kong Situation, 12 July 1967, CHI, Board for Missions, Supplement 10, box 2, "Hong Kong 1967 Situation"; "News from Hong Kong," *Lutheran Sentinel* 51 (11 January 1968): 23–24; Wisconsin Evangelical Lutheran Synod, Report to the Nine Districts, 1968, 58–59, WELS.

47. Board of Directors Minutes, Lutheran World Relief, 11 March 1968, ELCA, Lutheran World Relief 1, Board of Directors, box 6, "1968"; American Lutheran Church, Convention Minutes, 1968, 429–30, ELCA; Minutes of the China Advisory Committee, Lutheran Church in America, 6–8 September 1973, ELCA, LCA Division for World Mission and Evangelism, Secretary of East Asia, boxes 1 and 2.

48. Untitled, *Lutheran Women's Quarterly* 24 (April 1966): 14; Roy Karner to Paul H. Strege, 10 July 1967, CHI, Board for Missions, Supplement 10, box 2, "Hong Kong 1967 Situation."

Chapter Three

Has the Tiger Changed Its Stripes? Lutheran Debates about Domestic Communism

Although unified Lutheran antagonism toward the two Communist giants persisted from 1964 to 1975, other aspects of anticommunism divided Americans and demonstrated that they no longer agreed upon how to fight the Communist Other. In the early years of the Cold War, most Americans feared that monolithic communism intended to infiltrate U.S. institutions and ultimately take over the U.S. government. McCarthyism brought this dread to a peak when red hunters targeted thousands of innocent victims in an effort to purge the United States of any Communist tendencies. Named after Senator Joseph McCarthy from Wisconsin, McCarthyism became a label for extreme anti-Communist individuals and groups who assaulted that which they opposed by accusing its supporters of communism, thereby inspiring American fears in order to win political battles. McCarthy used this strategy to promote his career, in countless speeches and congressional hearings, assaulting Hollywood, universities, and even the U.S. Army. Indeed, his witchhunt ended embarrassingly when increasing numbers of faultless people found themselves under attack and when, during the infamous 1954 Army-McCarthy hearings, Americans saw on television red hunting at its most absurd, which humiliated McCarthy and those who had backed him. McCarthy claimed that Communists had infiltrated the U.S. Army, but his hearings showed no proof and instead exposed him to the nation as a fraud. But McCarthyism was a much broader movement than the man it was named for and persisted long after his demise. The anti-Communist crusade, which in the United States traced itself clear back to the late 1800s, continued even though many Americans came to question its antidemocratic tactics and smearing of innocent people during the 1950s. Christian institutions and leaders were part of this anti-Communist crusade. They linked it to their concerns about atheism as manifested in Communist nations around the world and therefore warned Americans to stop it before it infiltrated the United States. Whether coming from laypeople who worried that Communists had spies in America trying to promote atheism or denominations denouncing socialism in the United States, most Christians fought this alleged battle against an internal threat. No one embodied this anti-Communist zeal better than the evangelist Billy Graham. In crusades and sermons across the nation, he warned against Communist influences and cautioned that the mere presence of this ideology might signal the end times. Yet within religious circles and the larger public, decades of hunting for these domestic threats waned as more and more people recognized that it had become an irrational witchhunt. By the 1960s, Christians split over the belief in McCarthyism, a separation that often paralleled disagreements within the fundamentalist versus modernist debate. In other words, secular, political concerns generally aligned with theological controversies.[1]

By 1964, therefore, full-fledged efforts to eradicate communism in the United States subsided, and Americans debated what direction to take in combating this perceived threat. This debate took place in secular society and within the churches in much the same way. Conservatives insisted that Communists still plotted to instigate a revolution. Within conservative churches, this led to a continued mantra about the dangers of internal communism and the Christian responsibility to combat it. Conservative churches also used this to attack Christian counterparts with whom they disagreed, labeling liberal theology that called for welfare programs and interfaith dialogue "Communist inspired." Others felt less sure of such concerns but continued with their anxiety that Communists lurked in the background of left-leaning U.S. institutions, including Christian denominations. They also used this fear politically, by accusing anything with which they disagreed of being inspired by Communist agents in the United States. Other Americans, however, insisted that no internal Communist threat endangered the United States and pointed out how this not only harmed innocent people but also was an excuse to blast liberal programs with false accusations. The Christian campaign against anti-Communist zeal was led by the liberal mainline Protestant clergy because they disliked its constant condemnations and inability to allow for honest debate about many issues, including civil rights and poverty. Because of the religious component to their opposition to the USSR and PRC, this debate about McCarthyism also crept into American Lutheranism and continued throughout the 1960s and 1970s.

A survey of Lutherans demonstrates that some held onto their belief that Communists sought to extend their sway over the United States by infiltrating its institutions. Other Lutherans questioned this thinking but agreed that Communists could subversively try to undermine U.S. democracy. Despite their differences, both of these groups persisted with red scare fears when they wondered whether liberal theological arguments about the government and welfare programs were inspired by subversive Communist agents who had infiltrated the church; they at least felt that socialist-type programs played into Communist aims even when advocated by well-meaning Lutheran Americans. Although Americans had displayed a near consensus regarding the danger of communism both abroad and at home during the early Cold War years, McCarthyism's excesses convinced a large bloc of Lutheran Americans to counter anti-Communist crusaders with reasoned dissent. To this end, they criticized their rightist opponents for spreading unfounded rumors and defended those falsely attacked. Lutherans agreed during this entire decade that the Soviet Union and China posed a danger to world security but opposed one another on the issue of domestic Communist threats in theological and political debates. This Lutheran disagreement also proves interesting because it so infiltrated church discussions and documents, yet neither side spent much time placing this in a theological context. In other words, the churches debated the issue but skirted around explaining why the topic was of such interest to Lutheranism. It was simply important to Americans and therefore involved Lutherans without comment. And, much like Christians throughout the nation, the disagreement paralleled Lutheran infighting about theological concerns such as biblical criticism and unionism; those inclined toward a more conservative faith tended to harbor continued fears about internal communism while moderate theological believers shunned this reasoning that was often used against their use of biblical criticism and cooperation with other denominations.[2]

COMMUNISTS WITHIN THE UNITED STATES?

Because the church and Christian Americans had so involved themselves in the fear of Communist infiltrations into the United States during the 1950s, they had to grapple with this legacy in succeeding decades. This became the first sign of a serious split between conservatives and moderate/liberals about the Cold War because rightists insisted that communism still threatened U.S. institutions, including the church, well into the 1970s, while their counterparts came to argue that no real threat to the United States existed, either for the church or its citizens, from inside the nation. Lutherans debated the existence of a Communist threat on U.S. soil. Claiming that Communists wanted to inculcate U.S. society with totalitarian ideas, conservatives warned people to resist socialist thought or veiled Communist principles. And they often pointed out Communist atheism as a significant reason to battle this ideology in the United States, before it toppled the church. Their opponents responded with equally emphatic pronouncements, claiming embarrassment at the 1950s "witch-hunt" that to them proved the falsity of such claims. They also insisted that no viable Communist danger imperiled churches in the United States. Often, this disagreement about McCarthyism took place when Lutherans disagreed about political issues. Both sides talked about separating politics from the Lutheran churches, yet it was never easy to maintain clean lines of separation in this regard. They therefore fused conversations about U.S. secular and religious organizations and political matters with theological rhetoric to justify why they discussed it within the church. For conservatives, this sometimes meant accusing the opposition of sympathy with communism, while for moderates it meant justifying their advocacy of welfare programs on religious grounds.

Leading the conservative anti-Communist charge by declaring that Communist atheism still threatened the United States and its Christian institutions in the 1960s, ultra-right Lutheran journals depicted a Communist demon that prowled in the shadows; more than any other Lutherans, they combined politics with theology when they discussed domestic Communist concerns. Founded and edited by a former LCMS seminary student, *Christian News* warned that Communists tried to infiltrate Protestant denominations. Herman Otten championed a myriad of conservative causes in this periodical, most of which had to do with warning that the Lutheran Church–Missouri Synod had succumbed to liberalism and no longer adhered to true Christian principles. Yet his brand of politics and theology alienated even conservatives within the denomination, who continued to isolate him after the conservative takeover of the denomination in 1969. His constant mantra against Communist influences in the United States therefore matched his consistent far-right rhetoric against even traditional conservatism in the United States and his former church body. In particular, Otten insisted that Communists used Christian institutions in the United States to gain a foothold in the nation. For example, he warned that Communists often claimed that the church and communism had the same goals of supporting the poor and assisting those in need. But they did so to convert people to their ideology, not because any Communists really cared about people. For example, the Communist Party U.S.A. claimed that it and the churches both advocated poor relief. Otten and his journal cautioned readers against believing this ploy and asserted that the church truly wanted to help the poor while Communists only wanted to control them. In addition to targeting communism, this argument was a veiled attack on Lyndon B. Johnson's Great Society programs. Though couched in terms of protecting Lutheran churches from mistakenly adopting "socialist" ideals, it really aimed to get people to advocate eliminating welfare programs. However, so as not to appear cold-hearted or opposed to aiding the needy, it manufactured a religious reason for churches to fight against welfare by arguing that these socialist programs were inspired by Communist operatives. An American Lutheran Church (ALC) right-wing splinter group, Lutherans-Alert National (LAN), also dispensed such advice in its periodical, *Lutherans-Alert*. Much like Otten and his periodical, LAN came into being because of a disgruntled ALC pastor, Rueben H. Redal, who campaigned against his denomination and warned that it had been taken over by liberalism and moved away from God's message. In particular, LAN warned that the ALC had adopted biblical criticism and therefore no longer believed in the Bible. This naturally led to other rightist causes, including the idea that Communists threatened the United States politically and religiously or had been the inspiration behind biblical criticism. LAN counseled that Communists blended into U.S. life by acting like "average" citizens, even though they "are really enemies" and "doubly dangerous" because no one could easily detect their true sympathies. Indeed, LAN took this a step further and connected its crusade against communism to its denunciation of the ALC: the organization announced that Communist principles had led the ALC to abandon belief in biblical inerrancy. Because they felt that the ALC had become too theologically liberal, LAN officials asserted that "when the church forsakes the doctrine of an inerrant Bible, it can end up fellowshipping with atheistic Communism." Conservatives saw the fight against communism as both a political and religious battle. These two journals persisted with a passionate fear of all forms of communism; from 1964 to 1975, they led the rightist campaign that sustained a conservative horror about Communist plots to conquer the United States.[3]

But ultra-rightists had conservative Lutheran company when they argued that communism promoted the "devil's agenda" by undermining Christianity and democracy. It had become an easy ploy when conservatives disliked a liberal idea to accuse its adherents of communism because this linked their cause to a holy war against atheism instead of it simply being a political disagreement. For example, several denominations, church leaders, and other liberals had by the 1960s begun to dialogue with Communists and other far-left organizations in the United States and around the globe in order to foster better relations between people with varying ideologies. Conservatives who disliked this claimed that this spirit of cooperation aided Communists and therefore labeled any discussion with those with whom they disagreed as "satanic." A Lutheran Church in America (LCA) member asserted that "Communists have been trying to destroy our *freedom* to *worship*" by getting church leaders to talk to them. Conservatives therefore thought that the devil inspired Communist principles and urged Americans to guard against Communist influences, the "real poisons that threaten our country." More pointedly, conservatives stated that attempts to dialogue with Communists failed

Christianity because "when you compromise with the devil and his disciples [Communists]" you work against God's will. Indeed, they contended that "our Lord never debated with Satan, He put him down." Years of propaganda had convinced these Americans that "this monster would have us live on our knees—not in praise or worship of God but in service to an atheistic state." *Lutheran* editor G. Elson Ruff came under particular scrutiny in this regard because his editorials argued for Americans to ease their hatred of communism. He did so with the hope that it would foster better relations between people around the world and end the false accusations of communism in the United States. Conservatives disagreed. A minister, believing that Communist agents worked in the United States to undermine its institutions and churches and to inspire a revolution, chastised Ruff because "you may find out too late that the tiger has not changed his stripes." In other words, he despised the fact that McCarthy-era anticommunism had been debunked and stated that this fear had actually been correct but liberal claims against it now provided Communists with easy access to America. Conservatives saw the fight against alleged Communist infiltrations as a religious war that continued in the 1970s when they portrayed the enemy as the devil that combated God's message.[4]

Many conservative Lutherans truly believed that Communists plotted to infiltrate the United States. But their accusations came in general references to an unidentified threat and seldom included specific examples. Even young adults made these vague references. Again targeting the *Lutheran* editor for his moderate stance on world communism, a teenager wrote Ruff that "unless you live in your own little world and are completely uninformed you cannot deny the existence of a Communist influence in our daily lives." Typical of such warnings, he gave no examples. His was not, however, an isolated opinion. A conservative Lutheran journal, *Lutheran Spokesman*, of the small denomination Church of the Lutheran Confession, also cautioned that Communists "may have a vast network of spies and may be training traitors from our own midst." Some conservative Lutherans did claim to possess concrete evidence of Communist infiltration, but this information seldom held much merit. For example, they often mirrored the ultra-right journals by stating that Lyndon B. Johnson's Great Society programs were proof of communism in America. Even Americans who denounced Communists ended up supporting them if they naively endorsed welfare reform. As an LCA layperson stated, "Our nation is in dire peril of Communists today more so than ever. Unfortunately, these Communists are American citizens" who support socialist programs. These conservatives also blamed Communists for the 1960s unrest at various universities. The 1960s generation of college students regularly lashed out against the establishment for acquiescing to racism, sexism, outdated college curricula, and war. This had led to numerous campus demon-

strations across the nation and frequent clashes with police and other authorities. Conservatives tried to explain away this unrest, surmising that Communists were in part to blame because they fomented it as a tactic to undermine
democracy. A minister informed parishioners that "college campuses have
been put out of operation by Communists and Communist stooges." And an
LCMS layperson expanded this sentiment by blaming all of the nation's ills
on Communist agents: "All our country's major problems—pornography,
drugs, campus unrest, revolutionaries, anti-Vietnam war marches, criticism of
Nixon's war policies, etc. have either originated or [been] made worse by
Communist activity and influence in this country."[5]

Anti-Communist adherents had long accused churches of tacitly allowing
Communist influences into the United States because many Christian denominations advocated liberal social policies regarding race and poverty.
Such conservative accusations included Lutherans who insisted that their own
denominations harbored Communists. After the Lutheran Church–Missouri
Synod's (LCMS) *Lutheran Witness* voiced support for the Great Society, a
reader asserted that "if you are going to advocate Marxism at least have the
guts to call it what it is." Another LCMS member "heard rumors of the Missouri Synod itself going *Communistic*" because of such stances. People even
thought that biblical prophecies came true when Lutheran leaders advocated
social welfare programs, which they thought were Communist inspired: "Our
Lord warned that 'false prophets' would speak in His name, but it is a shock-
ing and saddening experience to find the 'ravening wolves' within the
'sheep's clothing' of our own church." But the LCMS was not alone in confronting these accusations. A member disliked a book by LCA President
Robert J. Marshall because "the doctrine of communism is inserted in a sly
manner"; Marshall's advocacy of social welfare programs had prompted this
response. Decades of fearing communism scarred people deeply. Conservative Lutherans in the 1960s and 1970s still placed a Communist label on anything that went against their beliefs and even accused their own church leaders of harboring Communist sympathies. As one man implored, "Please send
the Commie leaders of the Church and the [National] Council of Churches to
Red China where they MAY be happy."[6]

But not all conservatives made accusations that respected church leaders
aided communism, even though they persisted with a fear that communism
threatened the United States internally. A member of the ALC believed that
Communists undermined established institutions and asserted that even "anti-
Communist right-wing organizations are to some degree Communist infiltrated." Unlike far-right Lutherans, however, he isolated the possibility to a
few people. In addition, moderate conservatives stated that innocent people often joined Communist front organizations without realizing it. This included

liberal groups that advocated policies with which conservatives disagreed. Rather than attack organizations issue by issue, they made sweeping judgments against entire groups by stating that they unknowingly assisted Communists by fighting for liberal causes. Students for a Democratic Society, which fought for student rights, the National Organization of Women, which championed women's rights, any organizations that supported welfare programs, and liberal political lobbies were all imbedded with secret Communist agents according to these principles. Calling people who accidentally supported such "socialist" causes "naïve and misguided," the *Lutheran Digest* asked Lutherans to cease all activity with "Communist front organizations" and to stop participating in "movements that would destroy the most successful form of government the world has ever seen." LCMS President J. A. O. Preus stated that "certainly we want to have no dealings with communism in our church."[7]

Conservative Lutherans also distanced themselves from the far-right when they discussed the number of Communists already in the United States. While ultra conservatives saw agents lurking everywhere, other conservatives stated that attempts to infiltrate could only succeed if Americans stopped guarding against Communist ideas. A writer for the *Lutheran Digest* explained that Communists wanted to get inside "organized religion and use it to destroy that religion's own civilization." He asserted that this plan had not yet commenced inside the United States. But by outlining this alleged plot, he planted the idea in people's minds that the church at least *could* become a target if they were not diligent in guarding against it. An LCA member also cautioned that Communists might plan to invade the church *in the future*: "I doubt very much that we have actual communists in our churches, press, school, and government positions; at least very few if any." This individual, though, claimed that people would succumb to Communist ideals if conservatives dropped their guard. In other words, conservative Lutherans remained steadfast in shielding the United States from communism but did not believe a widespread Communist infiltration had commenced.[8]

Despite the differences between far-right fears of Communists and conservative warnings, the overall stance remained the same. Conservatives asserted that Communists sought to undermine U.S. democracy whenever they explained their positions. Each side thought that Communists wanted to take over the world, including the United States. They only disagreed on whether or not this infiltration had already started. This small variance also contained a theological difference: the most conservative Lutherans insisted that the church was in imminent peril while their more moderate conservative colleagues asserted that the church was safe so long as it guarded against the possibility of future Communist incursions. In contrast, their moderate/liberal counterparts denied any looming Communist threat to the United States or its Christian institutions.

Lutheran editor G. Elson Ruff illustrates the moderate view. In a 1964 *Lutheran* editorial, he criticized far-right accusations. Ruff took a number of moderate stands regarding domestic and foreign policy issues, including the notion of internal Communist threats. He was especially concerned by the wild assertions of right-wing political entities and people that also paraded as religious bodies crusading to protect Christianity in America. John Stormer's infamous *None Dare Call It Treason*, published in 1964 and which sold millions of copies, blamed a myriad of problems with U.S. leadership on Communist infiltrations. Stormer included several church bodies and leaders in these insinuations. Worried that LCA constituents would believe him, Ruff wrote that Stormer "deals in fantasies regarding infiltration of Communist influence among responsible American leaders." He claimed that such right-wingers "are reckless with truth, pander to frustrations which are inevitable in the long years of the cold war, [and] seek to arouse fanatic emotions." He later implored Americans to "get over our dreadful fear of a world-wide Communist conspiracy which is determined to destroy us."[9]

In addition to editorials, Ruff combated extreme anticommunism in his personal correspondence. As he did with Stormer, Ruff criticized the John Birch Society. Created in 1958 by Robert Welch, this organization claimed to want to save the United States from destruction but in reality aimed to help far-right people and ideas within America. As part of its campaign strategy and to get Americans to support it, the Society accused liberals of communism as a way to undermine their arguments without having to address the actual issue. Ruff asserted that this dependence on deception sought "to disrupt and destroy the prevailing institutions of our land." Yet, Ruff disdained communism when he stated that "we Americans must be steadily and wisely alert to the great danger of world communism, and can't afford to be distracted by the extremists who sow dissension and distrust. They pay almost no attention to the real dangers of communism, but concentrate on the imaginary infiltration into such institutions as the church, the press, the courts, [and] the presidency." He also defended himself against allegations that he supported Communist causes: "I simply can't understand the logic and motivation of folks who claim there are a lot of churchmen (including me, I suppose) who believe in socialism and the welfare state and who are using their church positions to promote such views." These people "have built up in their imagination a phantom who has no relation to reality." Furthermore, he accused staunch anti-Communist leaders of acting to gain notoriety by "frightening Americans who aren't well enough informed to know better." Ruff explained that the Communists "have met with complete defeat in their efforts to influence the

church." The *Lutheran* editor thus exemplified moderate Lutherans who despised McCarthyism's legacy and diligently worked to change people's minds
by exposing the extreme right's fraudulent claims and penchant for fear tactics. Ruff's statements represent liberal/moderate efforts in the 1960s and
1970s for a less-radical liberal agenda that promoted moderate patriotism. He
carefully balanced his opposition to the far-right with anti-Communist statements and support for American institutions so that conservatives who attacked him would not have sole claim to love for their country.[10]

Moderate to liberal LCA members came to Ruff's defense, demonstrating
that at least some laypeople agreed with their officials. One man wrote, "I
know what it costs to stand up to the extremists in our society," and therefore
thanked the editor for his efforts. Another reader urged Ruff to continue his
fight because "although it seems there are those who do not appreciate the ex-
posure of extremism much more is needed." More graphically, an LCA member stated that "God have mercy on us if too much of this trash gets into the
homes of poorly educated Lutherans who already are emotionally in the camp
of the right-wing nuts!"[11] Indeed, other Lutherans also supported this lib-
eral/moderate position. A fictional story in *One*, the ALC teenage magazine,
asserted that "the fanatics in Westgate [a fictional town] are not so much the
enemy of communism as they are of freedom. When intelligent citizens begin to tolerate unwarranted attacks on [the] loyalty of our leaders, then we do
indeed have cause to worry about the future of America." Agreement with
Ruff's stance also came from other Lutheran leaders. ALC President Kent S.
Knutson criticized those who saw Communists everywhere when he wrote,
"Pity those who find conspiracies behind every structure and procedure."
Ruff's successor, Albert P. Stauderman, mirrored his sentiments about the
John Birch Society to a reader: he declared in 1975 that "while most Ameri-
cans are opposed to Communist encroachment on our society in any form, the
Birchers' brand of blind anti-communism identifies anyone who does not
agree with them as 'Communist' and therefore loses its credibility. Your own
charge that 'whoever wrote this article is a "Communist"' is typical of this un-
thinking attitude."[12]

But what most motivated moderate Lutherans to defend against accusations of communism was the conservative assertion that the church harbored
Communists in its midst and advocated Communist policies. Ruff explained
that "to spread slanders that top men in . . . the church . . . are agents of the
Communist conspiracy is the best way to undermine the strength and loyalty
of Americans." He also had to defend himself from readers who claimed his
support for the Great Society proved his Communist sympathies. In a sar-
castic response to one accuser, Ruff apologized because he "got behind in my
correspondence due to a long journey in Europe in the fall, in which oddly

enough I was barred by the Communists from traveling in East Germany. Evidently they don't consider me as much their friend as you seem to think I am." But even the more conservative LCMS's *Lutheran Witness* editor had to defend himself from accusations of Communist sympathies. Martin W. Mueller wrote to a reader that an "examination of the facts established that such charges [of communism inside the Christian church] are unfounded." Conservatives not only targeted magazine editors but often went straight to the presidents of their Lutheran denominations with these concerns. Lutheran polity, which elects presidents at national conventions, allows members to feel that they can contact their leadership with any concerns. Thus, when they decided that their denomination had taken pro-Communist stances, they wrote to the president in protest. For example, ALC President Frederik A. Schiotz had to defend the church from such accusations. In response to a pastor's indictment that church policies regarding welfare contained Communist ideas, he asserted that "I had a long discussion with him about his deep fears regarding Communism and its alleged infiltration into the churches. I regard his evidence as poorly authenticated." These church leaders contended that no Communist threat imperiled the United States; they denounced anti-Communist attacks on the church and tried to demonstrate that claims that church leaders were Communists were unfounded rumors, not true facts. While their conservative counterparts continued to wage a religious battle against communism inside U.S. borders, they insisted that no Communists threatened American Christianity.[13]

To counter these charges of church and societal infiltration, moderate and liberal Lutheran leaders rationalized that no Communist demon had intruded upon the U.S. landscape. G. Elson Ruff explained that too many Americans adhered to simple-minded principles: "It so happens that our magazine doesn't reach any Communists or have influence on their sympathizers, but we do have within our readership a large variety of radical rightists who slander good people mercilessly and are creating serious problems in our churches." Ruff stated that "there are all sorts of lights and shadows in the Communist camp and constant change." By 1970, Ralph L. Moellering, a prominent Lutheran theologian, stated that "the prevailing concept of anti-Communism is outmoded and irrelevant in responding to events of our time." He emphasized that "at no time has a communist-instigated revolution been imminent in this country."[14]

A controversy within the Lutheran Church–Missouri Synod and the American Lutheran Church reveals even better this debate over Communist threats to U.S. internal security. In 1965, the LCMS youth organization, the Walther League, and in 1970 the ALC youth organization, the Luther League, held national gatherings. The young leaders at both conventions invited folksinger

Pete Seeger to perform. Seeger, a popular entertainer, came under fire because of allegations that he supported Communist causes and in the early 1960s had appeared before the House Committee on Un-American Activities. Although Seeger had ties to far-left groups and Communists, there is no evidence that he made any attempt to promote a Communist incursion into U.S. life. Seeger himself later explained that his leftist agenda regarding labor, environmental issues, racial justice, and the Vietnam War led to these false charges. False or not, his appearance at Lutheran youth gatherings outraged conservatives.[15]

Seeger's 1965 appearance angered people who insisted that his performance represented part of the Communist plot to brainwash U.S. children. An ALC laywoman framed her criticism in terms of the religious battle that Christians fought against communism when she called *One*'s reporting of the event "literary trash" that would lead to welcoming "satan to the pulpit." Another LCA constituent wanted the older generation to investigate why the youth decided to invite Seeger. He complained that Seeger's Communist ties were obvious but "too numerous for me to mention here." As the most conservative of the largest Lutheran bodies, LCMS members had the sharpest words about the decision. They condemned the young people's leadership and chastised LCMS officials for allowing a "Communist to poison the children's minds." A 1965 LCMS convention resolution summarized their feelings. The delegates voted to move beyond the debacle, but still declared that "we are troubled by instances of poor judgment and of faulty and inadequate communication." Although Seeger's appearance failed to convert young people to communism, conservatives still urged Lutherans to prevent such a "dangerous person" from ever again appearing at a Walther League convention.[16]

Conservative ALC constituents created a similar uproar when their youth organization invited Seeger to its 1970 gathering. A layperson insisted that Communists used Seeger's show to influence young people: "Although 15,000 Luther Leaguers might applaud the plaintive songs of Pete Seeger, they would not recognize subtle class-hatred propaganda; the down-grading of America, nor anti-Vietnam war appeal." A minister concurred that "it is really hard to imagine how the church would permit her enemies to poison the minds of her young people with such impunity to the dangers involved." Other readers claimed that Seeger intended to "tell our young people, as he told the Russians, how much better communism is than our country." Even a year after the convention, the ALC president's office received lamentations about Seeger's appearance. Conservative Lutherans thought that Communists gained ground because young leaders failed to note that "it has long been a principle [*sic*] strategy of the communist conspiracy to infiltrate and subvert."

Another ALC constituent warned that "the Communists have always been adept at using non-communist, well meaning, but naïve people, to further their cause." Like the clamor that greeted 1965 LCMS officials, conservative ALC members castigated the church for allowing Seeger to sing and thereby "advance the Communist goal of invading American minds."[17]

Liberal to moderate Lutherans defended themselves, the youth, and their church from these accusations. They first pointed out that "while Mr. Seeger is a controversial figure, it is not established that he is a Communist; he is not so designated by the FBI." ALC President Kent S. Knutson scolded the Seeger bashers, stating that "to accuse him of Communism is to perpetuate malicious gossip unbecoming to the Christian community," especially because they "offered no evidence to support this very terrible kind of accusation." These moderate to liberal people no longer feared that any sign of communism represented a threat to the United States, nor did they believe that Communists infiltrated U.S. institutions to convert innocent people. Yet Knutson's statement is an example of how liberal to moderate Lutherans distanced themselves from the far-left: his defense of Seeger not only denied the Communist allegations but called them "malicious" and "terrible" because he, too, saw Communists as undesirable. Regarding Pete Seeger's appearances, moderate to liberal Lutherans became impatient with false insinuations and demanded that conservatives stop accusing an innocent man.[18]

After twenty years of fearing that Communists wanted to plant spies in the United States, between 1964 and 1975 Lutherans no longer agreed that Americans had to worry about every form of communism. Rightist Lutherans clung to the domino theory and applied it even to the domestic front. More moderate conservative Lutherans stopped the constant accusations but still warned that the Communists might try to infiltrate the United States. Their moderate to liberal counterparts combated this rhetoric and defended people from attack. They saw no correlation between world communism and any threats to the United States and learned from McCarthyism that no massive Communist plot threatened domestic America. Thus, they declared that such indictments hurt the United States and innocent people, not Communist governments. Amazingly, this deliberation took place throughout Lutheranism without much mention of religion, theology, or why it belonged in the church. The war against communism had so imbedded itself in the churches that it seemed obvious—according to their theology, Lutherans had an obligation to both kingdoms, the earthly and heavenly, when they concerned themselves with worldly matters. But this debate was not limited to general discussions of communism within the United States; the controversy also manifested itself in more specific situations.

THE WORLD COUNCIL OF CHURCHES AND
NATIONAL COUNCIL OF CHURCHES OF CHRIST

American Lutherans' debate about internal communism persisted when they discussed more specific subjects. Within the Christian community, the World Council of Churches (WCC) and the National Council of Churches of Christ (NCC) became focal points in this controversy. Various Christian denominations formed the WCC and the NCC because they wanted to cooperate on certain endeavors on a worldwide and national level. The WCC was formed in 1948 as a global ecumenical body, created to bring Christians together in dialogue and to stand together on causes upon which all of the member bodies could agree, such as fighting racism and poverty. Established two years later, the NCC had the same general focus but included only churches within the United States. These bodies were created at a moment in Christianity that emphasized ecumenical notions of cooperation in order to make the world a better place, a movement inspired in part by the horrors of World War II and the Holocaust. By the 1960s, both organizations espoused liberal Protestant ideals and supported social policies that fostered equality. They also promoted the liberal agenda of dialoging with Communists in order to ease the century-long Marxist-Christian feud. The WCC especially had a softer stance on communism because some of its member churches hailed from Communist countries. Conservatives Christians charged both of these interdenominational bodies with promoting a socialist agenda, a convenient way to disregard their ecumenical spirit that went against insular theological thinking and anti-Communist politics. Like Christians around the nation, Lutherans debated whether or not the WCC and the NCC advocated a Communist program.[19]

Despite the reality that it was a genuine interdenominational organization dedicated to Christianity and social justice, the World Council of Churches' inclusion of Christian bodies from Communist nations led conservative Lutherans to insist that Communists controlled the organization. According to conservatives and without proof, the mere presence of someone from a Communist country proved collusion with communism. One member criticized President Frederik A. Schiotz for his participation with and the ALC's membership in the WCC because it "openly committed itself to the purposes of world communism." But he said nothing else to support this claim. Schiotz, an active WCC member, was hardly a Communist and knew almost all of the dedicated leaders who participated in the WCC. Even though the WCC only affected U.S. society on the periphery because it contained U.S. churches but did no relief work within U.S. borders, conservatives still worried that U.S. participation allowed WCC officials to brainwash church leaders and used hearsay to prove this claim. A *Reader's Digest* article that accused the WCC of promoting communism especially angered conservatives. Regarding the Lutheran Church in America's membership in the WCC, a lay member wrote that, even if the accusations of communism were only half true, "it is reason enough for the L.C.A. to divorce itself from the organization and to brand it as subversive and highly dangerous to the Church of Jesus Christ." This prompted some Lutherans to take action against their church body, including leaving the denomination. In the 1970s, a couple left the ALC upon learning that it worked with the WCC, which they believed promoted "the cause of our Communist enemies in the U.S. and abroad." LCA members, too, dropped out of their church body when they discovered that it cooperated with the WCC. A laywoman explained that "if the Communists want to rule the world they will have to do it without my contribution." Another layperson withdrew her tithe because she claimed that the WCC funded Communist revolutions: "If our Lutheran churches are spending money on riots, violence, and black militants, all of whom are communist sub-agents in America, then this is the last I want to hear from any Luth. Church." Baseless rumors of Communist sympathies fueled conservative beliefs that communism had infiltrated the church simply because some Christians from Communist countries belonged to the WCC.[20]

Conservatives therefore insisted that the WCC debate was both a theological battle to protect Christianity from Communist destruction and a political fight to save the world from Communist revolution. An ALC layperson told President Schiotz, "The association with Communists can only help to destroy the Church, as has been the case in all communist countries." LCA President Robert J. Marshall also received scathing attacks because of his WCC participation. A man stated that Marshall's affiliation aided the Communists and wondered, "Isn't it a dirty shame that laymen have to take time out to tell you how to save your skin and the Churches, too," from communism. He continued, "I'm sure it gives the Communists much cause for laughs over their vodka to see the spectacle of an American working diligently against America and for their God-less goals."[21]

The leaders of the Lutheran churches who challenged these red scare accusations called anti-WCC indictments preposterous. They pointed out that far-right leaders invented such charges to further their personal fame. An ALC leader from the national headquarters explained that "there are those in this country who devote themselves to generating unwarranted fears concerning Communistic influence in the World Council of Churches" but that the "Committee on Inter-Church Relations has checked into many of these allegations and has not found them to be factual." *Lutheran* editor Albert P. Stauderman bitterly denounced the accusations. After *Reader's Digest* declared that Communists ran the WCC, he stated that "the treatment given the World Council by the article in the Digest was a hatchet job, deliberately aimed at presenting a distorted picture." These church officials knew that the WCC did not advocate communism. They explained that conservatives perpetuated the fear of communism because it prompted people to listen to their message and contribute financially to their causes; in short, ultra-conservative leaders led people to believe that their ministry protected the United States from Communists. Thus, liberal to moderate leaders exclaimed that unethical fear mongers propagated misinformation merely to maintain their popularity.[22]

ALC President Frederik A. Schiotz provides an example of how liberal to moderate Lutherans defended the WCC from Communist accusations while also appealing to moderate patriotism by denouncing communism. After an ALC member alleged that WCC Eastern Bloc members supported communism, he retorted that "I know the bishops well in these churches. They are not fooled by the insidious nature of communism." Schiotz's statement reveals that, although he disregarded the fear that Communists controlled the WCC, he still despised communism. He also refuted conservative accusations that the WCC criticized non-Communist nations for humanitarian problems but ignored them in Communist countries. Having worked on numerous WCC boards, Schiotz knew that "concerns are . . . sent to all governments including those in Communist countries." More sarcastically, he stated that "I am a member of the Central Committee which is the governing body of the WCC between assemblies. I know the officers and the various staff members of the WCC and I can honestly say that they are not 'Communist-inspired.' However, it is true that they are not afraid of Communism to the point of paralysis."[23]

The dispute over internal Communist threats intensified when Lutherans discussed the National Council of Churches of Christ because the NCC operated within the United States. Its liberal rhetoric made conservatives especially uneasy and false allegations that the NCC harbored Communist believers had plagued the group from its inception. Conservative Lutherans therefore added their voice to a chorus of Americans who pummeled the ecumenical group with insinuations of communism simply because of its liberal policies regarding race, gender, and poverty. Liberals and moderates rebutted these accusations by pointing out that the Lutherans involved with the NCC knew that no Communists controlled it. They also disdained the fact that charges against the NCC closely resembled the attacks leveled against innocent Americans during the McCarthy era. The NCC debate demonstrates how Lutherans could join in criticizing the Soviet Union and China but oppose one another on other issues regarding communism.[24]

Conservative Lutherans often got their "proof" that Communists ran the NCC from ultra-rightist organizations. John A. Stormer's *None Dare Call It*

Treason especially fueled the anti-Communist hysteria because he named the NCC as a Communist front organization in his book. In truth, he and other conservatives made such specious allegations because the NCC adopted liberal political policies with which they disagreed. It was easy for them to dismiss the NCC as a Communist sympathizer and therefore get many Americans to ignore anything that the NCC advocated. An ALC constituent informed Schiotz that "Mr. Stormer gives several documented accounts of communist infiltration in the N.C.C." This made her "sick at heart" because her church supposedly supported a godless ideology. Another constituent stated that "charges against NCC, WCC, LWF, as understanding friends of the Communistic movement are well founded. *You* may call it vitriolic slander. A court would not." An LCA pastor complained to President Marshall that the church's NCC membership lost him prospective members. He enclosed a pamphlet that epitomized the right's shock methods. It dubiously linked the NCC directly to the Soviet Union, an accusation completely without foundation. Its cover sought to demonstrate the NCC's danger to the United States with red lettering, the Soviet hammer and sickle, a toppling cross, and the provocative title, "How Red Is the National Council of Churches?" Conservative Lutherans therefore exhorted that communism wanted to spread to the United States through the NCC.[25]

The NCC's liberal policies toward non-Western countries sparked further conservative assertions of Communist sympathies because they assumed that Communists inspired revolutions and unrest in these nations. When the NCC failed to denounce revolutionary turbulence around the world, a *Lutheran* reader insisted, "We can begin to understand [that] the World and National Council of Churches' [*sic*] ardently support totalitarian international communism and it's [*sic*] slaughter, plundering, burning and enslaving 1/2 of the world's people." Finally, someone exclaimed that the NCC had "gone from a Pro-Communist organization to a Pro-Revolutionary one." Buttressed by inaccurate observations and a continued belief that Communists sought to take over every nation, conservative Lutherans warned that the NCC threatened the United States because it espoused Communist doctrines.[26]

Although far-right Lutherans contended that the NCC knowingly promoted communism, less-severe conservatives claimed that the NCC mistakenly supported communism because guileful Communists persuaded its leaders to believe socialist rhetoric. An LCA layperson advised that "it would be a feather in the Red Cap to be able to dupe even one clergyman into following the Communist line and thus preaching it, however innocently, from the pulpit." A vehement NCC opponent, Harry H. Feistner, wrote in the ALC's *Commentator* that the NCC's backing of disarmament played into Communist hands by weakening U.S. defenses. The NCC had long supported any U.S. efforts toward arms limitation and cooperation with Communist countries and thus hailed the Nixon administration's talks with the Soviet Union in this regard. Like many conservatives, Feistner indicated that this was a religious war because it was part of the Communist "conspiracy which has as its sole purpose the destruction of the Bible." Although moderate conservatives avoided extreme accusations about the NCC's alleged communism, they insisted that the organization threatened the United States' internal security. They asserted that the NCC's liberal agenda played into Communist hands by converting people to socialist causes without exposing the Communists behind it.[27]

Conservatives ultimately avowed that Communists even used the NCC to infiltrate Lutheran churches. A layperson thought that the NCC's liberal "political policies are pure '*Red*' and under-mining the basic principles of the Lutheran Church." Feistner campaigned against the ALC's attempt to join the NCC by asking convention delegates to pray to keep the church "from going modernistic, from joining the N.C.C., and from being infiltrated with atheistic communist ideology." Indeed, his efforts worked because the ALC never joined the NCC. Conservatives also claimed that the devil used their church to further his aims; Lutheran cooperation with the NCC proved this fear to them. They listened to far-right rhetoric against the NCC that convinced them that it had socialist tendencies and then warned that these "evil" realities might seep into the ALC and LCA because of their NCC affiliation. This demonstrates that conservatives between 1964 and 1975 still believed that Communists sought to influence Americans by converting one person at a time until their ideology became the majority opinion.[28]

Moderate and liberal Lutheran leaders and laypeople countered the false accusations against the NCC by detailing how right-wing propagandists spread malicious rumors. They called such people "scaremongers" who preyed on insecure Americans. A moderate ALC member combated Feistner's NCC hatred by claiming that he only served to "aggravate, increase, and confuse and add to the turmoil." These Lutherans feared the continuation of an extreme anti-Communist hysteria when their colleagues irrationally accused a major Christian organization of communism. They also lamented the realization that many Lutheran Americans refused to change their minds. An LCA pastor expressed defeat: "I frankly don't feel that much arguing is going to convince" rightist anti-Communists "of anything else." These Lutherans fought to change conservatives' illogical thinking but feared that twenty years of extreme anticommunism doomed their efforts.[29]

Liberal/moderate Lutherans also accused their opponents of simple-minded and irrational beliefs. G. Elson Ruff wrote a curt letter to a constituent that read, in its entirety, "Thanks for your letter about Communist infiltration of the National Council of Churches. You have been thoroughly misinformed." His LCA colleague in the national office, George F. Harkins, explained to another layperson that "you take up an old, old charge and hurl it blindly against the National Council, and thus indirectly against your own church. And you do it in such a way as to give it a cutting edge while dropping the knife and disclaiming responsibility." He scolded still another person for accusing the NCC of communism and stated that "all that anyone needs to do to make life miserable for another person who holds a position of trust is to start the rumor" of communism. He continued that "some lives have been practically ruined by irresponsible and unsubstantiated charges."[30]

NCC supporters finally asserted that conservatives had no proof of their charges that the organization had ties to communism. An LCA official refuted the accusations by explaining that "I have been a member of the [NCC] General Board ever since 1954" and know that the people you accuse "are not Communists, nor 'fellow-travelers.'" An ALC leader stated that "many of the allegations are made which simply have no basis in fact and cannot be sustained." But Albert P. Stauderman best combined the belief that conservatives had no factual evidence with the assertion that they used irrational thinking in their judgments: "The National Council is an agency of the churches. It has no 'relationship' to the Communists anymore than your local congregation does. If the Communists say they stand for 'peace' and the Council says it also stands for 'peace,' this may be a source of hope for the world rather than for alarm." NCC champions cringed when they saw that red scare tactics continued to plague the United States and threatened the Lutheran churches' relationship with this ecumenical body. They saw no danger from its principles and knew that no Communists controlled its actions.[31]

The Lutheran debate about the World Council of Churches and the National Council of Churches of Christ reveals two distinct beliefs about communism. The most conservative Lutherans continued to think that any liberal policy led to communism. Therefore, they claimed that the WCC's and the NCC's liberal agenda made them Communist sympathizers. Less-ardent conservatives feared that the organizations' naive leadership accidentally aided Communists by failing to see the danger hidden in socialist causes. Both groups, though, believed that communism used the WCC and the NCC to subvert U.S. institutions. Their opponents displayed a different point of view. They doubted that massive numbers of Communists lurked within the United States and instead defended the two organizations. Although evidence suggests that both sides disliked Communist ideology and combated the two largest Communist giants, Lutherans split over the topic of internal Communist threats, especially in relation to the WCC and the NCC.

COMMUNISM AND THE CIVIL RIGHTS MOVEMENT

The debate over Communist infiltration into U.S. society also involved the civil rights and black power movements from 1964 to 1975. After World War II, the civil rights movement intensified its efforts to liberate African Americans from southern segregation and by the 1960s started to attack economic discrimination against blacks throughout the nation. But the movement was not immune from 1960s generational conflicts. Among younger blacks, a tendency grew toward more militancy that questioned Martin Luther King, Jr., and other civil rights leaders' commitment to nonviolent resistance. Blacks began to agitate for immediate equality and insisted that white Americans would not otherwise give it willingly. The more extreme form of this advocacy came with black power. With slogans such as "black is beautiful" and campaigns against economic segregation, the black power movement concerned moderate to conservative Americans with its harsh rhetoric, threats of violence, and strong stand against all forms of racism. Throughout this era, Christian institutions had been involved in the civil rights movement, especially among the clergy because of a commitment to social justice. They felt called to defeat discrimination and argued that Christian commitment demanded that they act on behalf of the oppressed. Not all Christians, however, agreed with this stance. Southern Christians especially defended segregation and condemned the largely northern clergy presence in the civil rights movement as interference. Because the churches had been deeply involved in the civil rights movement since the mid-1950s, Christians paid special attention to the developing rift in the civil rights movement in the 1960s.[32]

This civil rights feud included Lutherans on both sides by the 1960s. But by this time, most Lutherans either supported moderate civil rights efforts, such as those promoted by King, or tacitly accepted the reality of this new equality without comment. The leadership of the LCA, ALC, and LCMS in particular denounced racism and economic inequality. This put right-wing conservatives in a difficult position when they argued against black equality. In order to mask their prejudice in the face of accusations from fellow Lutherans of an un-Christian hatred of people based on race, they threw the debate into the political and foreign policy realm by claiming that Communists instigated the civil rights movement to foment a revolution in the United States. This gave them a more comfortable position from which to argue: instead of racial prejudice, they claimed that they defended the United States from ungodly Communist infiltrations when they denounced black leaders and their white supporters. In reality, they persisted with accusatory tactics when they discussed the civil rights movement because they disliked the changes it embodied. After twenty-plus years of blaming communism for every ill, far right-leaning Lutherans maintained that Communists inspired the civil rights movement in order to destabilize the United States. But their accusations escalated severely with the onset of the black power movement because this radicalization intensified their fear. Regarding this topic, however, ultraconservatives combated not only their traditional moderate and liberal foes but also conservatives who agreed that communism posed a danger in most other quarrels. The civil rights movement presents a poignant example of how anti-Communist terror became a convenient excuse for demeaning anything that attempted to change U.S. society, even when it promoted equality.[33]

Far-right Lutherans asserted that Communists targeted the black community and had gained entrance into the United States through the civil rights movement. A laywoman explained that civil rights advocates ignored that "the Socialists are *just using the negro* to get their votes, and frankly, look at all of these negro fronts—who started them???????????? Of course, the reds." The small and politically conservative *Lutheran Ambassador* of the Association of Lutheran Congregations concurred that "some Communists have likely infiltrated the civil rights movement." Conservatives often revealed these position when they attacked other Lutherans who supported civil rights policies. The politically moderate editors of church-related periodicals especially opened themselves to attack because they supported equality in their journals. The *Lutheran Witness* editor, Martin W. Mueller, came under fire for printing an article about racism. An anonymous reader ripped the story out and scribbled across it in blue magic marker, "'racism' is a term exploited by [an] Ungodly anti-Christian Christless Marxist Population. The word 'racism' does *not* belong in a Christian publication. As it aids and Abets the subversive communistic anti-Christian conspiracy." Arch-conservative Lutherans assumed that Communists lurked in the United States and preyed on people in the civil rights movement. Thus, a volatile anticommunism fueled the right-wing conspiracy theorists into more and more suspicion that Communists inspired racial unrest in the United States.[34]

Ultra-rightist Lutherans became even more convinced that Communists operated within black rights organizations as the civil rights movement evolved into black power. A *Lutheran* reader said that this "insurrection" would lead "into a godless Christless Communist dominated world." The *Black Manifesto* especially riled conservative opinions. In 1969, the Black Economic Development Conference demanded $500 million in reparations from Christian churches and Jewish organizations because of racist oppression dating back to the first Africans in America during the colonial era; they wanted the money to rehabilitate the black community and targeted churches because they assumed they would find a more sympathetic voice than they would from the government. This request for money rankled conservatives, who called it blackmail. These conservative Lutherans felt that "the black militants [*sic*] demand for 500 million is nothing but a Communist brainstorm and robbery without a gun." Another person claimed that the manifesto read "like it was written in the 20's by a Bolshevik." Condemnations of the manifesto reveal that conservatives still used the charge of communism against anything with which they disagreed. An LCA layperson best summarized this fact. In a letter to President Robert J. Marshall, a civil rights advocate, he wrote that "while I am not anti-Negro, in no manner will I support any man or group who is a revolutionary or even a mild or timid socialist or Communist."[35]

In addition, conservatives accused the civil rights leader, Reverend Dr. Martin Luther King, Jr., of Communist affiliations, false accusations that persisted until his assassination in 1968.[36] For example, King faced charges of communism after he came out against the Vietnam War, a position King had long deliberated for fear that his stance would alienate Lyndon B. Johnson and keep the president from supporting civil rights legislation to spite King. But King's conscience won this battle and in August 1965 he publicly called for a negotiated settlement to the war. By 1967, as the United States escalated the war and with no end in sight, King participated in several antiwar demonstrations, which gave conservatives their fodder. *Lutheran News* explained that "although King said he could not condone demonstration by-products including draft card burnings, the burning of the American flag and waving of Viet Cong flags, the fact remains that he knowingly worked with communists." *Jesus to the Communist World* joined these accusations. After King's assassination, Richard Wurmbrand lamented that "I was distressed about the shooting of Pastor Martin Luther King. I was also distressed about the flags in USA waved at half-mast not in honor of those who die for [the] Fatherland in Vietnam, not in honor of the Christian martyrs killed in the Communist camp, but in honor of a man who is dead now and beyond our judgment, but who organized the blocking of all the Government offices in Washington, D.C."[37]

Other Lutherans echoed this anticommunism. A Wisconsin Evangelical Lutheran Synod (WELS) pastor bemoaned that a man who fractionalized the United States "bears the name of the great Reformer" Martin Luther. He set his argument within the typical framework of Lutheran two kingdoms theology and obedience to the government when he insisted that Luther preached obedience to all government while King advocated disobedience. A pastor and his church asked ALC President Frederik A. Schiotz to rescind his "endorsement of and his request for our prayers on behalf of the work of this man, Martin Luther King and his organization, the Southern Christian Leadership Conference in the furtherance of their actions under the influence of known Communists." An LCMS layperson denounced president Oliver R. Harms's presence at a King memorial service because he "is an apostle of violence and lawlessness, a racist, a power hungry tyrant and an individual who has done more for the Communist Party than any other person in this decade."[38]

Far-right Lutherans more pointedly labeled King himself a Communist. For example, a couple disliked his association with Bayard Rustin. Rustin was a long-time civil rights advocate who worked behind the scenes while allowing others to accept public recognition. Rustin was one of the prime movers behind the 1964 March on Washington yet still today seldom gets the credit he deserves for his influence. Rustin's affiliation with known Communists and his once having belonged to the Young Communist League prompted even his allies and friends to hide him in the background. Indeed, this fact and his being "convicted of sex perversion in Pasadena" prompted this couple to criticize King's affiliation with Rustin. They decided that King's appearance with a homosexual and admitted Communist meant that he, too, condoned communism. Others simply hurled blind accusations: a *Lutheran* reader stated that King "is a member of 22 Communist front organizations and has had 3 proven Communists as his aid[e]s." Again because he publicly supported King and the civil rights movement, *Lutheran Witness* editor Martin W. Mueller received even more frightening allegations of King's communism. An LCMS layman defended King's assassin because he "was courageous enough to risk his own life to execute a Communist subversive who openly threatened the very existence of our nation." He continued that the killer "has carried out the will of all true Americans. Martin Looter King's brand of 'Peace' was the same as that which was peddled by prohibition racketeers." Some even called King the anti-Christ. They asserted that "with one hand he preached peace and to pretend he was God-fearing—while on the other hand, he prepared his evil, diabolical work—the work of evil Communism." Radical right Lutherans sought an excuse for their opposition to King's legacy and found it in the decades-long battle against Communist infiltration into the United States. They looked for signs of Communist incursions into U.S. life and thought they had proof because of King's activism.[39]

But ultra-rightist Lutherans stood alone in their extremist King condemnations because even most conservatives took a softer stance. Conservatives distrusted King but presumed that he merely failed to see how his work aided communism. In other words, some Lutherans opposed the civil rights movement and King but did not claim he was a Communist; they implied that he accidentally championed communism. An LCA layperson stated that King was not a Communist, but "he is certainly playing into their hands." Some LCMS members maintained that "this man has been a tool of the Communists and engaged their methods to create anarchy in our land." Another layperson explained that the Communists always mentioned King "as the man that all Communists should support and should look up to in the leadership of the forthcoming struggles." In short, King "has by his demonic philosophy of civil disobedience done more than any other . . . to promote a socialist communist ideology in our midst." Less-radical conservatives used milder rhetoric when condemning King but still displayed anti-Communist prejudices when they claimed that he inadvertently assisted communism.[40]

While this rhetoric insinuated that Communists targeted African Americans because they were easily swayed, extremists within conservative Lutheran ranks more bluntly called blacks "thriftless Communists dupes." An LCA layman questioned the National Council of Churches of Christ for funding "black development aid" because it bordered on communism. While he thought the money might assist a few black people "who are really trying to help themselves," he doubted that the majority would do so; rather, he feared that they would adopt Communist thinking and expect socialist welfare programs to assist them. Claiming that more African Americans demanded free handouts, something he associated with communism, than worked to provide for themselves, he used the stereotype of African Americans being lazy to argue that they were therefore more susceptible to communism. A *Lutheran* reader put it more bluntly when he called King a Communist thief and declared that "instead of marching and singing little ditties he could at least insist that his people stay in school, work hard like the rest of us and be able to hold a job." An LCMS laywoman also thought that Communists brainwashed African Americans too easily. She assumed that King was a Communist and thus asked "will Americans and the Negroe community in particular . . . summarily reject this demagogic leadership or will they continue to be brainwashed?" She predicted the former.[41]

Such conservative accusations of communism also contained overt racism. An LCA laywoman sent the LCA's *Lutheran* editor G. Elson Ruff a series of questions as a test to see if he supported communism; answering yes to any of them meant that he did. Question five read, "Am I promoting consciously or unconsciously miscegenation?" For her, interracial marriage was something only "evil" Communists supported. An LCMS member lamented that Communists used African Americans because they were not as intelligent. As proof, he asserted that blacks "have consistently gravitated to the level of their aboriginal ancestors. Look at Africa." Another person told LCMS President Oliver R. Harms that Martin Luther King, Jr., and "his henchmen" acted like animals during their protests in Selma, Alabama, and expressed disgust at the alleged "sex that took place there." The presence of Concordia College, an LCMS institution, in Selma led to some of this hostility. Supporters, faculty, and students marched against southern segregation and angered ultra-conservatives within that denomination. A laywoman best shows the connection to racism and anticommunism: she proclaimed that Communists used blacks and their money to foment revolution when they should have been using the funds for farming: "The ant has much sense, it seems pathetic that the negro is not as intelligent as a little busy ant."[42]

Not all Lutherans were so racist. From across the political and theological spectrum, including conservatives, moderates, and liberals, others reacted indignantly to allegations that likened the civil rights movement to communism. They avoided making a sharp distinction between the civil rights and black power movements and instead defended African-American organizations and leaders from charges of communism. Although a variety of lay-Lutherans and leaders responded similarly, the clergy more eloquently voiced these views. After Los Angeles erupted into mob violence in 1965 in the Watts neighborhood, a crisis precipitated by poor economic conditions and a legacy of mistrust and antagonism with white police officers, ALC President Frederik A. Schiotz admitted that some Communists might have participated in the rioting but did not want "the confusion occasioned for many by the Los Angeles riots [to become] the incentive for rash judgments and comment." Schiotz also defended Martin Luther King, Jr.'s, reputation. An ALC investigation of King prior to his appearance at a Luther League convention found no connection to communism. But Schiotz lamented that "in certain circles in this country today, when you want to be sure to stop someone's work, then the technique is to try to smear that person as a Communist." He recognized the damage of false accusations and refuted them with factual evidence. Martin W. Mueller also pointed out that "if there had been any real substance to the allegation that Dr. King's activities were communist-inspired and communist-supported, the President of the United States would not have ordered the U.S. flag flown at half staff" after his death. These Lutherans found it preposterous that their opponents called King and his followers Communists. They contended that no significant Communist effort to infiltrate the United States existed and therefore considered these accusations another form of reactionary politics.[43]

Still, the defense of the civil rights movement also demonstrated that even liberal and moderate Lutherans continued to distrust communism. For example, G. Elson Ruff balanced his civil rights advocacy with a suspicion of communism. He stated that "the second high-priority target of the Reds in the U.S. was the Negro people, and here the Reds have suffered a great defeat. The representative leaders among the Negroes are anti-Communist." Ruff therefore revealed that he backed black equality but disliked communism. Significantly, he simultaneously shunned the notion that Communists had gained a foundation into U.S. society. He explained that "I do not think you will find the slightest trace of Communist influence [in Martin Luther King, Jr.'s, writings]. My own opinion is that these charges against him are untrue." He endorsed King by recognizing that red scare tactics falsely implicated him; but he did so only after he knew this for certain.[44]

The Lutheran disagreement about internal Communist threats included emotional debates about the civil rights movement. Racist Lutherans linked the entire movement to communism. Their intense fear of internal Communist threats also affected their opinion of the civil rights and black power movements. Faced with calls for Christian understanding about the plight of minorities in the United States, these Lutherans sought a religious counterpoint and found it in anticommunism. They asserted that communism was an "evil" force and, since they insisted that Communists controlled black efforts for equality, they were also "evil." By framing their civil rights opposition in the jargon of a theological battle versus evil communism, they, at least in their minds, justified their opposition to a movement that sought racial equality. Liberal to moderate Lutherans rebutted these notions with continued proof that no Communist conspiracy threatened the United States and denounced anyone who thought that Communists led the civil rights movement. Rather, they saw the movement and its leaders pining for equality, promoted its agenda, and denied that Communists infiltrated black organizations.

REVEREND RICHARD WURMBRAND

A case study of a Lutheran immigrant pastor even more pointedly demonstrates Lutheran differences regarding internal Communist threats. The Reverend Richard Wurmbrand, a Romanian immigrant, exemplified conservatives who insisted that Communists wanted to take over the world, including the United States. He spoke at many Lutheran churches against Communist tyrannies and displayed an intense hatred of anything Communist.

Richard Wurmbrand's public life in Romania began, ironically, as a Communist propagandist before World War II. He studied at a Moscow party school, returned to Romania, and served as secretary of the Young Communists until his first arrest because the government had outlawed communism. After his release, Wurmbrand denounced his party affiliation and Jewish heritage to convert to Christianity. He affiliated with a number of different churches, was ordained by the German Lutheran minority church, and served as a professor at the only Protestant seminary in the country. In 1947, the Communist government arrested him on the charge of crimes against humanity because he had betrayed his former Communist colleagues prior to the

Communist takeover of Romania. He remained in jail until 1956 when a wave of anti-Stalinism swept across Europe and led to the liberation of many political prisoners. Upon release, he immediately demanded his own congregation, but the Romanian churches felt he aggravated the Communist government too much and therefore put the church at risk. They refused his demand and so he publicly denounced the church leadership. Wurmbrand therefore evangelized on his own until his rearrest in the late 1950s, this time on the vague charge of religious activism. The authorities released him in 1964, and shortly thereafter he left Romania with the help of the Norsk Israel Society, for which he had previously worked. He traveled to Norway, began a career of speaking against communism, and first encountered the American Lutheran Church through its Oslo congregation. Pastor Myrus L. Knutson encouraged Wurmbrand to take his message to the United States and introduced him to ALC officials. The ALC wanted him to visit the United States on a one-year evangelist stint, but these plans fell through because Wurmbrand refused to take a physical and sign papers that would have accounted for the money he raised. He traveled to the United States in the spring of 1966 without denominational backing, and trouble immediately began. At gatherings that took place in local Lutheran churches of every denomination, he chastised Lutheran leaders for failing to promote his agenda and declared that Lutherans ignored those persecuted by the Communists. Although the ALC national leadership had no control over who individual congregations invited to their churches, Wurmbrand's outbursts prompted Frederik A. Schiotz to advise ALC clergy against having him speak. Wurmbrand denounced Lutheran leaders in every denomination, frightened Lutherans with assertions that Communists controlled their churches, and split the churches between conservatives and moderate/liberals.[45]

Wurmbrand published a number of books and tracts that promoted his agenda and counseled that communism might infiltrate the United States. He tried to convince people to aid Christians imprisoned inside communism's borders by sending him money, but he never detailed how he intended to use these funds. His books outlined *ad nauseam* how the Communists had tortured him and sought to purge the world of all religion. Amid this material, he included admonitions that Communists wanted to conquer the entire world and threatened the United States. For example, he wrote subtle phrases such as "God may use the communists to punish you [Americans] for a sin" and continually warned that more and more people were victimized by this "creeping" force. He also claimed that "Americans must know that they have at times unwittingly assisted the Russians in imposing upon us a regime of murder and terror." Each of Wurmbrand's books belabors the point that Communists kill Christians, describes methods of torture, beseeches Americans to assist their brethren in chains, and instills a tremendous fear of communism with suggestions that its plan to take over the world was working. Furthermore, Wurmbrand is a good example of how politics, diplomacy, and theology merged into one for conservative Lutherans when they considered the battle against communism. For Wurmbrand it was a crusade.[46]

Wurmbrand's periodical, *Jesus to the Communist World*, mirrored his books' charges but more directly warned that Communists had infiltrated U.S. institutions. He especially cautioned that the Russian Orthodox Church "*in USA with a membership of one million American citizens has just recognized the Moscow Patriarchate, nominated by the Communist butchers*. The Red propagandists of this Patriarchate will have free access to these American churches." He alleged that Communists used the Russian Orthodox Church's U.S. presence to undermine democracy. He also explained why Communists targeted the United States: "The fall of the States would mean the destruction of Christian civilization, the end of liberty everywhere and a terrible blow to the church of Christ."[47]

Wurmbrand relied on fear to convince people of his cause. One of his postcards showed a Soviet guard tower watching over several graves marked with crosses that represented the various Soviet-controlled countries. The message was that the Soviets killed these countries' freedom and spirituality, and the crosses emphasized the religious war taking place. Wurmbrand's public appearances evinced the same passion because his dramatic preaching shocked people and created an atmosphere of terror by blaming Communists for evil. A minister described a presentation in which "with realistic screams, Wurmbrand imitated the voice of a woman being beaten in the next cell." His talk focused on his Romanian ordeal but frightened U.S. audiences with the implication that Communists meant to torture people around the world. Wurmbrand also utilized scare tactics in a letter to ALC President Frederik A. Schiotz protesting Schiotz's recommendation that pastors resist allowing Wurmbrand to speak. Wurmbrand explained that "Red China ministers are buried alive now, that Christians with whom they find hidden a Bible are stripped naked, anointed with honey, and exposed to the scorching sun," and that "in Northern Korea children who attended secret Sunday schools in which they were told about Christ had chopsticks rammed through both ears." After invoking these ghastly images, he asked Schiotz, "Will you be able to answer before God when He asks you, 'Why did you beware of the danger of inviting Wurmbrand to speak and never beware of the danger of inviting those who poison the youth of America with the Communist doctrine, a doctrine of hatred and mass murder?'" Because ALC leaders disparaged his ministry, by 1974 Wurmbrand alarmed people with claims that the American Lutheran Church knowingly worked with Communists. He refused to associate with the ALC leadership because "I would have had to participate at such receptions" in which ALC people mingled with the "Communist influenced" Lutheran World Federation. Although he shunned ALC national authorities, he continued to preach in local congregations and regularly sought to persuade laypeople to question their ALC leaders because he so passionately saw the war against communism as a crusade to save Christianity.[48]

Wurmbrand made false accusations against anyone who challenged him, most commonly by accusing church leaders of promoting a Communist agenda. Lutheran World Federation (LWF), the international body of Lutherans that coordinated conferences and relief efforts, especially received criticism because it cooperated with the Lutheran churches inside Soviet satellite nations. Wurmbrand claimed that the staff of "the Lutheran World Federation is infiltrated by Communism." After making these allegations, Wurmbrand insisted that "the truth about what happens in Communist countries must be gotten from Wurmbrand, and only from Wurmbrand." A non-Lutheran example provides further proof about his tactics. The far-right Christian organization Underground Evangelism (UE) supported Wurmbrand for a few years but eventually fell out of the Romanian's good graces when it questioned his motives. Thereafter, Wurmbrand and his son, Mihai, sued two UE leaders because of their "conspiracy to commit [the] murder" of Wurmbrand, the "crime of rape," and their "gross immorality." Wurmbrand sent these allegations around the world in letters to his supporters and only stopped when the two men countersued for defamation of character.[49]

Ultra-conservative Lutheran entities came to Wurmbrand's defense. The *Lutheran News* defended Wurmbrand from Schiotz's criticism and quoted him: "I accuse you [Schiotz] . . . to have brought the wolf [communism] in the stable of the sheep [Christians], with the result that the sheep will be destroyed." The article stated that "according to Wurmbrand, some American churchmen are associated with 'Communist spies' in the World Council of Churches" and never refuted this claim. Once again, evidence already presented proves the falsity of these claims because Schiotz himself opposed communism. The periodical also favorably reviewed each of Wurmbrand's books, published articles he authored, and supported statements that he made against the three largest Lutheran churches. Wurmbrand therefore supplemented his own publicity machine with other far-right presses. And in each release he emphasized that communism was attacking the church and not just political entities.[50]

Testimonies from people who read Wurmbrand's literature and heard him speak demonstrate his effect on conservative Lutherans. Wurmbrand's Christian witness dazzled people into believing him without question. One pastor invited Wurmbrand to speak because "he will breathe a fresh spirit into preaching evangelism." ALC constituents felt inspired by Wurmbrand and tried to change Schiotz's mind about condemning him. A woman exclaimed that "this man has been a cross in my life since I first heard him preach many, many months ago." An LCA layperson explained that "when a person such as myself reads a book like that [*Christ in the Communist Prison*], it is assumed that the contents are reliable." Conservative Lutherans thus believed "that God spared this man's life to bring the free-world the truth."[51]

After Wurmbrand entranced conservative Lutherans with his emotional faith, he seduced them into accepting harsh anticommunism. An ALC member stated that "he believes that the Gospel of Jesus Christ includes warning against Satan and his most widespread and insidious conspiracy: communism." Another layperson stated that Wurmbrand's testimony before the House Committee on Un-American Activities proved "that whenever Communists come to power, they torture and kill Christians." Wurmbrand exploited the United States' anti-Communist hysteria to convert people to his radical anticommunism. In addition, he brainwashed people with even more outrageous claims. He convinced a laywoman that Communists hid in Christian churches to subtly convince Americans to promote socialism. She told LCMS President Preus that "my own personal experience attests to this without realizing it. I often fell pray to humanistic teaching under the guise of Christianity." Years of believing Cold War rhetoric about sly Communists made conservative Lutherans susceptible to Wurmbrand's fear tactics, which further convinced them that Communists wanted to infiltrate the United States and vanquish Christianity. Wurmbrand fueled their insistence that the Cold War was both a political confrontation and a war to preserve Christianity.[52]

In contrast to Wurmbrand's advocates, moderate to liberal Lutherans feared that he would create another McCarthy-type campaign within Lutheranism. The ALC pastor in Norway, who first promoted Wurmbrand's coming to the United States, later stated that he was "deeply disturbed by Wurmbrand's continued projection of negativism and 'vicious' provocations." These Lutherans especially disliked Wurmbrand's accusations against Lutheranism. ALC President Kent S. Knutson lamented that "he conducts an intensive campaign of vilification against his own church" and continued, "I believe he accuses falsely." An article in the Evangelical periodical *Christianity Today* best summarized Wurmbrand's opponents' view. It asserted that "the world should be kept aware of atrocities, but excessive repetition instills hatred. This is an immoral antidote that perpetuates the original evil by extending it to innocent people." Or, as Schiotz asserted, "No, our church is not a front for Communist propaganda, nor must we yield to the fear paralysis that a man like Wurmbrand seeks to disseminate."[53]

ALC pastors provide a good example of why moderate Lutherans opposed Wurmbrand's rhetoric. They explained that he incited far-right elements in their congregations to advance his agenda. Reverend Obert J. Landsverk stated that "he has caused quite a 'stir' with our Rightists" during his "rather lengthy tirades on Communism." Although ministers admitted that "we can't help but appreciate this man's burning zeal," they also stated that "his methods are appalling." An Iowa pastor asked Schiotz for advice after a John Birch Society member of his congregation organized a "Congress of Freedom" convention at which he asked Wurmbrand to speak. The pastor wanted to prevent Wurmbrand's appearance but feared a conservative backlash if he protested. These and a myriad of other letters detail how Wurmbrand inspired the radical right and placed Lutheran leaders in the awkward position of refuting his claims without alienating their conservative constituents.[54]

Wurmbrand's rivals also wondered about his psychological instability. Frederik A. Schiotz pointedly advised him to "get the long period of physical rest which the Norwegian Israel Mission had wished" upon his release from prison because fatigue heightened his paranoia. Schiotz admitted that his first contact with Wurmbrand went well but that "since then we have seen another Wurmbrand" who claimed that Communists lurked everywhere. Others more openly charged that Wurmbrand was mentally ill. Myrus L. Knutson cautioned that "a psychiatrist who observed him casually from a distance recently said that he was getting dangerously near a messiah complex." He later asserted that "without a doubt if anything went to court psychiatrists would have little difficulty in proving his unbalanced state." A Lutheran World Federation official maintained, "He may no longer be capable of calm, objective judgment" and stated that "martyrdom has also left him with a degree of imbalance in good judgment and tactful procedure." Schiotz heightened his doubt about Wurmbrand's mental health after the immigrant pastor sued the ALC president for defamation of character because Schiotz advised ALC pastors against allowing Wurmbrand to speak to their congregations. Schiotz's lawyer therefore advised him not to answer Wurmbrand's letters; Schiotz responded that "I regret to be in this position but what I consider an illness in him requires it." This public evidence, combined with his correspondence to many Lutheran leaders, convinced them that he suffered from mental instability.[55]

Lutheran leaders questioned Wurmbrand's financial motives as well. Wurmbrand never accounted for the donations he collected or detailed how the money helped Christians in Communist countries. In fact, Lutheran leaders knew that he used it to fund his U.S. propaganda machine and maintain his livelihood, and this knowledge led them to censure Wurmbrand's fund-raising. A Lutheran Council U.S.A. leader asserted that he "would not encourage the giving of funds until I could assure the donors that I, at least, on a confidential basis know precisely how the funds are going to be used." Schiotz worried that Wurmbrand's "approach was that of a typical money raiser." Furthermore, a Lutheran World Ministries report stated that "Richard Wurmbrand himself . . . admits [neither] he nor his missions do any work in Rumania. *This is from his own pen!* He states: 'I have not sent anything to anybody.' He further states, 'that goes for my organization.'" Wurmbrand solicited money in his speeches and written literature and claimed that it helped Christians behind the Iron Curtain. But no proof existed that he dispersed the money in those countries, and his slow-growing U.S. empire indicated that he kept the funds for himself and his U.S. operations. His detractors thought that he gained financially by exploiting American fears of communism.[56]

Moderate to liberal Lutherans coupled their efforts against Wurmbrand with a continued stance against communism. In part, they were defending themselves against the inevitable conservative charges that their denunciation either naively assisted Communists or revealed their "Communist leanings." But their response also demonstrates an unwillingness to yield patriotism to the far-right; they supported the United States in its Cold War endeavors and took pains to prove it. G. Elson Ruff maintained that he disliked Communist governments but called the preacher's claims about Romania dubious and insisted that Wurmbrand offered no proof for his torture stories. Schiotz's denunciations often stated that "I conclude that more is accomplished for people in Communist countries through LWF gifts because we, too, have channels and we know what the money accomplishes." Schiotz desired to help Christians inside Communist borders just as much as Wurmbrand but did so without fomenting fears of Communists taking over America. Other ALC leaders mirrored the thought that "funds expended through Lutheran World Federation, . . . for which there must be regular audits, will accomplish more per dollar than anything a private individual might do." Wurmbrand's antagonists deplored his depiction of a demonic force creeping across the world and insisted that no Communists imminently endangered U.S. security. They still disliked communism and therefore supported the Cold War but relegated McCarthy-era fears to the past.[57]

Richard Wurmbrand's U.S. ministry provides a good example of how Lutherans debated the issue of domestic Communist threats between 1964 and 1975. Ardent Cold Warriors listened to Wurmbrand's message, convinced others to follow him, spread his propaganda, and blasted Lutheran leaders for ignoring him. Rightists even convinced some less-zealous moderates to believe Wurmbrand. Underneath the surface of Wurmbrand's denunciations of Communist nations lay the peril of a U.S. infiltration if Christians failed to heed his call. But other Lutherans asserted that it was Wurmbrand who threatened the nation. They knew no Communists ran the Lutheran churches, questioned Wurmbrand's mental stability, and detailed how he misspent the funds he collected. A subtle dispute about how to fight communism was woven into each side's rhetoric. Conservatives believed Wurmbrand's claim that Communist agents worked to crush the entire world while their counterparts denounced such notions based on the reality that the United States remained safe from internal threats.

CONCLUSION

The Cold War legacy of fearing that Communists infiltrated the United States to subvert democracy persisted from 1964 to 1975 but no longer enjoyed near-unanimous support. Ultra-conservatives continued to accuse innocent people and institutions of communism, labeled anything that went against their philosophies Communist, and depicted this as a battle against Satan. Other conservatives agreed that communism posed a danger to the domestic United States without making such radical charges. In both of these instances, however, any Communist believer threatened world freedom, and Communists worked throughout the world to undermine democracy. But many Lutherans denounced such rhetoric. They explained that illogical fears, not real dangers, led to these accusations. They disdained the Communist giants but no longer saw them hiding inside the United States. Domestically, they refuted claims that Communists worked secretly within U.S. institutions and the civil rights movement, defended Christian organizations from attack, and tried to convince people that no Communists threatened U.S. security. This entire conversation took place within the Lutheran denominations but seldom included a theological component: religion lay under the surface and spiritual language crept into the conversation, but it was seldom exclusively concerned with Lutheran theology. Rather, Lutherans were participating in a public debate in which the lines between the separation of church and state blurred. All Americans, including the churches, felt a responsibility to discuss the fear of internal communism. Those who feared that Communists operated inside the United States clung to traditional beliefs that all Communists threatened the United States while their opponents labeled this an irrational and non-provable suspicion; this argument also occurred in other debates, especially in reference to the Vietnam War.

NOTES

1. Because scholars generally agree that a Red scare swept across America during the Cold War and even before, only a quick highlight of an abbreviated list of secondary sources from an

extensive historiography seems appropriate. For a larger selection, see the bibliography. The best red-scare history is Ellen Schrecker's *Many Are the Crimes: McCarthyism in America* (Boston: Little, Brown and Company, 1998). Peter H. Buckingham's *America Sees Red: Anticommunism in America, 1870s to 1890s* (Claremont, CA: Regina Books, 1988) provides a survey of anti-Communist activities. Two excellent studies of McCarthyism's impact on the 1950s are David M. Oshinsky's *A Conspiracy So Immense: The World of Joe McCarthy* (New York: Free Press, 1983) and Richard H. Pells's *The Liberal Mind in a Conservative Age: American Intellectuals in the 1940s and 1950s* (New York: Harper and Row, 1985). To see that Christians played a role in the anti-Communist hysteria but ultimately debated about it, see Patrick Allitt, *Religion in America since 1945: A History* (New York: Columbia University Press, 2003); Martin E. Marty, *Modern American Religion*, vol. 3, *Under God, Indivisible, 1941–1960* (Chicago: University of Chicago Press, 1996); Randall Dean Austin, "Caution Christian Soldiers: The Mainline Protestant Churches and the Cold War" (Ph.D. diss., University of Arkansas, 1997); James Hudnut-Beumler, *Looking for God in the Suburbs: The Religion of the American Dream and Its Critics, 1945–1965* (New Brunswick, NJ: Rutgers University Press, 1994).

2. To examine the larger Lutheran context of debate and fighting, see Mary Todd, *Authority Vested: A Story of Identity and Change in the Lutheran Church–Missouri Synod* (Grand Rapids, MI: William B. Eerdmans, 2000); Lawrence L. Kersten, *The Lutheran Ethic: The Impact of Religion on Laymen and Clergy* (Detroit: Wayne State University Press, 1970); L. Deane Lagerquist, *The Lutherans* (Westport, CT: Greenwood Press, 1999); W. Kent Gilbert, *Commitment to Unity: A History of the Lutheran Church in America* (Philadelphia: Fortress Press, 1988).

3. "U.S. Red Leader Says Party and Church Have Common Goals," *Christian News* 1 (22 July 1968): 1; "Meditation," *Lutherans-Alert* 2 (December 1967): 11; "A Marxist Textbook," *Lutherans-Alert* 7 (November 1972): 17. Although conservatives regularly made these outrageous claims, no evidence suggests that any Communists ever truly threatened U.S. Christian institutions. Although some studies prove that Communists tried to infiltrate America, they also demonstrate that these efforts were unsuccessful. Unfortunately, none of these books ably examine the CPUSA after 1960 because its influence had dwindled. Harvey Klehr, John Earl Haynes, and Fridrikh Igorevich Firsov, *The Secret World of American Communism* (New Haven, CT: Yale University Press, 1995).

4. Nancy Kuschke to G. Elson Ruff, 6 January 1965, Evangelical Lutheran Church in America Archives, Chicago, Illinois (hereafter ELCA), G. Elson Ruff Papers, box 82, "Extremists, 1965" (emphasis in original); Martha B. Carroll to G. Elson Ruff, 22 January 1965, ELCA, G. Elson Ruff Papers, box 82, "Extremists, 1965"; Murl S. Cahn to G. Elson Ruff, 13 January 1965, ELCA, G. Elson Ruff Papers, box 82, "Extremists, 1965"; Herman A. Nelson to Jacob A. O. Preus, 27 June 1970, Concordia Historical Institute, St. Louis, Missouri (hereafter CHI), Executive Office, box 12, "Conscientious Objectors, 1970–71"; Anne Anzini to G. Elson Ruff, 17 January 1965, ELCA, G. Elson Ruff Papers, box 82, "Extremists"; Carl A. Zimmerman to G. Elson Ruff, 18 April 1968, ELCA, G. Elson Ruff Papers, box 22, "Y-Z."

5. F. Lamont Heppe, Jr., to G. Elson Ruff, January 1965, ELCA, G. Elson Ruff Papers, box 82, "Extremists, 1965"; N. Harms, "What of the Communist Threat?" *Lutheran Spokesman* 8 (January 1965): 14–16; Donald H. Glass to G. Elson Ruff, 20 April 1968, ELCA, G. Elson Ruff Papers, box 18, "G"; Harry H. Feistner to Frederik A. Schiotz, 17 March 1970, ELCA, Frederik A. Schiotz Papers, box 43, "Feistner, Harry H."; Mel Iversens to J. A. O. Preus, 5 February 1972, CHI, Executive Office, box 10, "Communism, 1962–1972."

6. Jack Pope to Martin W. Mueller, 19 March 1968, CHI, Lutheran Witness Letters, box 4, "Letters from Readers 1968"; George D. Spoor to Martin W. Mueller, March 1969, CHI, Lutheran Witness Letters, box 3, "Se-Su" (emphasis in original); Frances Brown to J. A. O.

Preus, 8 July 1969, CHI, Executive Office, UPN box 81, "World Council of Churches Correspondence, 1969–1973"; Alice S. Shaner to G. Elson Ruff, 30 December 1964, ELCA, G. Elson Ruff Papers, box 82, "Extremists, 1965"; Howard Murphy to G. Elson Ruff, 16 January 1965, ELCA, G. Elson Ruff Papers, box 82, "Extremists, 1965"; Joe Yugo to G. Elson Ruff [1965], G. Elson Ruff Papers, box 82, "Extremists, 1965"; Walter S. Berger to G. Elson Ruff, 12 April 1968, ELCA, G. Elson Ruff Papers, box 17, "B"; Ralph W. Cowden to Albert P. Stauderman, 19 February 1971, ELCA, Albert P. Stauderman Papers, box 86, "C."

7. Tyler Thompson, "A Look at the Left," *One* 14 (July–August 1964): 14–20; "Don't 'Squawk' before You Know the Facts," *Lutheran Digest* 16 (Summer 1968): 61–62; J. A. O. Preus to Jacob Bauer, 20 November 1969, CHI, Executive Office, box 10, "Communism, 1962–1972."

8. I. E. Howard, "Communism Can't Win," *Lutheran Digest* 12 (Fall 1964): 59–60; J. N. Bourque to G. Elson Ruff, 7 March 1965, ELCA, G. Elson Ruff Papers, box 2, "O"; George Hedley, "The Easy Way Out," *Lutheran Digest* 16 (Fall 1968): 1–4.

9. G. Elson Ruff, "Some Call It Poison," *Lutheran* 2 (30 December 1964): 17–21; Ruff, "Editor's Opinion," *Lutheran* 8 (10 April 1968): 50.

10. Jonathan M. Schoenwald's *A Time for Choosing: The Rise of Modern American Conservatism* (New York: Oxford University Press, 2001) contains an excellent history of the John Birch Society. G. Elson Ruff to George A. Palm, 3 December 1964, ELCA, G. Elson Ruff Papers, box 11, "Pa"; Ruff to Erland L. Borg, 26 February 1965, ELCA, G. Elson Ruff Papers, box 2, "Bo"; Ruff to R. M. VanHorn, 6 May 1966, ELCA, G. Elson Ruff Papers, box 15, "Va"; Ruff to R. M. VanHorn, 26 May 1966, ELCA, G. Elson Ruff Papers, box 15, "Va."

11. Kingsley D. Holmes to G. Elson Ruff, 4 January 1965, ELCA, G. Elson Ruff Papers, box 82, "Extremists, 1965"; H. B. Johnson to G. Elson Ruff, 28 January 1965, ELCA, G. Elson Ruff Papers, box 82, "Extremists, 1965"; J Wilson Harner to G. Elson Ruff, 2 February 1965, ELCA, G. Elson Ruff Papers, box 6, "Hal-Han."

12. Phyllis Naylor, "Sweet Freedom's Song," *One* 15 (November 1965): 38–43; F. Dean Lueking, "Roots of the Radical Right," *Lutheran Quarterly* 28 (August 1966): 197–204; Kent S. Knutson, "Dear Fellow Ministers," *Commentator* 11 (April 1971): 4–7; Albert P. Stauderman to N. Bailey, 4 April 1975, ELCA, Albert P. Stauderman Papers, box 96, "A-Be 1975."

13. G. Elson Ruff to Mrs. T. Franks, 3 December 1964, ELCA, G. Elson Ruff Papers, box 5, "Fra"; G. Elson Ruff to Paul G. Erickson, 6 March 1968, ELCA, G. Elson Ruff Papers, box 18, "E"; Martin W. Mueller to George D. Spoor, 13 March 1969, CHI, Lutheran Witness Letters, box 2, "Se-Su"; Frederik A. Schiotz, n.d., ELCA, Frederik A. Schiotz Papers, box 43, "Feistner, Harry H."

14. G. Elson Ruff to Courtney W. Anderson, 26 March 1965, ELCA, G. Elson Ruff Papers, box 1, "A-An"; G. Elson Ruff to Fred Schwarz, 10 June 1966, ELCA, G. Elson Ruff Papers, box 12, "Scho"; Ralph L. Moellering, "Anti-Communism is Outmoded," *Lutheran Forum* 4 (November 1970): 9–11.

15. One other historian has probed Seeger's 1965 appearance at the Walther League's convention, and many of the findings in this book mirror his arguments. See Jon Pahl, *Hopes and Dreams of All: The International Walther League and Lutheran Youth in American Culture, 1893–1993* (Chicago: Wheat Ridge Ministries, 1993), 266–71. For other information on Seeger, see Griffin Fariello, *Red Scare: Memories of the American Inquisition* (New York: Avon Books, 1995), 362–67; Schrecker, *Many Are*, 311–12; and Charles DeBenedetti and Charles Chatfield, *An American Ordeal: The Antiwar Movement of the Vietnam Era* (Syracuse, NY: Syracuse University Press, 1990), 377–78.

16. Mrs. David E. Williams to Charles Lutz, 5 June 1965, ELCA, Frederik A. Schiotz Papers, box 25, "Youth Activity—David Brown"; Charlene Hall to G. Elson Ruff, 6 June 1965,

ELCA, G. Elson Ruff Papers, box 6, "Hal–Han"; Lutheran Church–Missouri Synod, 1965 Convention Minutes, 161–62, Young People's Committee, CHI.

17. Carl H. Amelung to Frederik A. Schiotz, 15 July 1970, ELCA, Frederik A. Schiotz Papers, box 103, "Youth Activity, 1970, Luther League Convention"; Ernie E. Brown to Frederik A. Schiotz, 23 July 1970, ELCA, Frederik A. Schiotz Papers, box 103, "Youth Activity, 1970, Luther League Convention"; Floris K. Springer to Frederik A. Schiotz, 5 August 1970, ELCA, Frederik A. Schiotz Papers, box 103, "Youth Activity, 1970, Luther League Convention"; Lloyd Trygestad, Oscar Bakken, and Harley Ostrem to Kent S. Knutson, 8 February 1971, ELCA, Kent S. Knutson Papers, box 1, "Li"; Lloyd Trygestad to Kent S. Knutson, 11 February 1971, ELCA, Kent S. Knutson Papers, box 1, "Li."

18. H. Nottbohm to Donna Brager, 24 August 1970, ELCA, Frederik A. Schiotz Papers, box 103, "Youth Activity, 1970, Luther League Convention"; Kent S. Knutson to Lloyd Trygestad, Oscar Bakken, and Harley Ostrem, 8 February 1971, ELCA, Kent S. Knutson Papers, box 1, "Li"; Kent S. Knutson to Lloyd Trygestad, Oscar Bakken, and Harley Ostrem, 1 March 1971, ELCA, Kent S. Knutson Papers, box 1, "Li."

19. The Lutheran Church in America belonged to both the WCC and the NCC, the American Lutheran Church belonged only to the WCC but participated in some operations of the NCC, and the Lutheran Church–Missouri Synod belonged to neither. For histories of the ecumenical movement, see Robert A. Schneider, "Voices of Many Waters: Church Federation in the Twentieth Century," in William R. Hutchison, ed., *Between the Times: The Travail of the Protestant Establishment in America, 1900–1960* (Cambridge: Cambridge University Press, 1989), 95–121; Jean Miller Schmidt, *Souls or the Social Order: The Two-Party System in American Protestantism* (New York: Carlson Publishing, Inc., 1991), 210–17; and Owen Chadwick, *The Christian Church in the Cold War* (New York: Penguin Books, 1992).

20. Mrs. Vernon Drake to Frederik A. Schiotz, 15 February 1969, ELCA, Frederik A. Schiotz Papers, box 66, "Wurmbrand"; Frances Brown to J. A. O. Preus, 4 January 1970, CHI, Executive Office, UPN box 81, "World Council of Churches Correspondence, 1969–1973"; John W. Olson to G. Elson Ruff, 1 November 1971, ELCA, Albert P. Stauderman Papers, box 87, "N-O"; Mr. And Mrs. Herbert Fooks to David W. Preus, 4 February 1973, ELCA, David W. Preus Papers, box 24, "?"; Ingeborg Brown to Robert J. Marshall, 17 November 1971, ELCA, Robert J. Marshall Papers, box 112, "Readers Digest Article-WCC"; Mrs. K. Simms to Albert P. Stauderman, November 1971, ELCA, Albert P. Stauderman Papers, box 88, "Sa-Si."

21. Wayne C. Jenkins to Frederik A. Schiotz, 24 March 1969, ELCA, Frederik A. Schiotz Papers, box 58, "Possible Membership-ALC"; Andrew D. Tomko to Robert J. Marshall, 29 November 1971, ELCA, Robert J. Marshall Papers, box 112, "Readers Digest Article-WCC."

22. H. Nottbohm to Wayne C. Jenkins, 27 March 1969, ELCA, Frederik A. Schiotz Papers, box 58, "Possible ALC Membership"; Albert P. Stauderman to R. K. Davis, 29 November 1971, ELCA, Albert P. Stauderman Papers, box 86, "D."

23. Frederik A. Schiotz to Paul Stendal, 10 March 1969, ELCA, Frederik A. Schiotz Papers, box 58, "NCC"; Frederik A. Schiotz to Mrs. W. R. Leininger, 14 May 1969, ELCA, Frederik A. Schiotz Papers, box 47, "WCC Reactions to 1968 Assembly I."

24. For an overview of the NCC that includes this and other information, see Jill Kristine Gill, "'Peace Is Not the Absence of War but the Presence of Justice': The National Council of Churches' Reaction and Response to the Vietnam War, 1965–1972" (Ph.D. diss., University of Pennsylvania, 1996), 58–60.

25. Mrs. William Wayne Huff, Jr., to Frederik A. Schiotz, 10 July 1968, ELCA, Frederik A. Schiotz Papers, box 58, "Possible Membership ALC"; John G. Hansen to Arnold Mickelson, 5 April 1969, ELCA, Frederik A. Schiotz Papers, box 58, "NCC" (emphasis in original); H. D.

Hammer to Robert J. Marshall, 4 October 1971, ELCA, Robert J. Marshall Papers, box 112, "Readers Digest Article-WCC."

26. William L. Howe to G. Elson Ruff, 7 April 1969, ELCA, G. Elson Ruff Papers, box 19, "Hoc-Hz"; Harold W. Loomis to David W. Preus, 2 October 1974, ELCA, David W. Preus Papers, ?, "?".

27. Mrs. Donald W. Nyberg to G. Elson Ruff, 14 March 1967, ELCA, G. Elson Ruff Papers, box 10, "N"; Harry H. Feistner to *Commentator* editor, 17 March 1970, ELCA, Frederik A. Schiotz Papers, box 43, "Feistner, Harry H."

28. Norman C. Haase to Franklin Clark Fry, 18 March 1968, ELCA, George F. Harkins Papers, box 211, "?" (emphasis in original); Harry H. Feistner to All ALC Pastors and Church Councils, 29 December 1969, ELCA, Frederik A. Schiotz Papers, box 43, "Feistner, Harry H."

29. George F. Harkins to John Yost, Jr., 4 December 1968, ELCA, George F. Harkins Papers, box 211, "?"; C. Hartmann to Harry Feistner, 16 January 1970, ELCA, Frederik A. Schiotz Papers, box 43, "Feistner, Harry H."; W. Walter Betz to Robert J. Marshall, 4 June 1970, ELCA, Robert J. Marshall Papers, box 105, "?".

30. G. Elson Ruff to Robert W. Fischer, 11 February 1966, ELCA, G. Elson Ruff Papers, box 4, "Fc"; George F. Harkins to St. John's Lutheran Church, September 1966, ELCA, George F. Harkins Papers, box 211, "?"; George F. Harkins to Mrs. F. J. Eckert, 8 June 1967, ELCA, George F. Harkins Papers, box 211, "?".

31. Melvin H. Lundeen to Mrs. James W. Olson, 26 January 1966, ELCA, George F. Harkins Papers, box 211, "?"; H. Nottbohm to Mrs. William Wayne Huff, Jr., 16 July 1968, ELCA, Frederik A. Schiotz Papers, box 58, "Possible Membership ALC"; Albert P. Stauderman to Carl B. Gift, 12 June 1975, Albert P. Stauderman Papers, box 96, "F-G 1975."

32. Good studies of Christian participation in the civil rights struggle are Michael Brooks Friedland, *Lift Up Your Voice Like a Trumpet: White Clergy and the Civil Rights and Antiwar Movements, 1954–1973* (Chapel Hill: The University of North Carolina Press, 1998); James F. Findlay, Jr., *Church People in the Struggle: The National Council of Churches and the Black Freedom Movement, 1950–1970* (New York: Oxford University Press, 1993). An excellent examination of the LCMS and civil rights is Kathryn M. Galchutt, *The Career of Andrew Schulze, 1924–1968: Lutherans and Race in the Civil Rights Era* (Macon, GA: Mercer University Press, 2005).

33. Jeff Woods's *Black Struggle, Red Scare: Segregation and Anti-Communism in the South, 1948–1968* (Baton Rouge: Louisiana State University Press, 2004) provides an excellent study about how the South used anticommunism to combat the civil rights movement; as will be shown in this section, Lutherans who opposed the civil rights movement mirrored the South in Woods's analysis in many ways. Ample other historiographic evidence challenges conservative claims regarding communism and the civil rights movement: Earl Ofari Hutchinson, *Blacks and Reds: Race and Class in Conflict, 1919–1990* (East Lansing: Michigan State University Press, 1995); Gerald Horne, *Black Liberation/Red Scare: Ben Davis and the Communist Party* (Newark: University of Delaware Press, 1994); Daniel Levine, *Bayard Rustin and the Civil Rights Movement* (New Brunswick, NJ: Rutgers University Press, 2000); Schrecker, *Many Are*, 389–95.

34. Mrs. H. Winquist to G. Elson Ruff, September 1964, ELCA, G. Elson Ruff Papers, box 16, "Win" (emphasis in original); Raynard Huglen, "The Struggle for Rights," *Lutheran Ambassador* 3 (6 April 1965): 9–10; Anonymous to Martin W. Mueller, September 1968, CHI, Lutheran Witness Letters, box 1, "Dr. Martin Luther King, Jr" (emphasis in original).

35. Orville C. Hillman to G. Elson Ruff, 20 February 1968, ELCA, G. Elson Ruff Papers, box 19, "Her-Hoc"; Clarence Ramming to Albert P. Stauderman, 18 June 1969, ELCA, Albert P. Stauderman Papers, box 86, "P to R"; Alfred J. Coutu to G. Elson Ruff, 20 October 1969, G. Elson Ruff Papers, box 3, "Co"; Carl F. Mikolita to Robert J. Marshall, 29 October 1971,

ELCA, Robert J. Marshall Papers, box 112, "Readers Digest Article-WCC." As noted above, numerous conservative Americans, not only Lutherans, asserted that Communists inspired the civil rights movement, despite their lack of proof: Schrecker, *Many Are*, 389–95; Richard Gid Powers, *Not without Honor: The History of American Anticommunism* (New York: Free Press, 1995), 100–103, 281–83; Richard Reeves, *President Kennedy: Profile of Power* (New York: Simon and Schuster, 1993), 530–31, 571.

36. Numerous scholars have shown the fallacy of Communist accusations against King: Reeves, *President Kennedy*, 502, 530–31; David J. Garrow, *The FBI and Martin Luther King, Jr.: From "Solo" to Memphis* (New York: W. W. Norton, 1981); and Kenneth O'Reilly, *"Racial Matters": The FBI's Secret File on Black America, 1960–1972* (New York: Free Press, 1989).

37. "The Peace March and the Misled," *Lutheran News* 5 (1 May 1967): 5; "Turret of the Times," *Christian News* 1 (11 March 1968): 3; Richard Wurmbrand, "Our Beloved Ones," *Jesus to the Communist World* (May 1968): 1.

38. Joel C. Gerlach, Report to His Congregation in Garden Grove, California, 16 April 1967, Wisconsin Evangelical Lutheran Synod Archives, Mequon, Wisconsin (hereafter WELS); David V. Sieberg to Frederik A. Schiotz, 27 December 1967, ELCA, Frederik A. Schiotz Papers, box 155, "Sieberg, David"; Mrs. Melvyn Coleman to Oliver R. Harms, 22 April 1968, CHI, Executive Office, box 28, "King, Martin Luther, Correspondence 1968."

39. Mr. and Mrs. Grant Bull, Jr., to Martin W. Mueller, 15 November 1964, CHI, Executive Office, box 28, "King, Martin Luther, Correspondence 1968"; Victor V. Rosenberg to G. Elson Ruff, 4 January 1965, ELCA, G. Elson Ruff Papers, box 82, "Extremists 1965"; Erwin J. Marynowski to Martin W. Mueller, 29 April 1968, CHI, Lutheran Witness Letters, box 1, "Dr. Martin Luther King, Jr."; Joseph Draper to the *Lutheran Witness Reporter*, 7 May 1968, CHI, Lutheran Witness Letters, box 1, "Dr. Martin Luther King, Jr." For an excellent discussion of Rustin's contentious relationship with the Communist Party and his homosexuality, see Levine, *Bayard Rustin*, and John D'Emilio, *Lost Prophet: The Life and Times of Bayard Rustin* (Chicago: University of Chicago Press, 2003).

40. Joseph Scholtes to G. Elson Ruff, 26 August 1965, ELCA, G. Elson Ruff Papers, box 12, "Scho"; Robert E. Valgren to G. Elson Ruff, 24 February 1968, ELCA, G. Elson Ruff Papers, box 22, "Tu-V"; William B. Welshonce to Martin W. Mueller, 17 May 1968, CHI, Lutheran Witness Letters, box 1, "W"; Gale J. McVay to J. A. O. Preus, 6 February 1971, CHI, Executive Office, box 28, "King, Martin Luther, Correspondence 1969–1973"; William A. DeJange to J. A. O. Preus, 12 February 1971, CHI, Executive Office, box 28, "King, Martin Luther, Correspondence 1969–1973."

41. Alfred J. Coutu to G. Elson Ruff, 20 October 1969, ELCA, G. Elson Ruff Papers, box 3, "Co"; Robert E. Valgren to G. Elson Ruff, 24 February 1968, ELCA, G. Elson Ruff Papers, box 22, "1970–72 Last Letters"; Mrs. Vera E. Shands to the *Lutheran Witness*, 15 May 1968, CHI, Lutheran Witness Letters, Department of Communications, box 1, "Dr. M. L. King, Jr.: Racism."

42. Mary T. Kearfott to G. Elson Ruff, 27 September 1965, ELCA, G. Elson Ruff Papers, box 8, "Ke"; Erwin J. Marynowski to the editor, April 1968, CHI, Lutheran Witness Letters, Department of Communications, box 1, "Dr. M. L. King, Jr.: Racism"; Mr. And Mrs. E. J. Brandt to Oliver R. Harms, 2 May 1968, CHI, Executive Offices, box 28, "King, Martin Luther, Correspondence, 1968"; Mrs. Gilbert Kapke to the editor, May 1968, CHI, Lutheran Witness Letters, Department of Communications, box 1, "Dr. M. L. King, Jr.: Racism."

43. Frederik A. Schiotz, "Blind to the Things that Make for Peace," *Lutheran Standard* 5 (21 September 1965): 12; Frederik A. Schiotz to David V. Sieberg, 23 September 1966, ELCA, Frederik A. Schiotz Papers, box 155, "Sieberg, David"; Martin W. Mueller to Elsie Schneider, 24 May 1968, CHI, Lutheran Witness Letters, box 1, "Dr. Martin Luther King, Jr."

44. G. Elson Ruff to Joyce Ryan, 12 January 1965, ELCA, G. Elson Ruff Papers, box 12, "Ru"; G. Elson Ruff to Mrs. Aubry Mauney, 1 October 1965, ELCA, G. Elson Ruff Papers, box 10, "Ma."

45. Myrus L. Knutson and Frederik A. Schiotz Correspondence, 1966, ELCA, Frederik A. Schiotz Papers, box 149, "Knutson, Myrus L."; Conrad M. Thompson to American Lutheran Church Council on Evangelism, 10 June 1966, ELCA, Frederik A. Schiotz Papers, box 66, "Wurmbrand"; Frederik A. Schiotz to ALC Clergy, 12 October 1966, ELCA, Frederik A. Schiotz Papers, box 66, "Wurmbrand"; P. Deak, "Richard Wurmbrand Report," March 1967, ELCA, Frederik A. Schiotz Papers, box 67, "Wurmbrand"; Paul Hanson to G. Elson Ruff, 26 May 1966, ELCA, Frederik A. Schiotz Papers, Church Files, "Norway, Oslo; American."

46. Richard Wurmbrand, *With God in Solitary Confinement* (Bartlesville, OK: Living Sacrifice Book Company, 1969), 49; Richard Wurmbrand, *Tortured for Christ* (Bartlesville, OK: Living Sacrifice Book Company, 1998), 15; *Christ on the Jewish Road* (Bartlesville: Living Sacrifice, 1970); Richard Wurmbrand, *In God's Underground* (Bartlesville, OK: Living Sacrifice Book Company, 1968).

47. "Communists Infiltrating in USA Churches," *Jesus to the Communist World* (February 1970): 2 (emphasis in original); "Win American Leftist Youth for Christ," *Jesus to the Communist World* (October 1970): 2.

48. Nate Bickel to J. A. O. Preus, May 1971, CHI, Executive Office, UPN box 63, "Prisoners of War—Laymen"; W. F. Murdie, "Suffering Christians," *Lutheran Sentinel* 51 (24 October 1968): 374–75, 385–86; Richard Wurmbrand to Frederik A. Schiotz, 4 March 1969, ELCA, Frederik A. Schiotz Papers, box 66, "Wurmbrand"; Richard Wurmbrand to Maurice Sorenson, 28 May 1974, ELCA, Division of World Ministry, box 10, "Voice of the Martyrs."

49. Richard Wurmbrand to Frederik A. Schiotz, 15 December 1969, ELCA, Frederik A. Schiotz Papers, box 66, "Wurmbrand"; Far East Broadcasting Company Board Meeting Materials, Statement of 23 November 1977, Billy Graham Center Archives, Wheaton, Illinois (Hereafter BGCA), Bertermann Papers, FEBC, box 5, "File 4." No quality study of the Lutheran World Federation exists, but primary material in the ELCA archives suggests that it suffered from the same false accusation that plagued the WCC. Americans belonged to every LWF board, and nothing indicates that Communists had any influence over the organization.

50. Ralph F. Baumbach to Frederik A. Schiotz, 23 March 1967, ELCA, Frederik A. Schiotz Papers, box 67, "Wurmbrand"; "Wurmbrand Says WCC Leaders Bring Wolf to Sheep," *Lutheran News* 4 (14 November 1966): 1.

51. Conrad M. Thompson to Committee on Evangelism, 10 June 1966, ELCA, Frederik A. Schiotz Papers, box 66, "Wurmbrand"; June Jones to Frederik A. Schiotz, 23 August 1967, ELCA, Frederik A. Schiotz Papers, box 66, "Wurmbrand"; Garfield Remus to G. Elson Ruff, 13 May 1969, ELCA, G. Elson Ruff Papers, box 21, "R-Ri"; Mrs. Clyde E. Roberts to J. A. O. Preus, 18 March 1971, CHI, Executive Office, UPN box 63, "Prisoners of War—Laymen."

52. Miss Anne Reid to Unknown, 7 February 1966, ELCA, Frederik A. Schiotz Papers, box 66, "Wurmbrand"; Mrs. Ray L. Catudal to Frederik A. Schiotz, 18 June 1968, ELCA, Frederik A. Schiotz Papers, box 66, "Wurmbrand"; Mrs. Jeren Keller to J. A. O. Preus, 27 August 1974, CHI, Executive Office, UPN box 108, "Wurmbrand, Reverend Richard."

53. Myrus L. Knutson to Frederik A. Schiotz, 22 December 1966, ELCA, Frederik A. Schiotz Papers, box 66, "Wurmbrand"; Kent S. Knutson to Kay L. Moldenke, 1 February 1972, ELCA, Kent S. Knutson Papers, box 1, "Mo"; "The Immoral Antidote," *Christianity Today* 16 (7 July 1972): 23; Frederik A. Schiotz to K. C. Grundahl, 19 September 1967, ELCA, Frederik A. Schiotz Papers, box 151, "Grundahl, Kermitt C."

54. Obert J. Landsverk to Charles Schmitz, 30 November 1966, ELCA, Frederik A. Schiotz Papers, box 66, "Wurmbrand"; Charles Schmitz to Obert J. Landsverk, 12 December 1966,

ELCA, Frederik A. Schiotz Papers, box 66, "Wurmbrand"; John D. Deines to Frederik A. Schiotz, 20 March 1968, ELCA, Frederik A. Schiotz Papers, box 66, "Wurmbrand."

55. Frederik A. Schiotz to Richard Wurmbrand, 3 November 1966, ELCA, Frederik A. Schiotz Papers, box 66, "Wurmbrand"; Frederik A. Schiotz to Rosemary Harris, 11 November 1966, ELCA, Frederik A. Schiotz Papers, box 66, "Wurmbrand"; Myrus L. Knutson to Joseph Bass, 17 August 1966, ELCA, Lutheran World Ministry, LWM 314, General Secretary, Country Files, box 46, "Rumania, Wurmbrand, Richard 1972"; Myrus L. Knutson to Frederik A. Schiotz, 29 November 1966, ELCA, Frederik A. Schiotz Papers, box 66, "Wurmbrand"; Werner Kuntz to Victor L. Behnken, 9 January 1967, ELCA, Lutheran World Relief 3, Administrative Files, box 5, "Lutheran Church–Missouri Synod"; Frederik A. Schiotz to Myrus L. Knutson, 12 December 1966, ELCA, Frederik A. Schiotz Papers, box 66, "Wurmbrand."

56. Paul C. Empie to Myrus L. Knutson, 9 June 1966, ELCA, Lutheran World Ministry, LWM 314, General Secretary, Country Files, box 45, "Rumania, Wurmbrand, Reverend Richard, 1966"; William Larsen to Conrad M. Thompson, 21 July 1966, ELCA, Frederik A. Schiotz Papers, box 66, "Wurmbrand"; Lutheran World Ministries Report, 1971, ELCA, Lutheran World Ministries, LWM 314, General Secretary, Country Files, box 46, "Rumania, Wurmbrand, Reverend Richard, 1972 (emphasis in original)."

57. G. Elson Ruff to William J. Kull, 17 May 1966, ELCA, G. Elson Ruff Papers, box 9, "Kr"; Frederik A. Schiotz to Mrs. Vernon Drake, 25 February 1969, ELCA, Frederik A. Schiotz Papers, box 66, "Wurmbrand"; H. Nottbohm to Ernest B. Bittner, 9 May 1973, ELCA, Frederik A. Schiotz Papers, box 158, "Wurmbrand, Richard."

Chapter Four

Lions Loose in the World: Pro-Vietnam War Lutherans

The Vietnam War took place in the context of the Cold War battle against the Soviet Union and People's Republic of China and the debate about the threat of domestic communism within the United States. The U.S. government and its civilian allies, which included a number of prowar Lutherans, both theologically and politically moderate to conservative, advocated the fighting in Vietnam because of the fear of Communist expansionism. The United States had become heavily involved in the war when the French pulled out in 1954 after their defeat by North Vietnamese Communists at the battle of Dien Bien Phu. The United States sent military advisors and supported the anti-Communist government in South Vietnam economically thereafter, even through a series regime changes that had American backing due to their anti-Communist stance but that had simultaneously lost the support of South Vietnamese citizens because of dictatorial tactics and suppression of those who disagreed with the government. The Tonkin Gulf Resolution passed by Congress in August 1964 gave President Lyndon B. Johnson authorization to carry out military programs against the Communist North without actually declaring war. Richard Nixon continued this war and even escalated the bombing of the North and expanding the bombing into the neighboring nations of Cambodia and Laos because of Communist activity there.

But despite U.S. claims that it fought in Vietnam to protect South Vietnam from communism, reality provides a much more complex picture. True, the North Vietnamese attacked the South and wanted a reunited Vietnam, but a civil war brewed in the South as well between non-partisan dissenters of the South Vietnamese government allied with peasants and Communists and, on the other side, the United States and South Vietnamese government. The National Liberation Front, created in the early 1960s, included Communists and North Vietnamese agents with non-Communist South Vietnamese and Buddhists who simply wanted a freer form of government. But pro-Vietnam thinking in the United States, both within the government and general population, so feared communism that it failed to see this complexity. Rather, it divided the world into pro- and anti-Communist factions and therefore saw the South Vietnamese as good allies of the United States and all of its enemies as Communists. This thinking did not end when the United States withdrew its military troops in January 1973. The Nixon administration brokered a peace that withdrew U.S. forces in return for a promise from North Vietnam not to invade the South. Nonetheless, the civil war continued and in April 1975 finally came to an end when Communist forces captured the South Vietnamese capital of Saigon. This defeat actually fueled conservative claims about communism: to them, it verified the domino theory.

Prowar Lutherans backed the Vietnam War for a number of reasons, all of which pertained to their disdain for communism and mirrored the government's reasons for fighting there. Because they persistently portrayed communism as a monolithic force creeping across the earth, they naturally feared that the loss of Vietnam signaled another step in this Communist conquest. Conservative and moderate Lutherans carefully outlined that Vietnam was another "domino" and insisted that the Soviet Union directed the Vietnamese revolution. Because they made no distinction between the Soviet Union and People's Republic of China, they assumed that Red China agreed with and assisted this Soviet effort. In other words, they thought that communism radiated out from Moscow, into Peking, and finally to Vietnam. To further link the war to a worldwide conspiracy, they used the same depictions in describing North Vietnam as an evil government as they did when they discussed the Communist giants. Indeed, they did not see the Vietnam War as a war for national liberation but rather insisted that it was part of a larger Communist manipulation and conquest. In short, the war against North Vietnam was part of the religious war against atheistic communism. Conservative Lutherans also supported the fighting in Southeast Asia with patriotic defenses of the U.S. government and a theological justification of the Vietnam War. Some even suggested that God ordained U.S. actions. Finally, they favored the war because they wanted to support U.S. soldiers. For prowar Lutherans, a loss in Vietnam might ultimately doom much, if not all, of the world to life under the Communist yoke.[1]

VIETNAM AND COMMUNIST EXPANSIONISM

Prowar Lutherans often described Vietnam as an important cog in the atheistic Communist plan for world domination. Containment theory claimed that communism spread throughout the world by taking one country at a time, and conservative Lutherans believed this without question. These prowar Americans insisted that each nation that "fell" to communism endangered the United States and imperiled Christianity. Thus, the domino theory extended into their religious beliefs because they felt that communism's atheistic agenda expanded with it. A military stand in Vietnam meant the protection of democracy and religion around the globe. This also led some conservatives to a paternalism regarding Vietnam when they viewed it as a weaker nation that needed American protection. Oddly, given the religious nature of much of their discussions, few conservative Lutherans considered in detail whether or not Vietnam represented a just war. It was obvious to them in the context of their anticommunism that any effort to eradicate this irreligious ideology deserved the churches' backing.

Prowar Lutherans used a rhetoric that clearly demonstrated their faith in containment and fear of Communist expansionism. As the far-right *Christian News* asserted, "The overall plan for world victory is to use the power of the Communist countries, the so-called national-liberation wars and the people within non-Communist countries whom they can either convert or manipulate to do those things which will be helpful to communism." One Lutheran Church in America (LCA) member used a religious motif to describe alleged Communist expansionism. He asserted that "as long as there are lions loose in the world seeking to prey on the lamb there must be people willing to do some sacrificing to maintain their freedom and security." His comment referred to the fact that the Communist lions had invaded the lamb of South Vietnam in order to conquer it. A Lutheran Church–Missouri Synod (LCMS) publication explained that pulling out of Vietnam meant that "we will have to meet the threat elsewhere." Even the moderate LCA passed a 1966 convention resolution imploring Americans not to "ignore or underestimate international Communism's declared purposes of aggression, conquest, and destruction of freedom." But a *Lutheran Forum* article best summarized this belief: "Communism is the great present-day enemy of the Church, as has been shown by its machinations in lands it has overrun. Conservative Christians know you cannot compromise with evil, so they oppose this world-wide movement strongly, even if it calls for the use of arms as in the case of Vietnam."[2]

Further rhetoric applied the domino theory directly to Southeast Asia. A pastor wanted the United States to fight the Vietnamese Communists because "in South Vietnam the Communist movement is making another major effort to breach the wall of containment." Such thinking demonstrates how conservatives felt that the mere presence of Communists in Vietnam connected the war to a worldwide Communist conspiracy. They did not always relate this directly to Christianity and their campaign against Communist atheism, but

given the simultaneous discussions about Soviet and Chinese efforts to eradicate Christianity, the connection is obvious. Simply put, Lutherans who supported the war thought that a U.S. loss would doom all of Southeast Asia. For
example, an LCA member questioned *Lutheran* editor G. Elson Ruff's antiwar stance on these grounds: "Since you don't want to fight a war in Vietnam,
neither will you want to fight a war in Laos or Malaysia. After that all of
South East Asia would be under Communist control." Another reader made
this same point: "If we withdraw from South Vietnam, all Asia will follow
into the Communist camp in just a few years." Even after the United States
pulled out of the war in 1973 when the Nixon administration negotiated a settlement with North Vietnam that promised to evacuate U.S. troops from the
war in return for a pledge by the North not to invade South Vietnam, conservative Lutherans persisted in their belief that Vietnam signified the first of
many countries in danger: "The darkness of Communism is settling down
over the nations of South Vietnam and Cambodia" and showed no sign of
stopping its expansionism.[3]

Conservative Lutherans also asserted that if the United States failed in
Vietnam the Communists would attack the United States. This provides the
ultimate proof of their abiding faith in Communist expansion because they really feared an American invasion would occur. For example, an LCA member stated that "if we do not fight the Communist in Viet Nam, then in a few
years we will fight him in San Francisco, or Los Angeles." An Army chaplain
proclaimed that Communists had promised to "destroy us [Americans]" by
first taking Vietnam. He urged Americans to support the Vietnam War before
the Communists arrived in the United States because "I would rather have my
family cinderized in a nuclear holocaust than to have them subjected to Communist tyranny." Nothing in their conversation in this regard directly related
their fears to Christianity, Lutheranism, or religion. One could even wonder
why this vibrant dialogue took place in religious journals and settings if they
did not somehow relate it to their belief system. But, once again, the context
of the time becomes crucial to understanding their motivation. The Cold War
so obviously included an element of religious warfare that it went without
saying. The Communist threat to Christianity was so imbedded in their thinking that they presumed everyone comprehended this connection. Conservatives even furthered their defense of containment when they explained that
Communists would easily take over Asia after the United States pulled out of
Vietnam, which would ultimately threaten America. Years of anti-Communist
hatred led conservative Lutherans to conclude that a loss in Vietnam doomed
the United States.[4]

Yet international circumstances provided fuel for this conservative thinking, especially because both the Soviet Union (USSR) and People's Republic

of China (PRC) provided economic assistance and armaments to North Vietnam. This reality intensified conservative concerns about a Communist monolith, despite the fact that they did not know what kind of assistance was provided and ignored the fact that, in part, the two Communist superpowers did so to gain leverage against one another by getting North Vietnam's loyalty. The USSR and PRC had long feuded over leadership of world communism and their shared border. Ho Chi Minh and North Vietnam played off of this tension and therefore received assistance from both allies who did not want to lose their international support. For conservatives, this Communist alliance system heightened their fear that these nations "supply arms, explosives, technicians, economic help and training to the Communists in North Vietnam." A wounded Lutheran soldier explained that the bullet that hit him was "transported from Red China through North Vietnam, down the Ho Chi Minh Trail, into Laos and finally to the sanctuary of Cambodia. From there it was issued to a North Vietnamese soldier, who put the bullet into his weapon, slipped across the border into South Vietnam . . . and shot me." Another person scolded an antiwar demonstrator for not understanding that "the war he was protesting was not against a small Asian tribe in Vietnam, like the Marxistic liberals insisted but against the World's Communist Power—Moscow." At the war's end, conservatives still insisted that the USSR and the PRC "started the damn war."[5]

Conservative Lutherans also linked the U.S. antiwar movement to a Communist plot. Begun after the United States escalated its involvement in Vietnam following the August 1964 Gulf of Tonkin Resolution, the peace movement began as a small group of intellectuals and students but gradually grew to include more and more Americans who opposed the war. Conservatives saw this as playing into Communist hands and even speculated that Communists were behind the peace movement. They alleged that the Communists planted people in the United States to foment antiwar sentiment, convince the U.S. government to exit the war, and allow them to conquer Vietnam. A *Lutheran* reader asserted that the "leftist attitude shown in regards to this country helping defend South Vietnam came from the ruthless, atheistic communists." The My Lai massacre intensified these beliefs. In March 1968, American troops under the command of William L. Calley, Jr., massacred the civilian population of the My Lai hamlet. This illegal act outraged many Americans and led to the conviction of Calley by a military court in March 1969. Conservative Americans, however, refused to believe that U.S. soldiers could commit such atrocities and insisted that Communists manufactured the story entirely. An American Lutheran Church (ALC) member declared that "the REDS needed a real spark to trigger the emotions of the American people to withdraw from Viet-Nam thus assuring a Communist victory." In short, he claimed that the Communists instigated the massacre, publicized it in the United States, and convinced Americans to condemn the war on the basis of this fabricated event.[6]

Conservatives also claimed that the United States had to fight to defend South Vietnam's right to self-determination. Much of the United States' argument for its Cold War posturing in civil wars such as Vietnam maintained that all nations had the right to determine their own government. Assuming that all Communist governments were ill-gotten, conservatives insisted that the South Vietnamese needed American protection. They stated that the United States fought the war "to preserve for the people of South Vietnam the right of a government of their own choosing." According to an LCA pastor, therefore, denouncing any attempt to get the United States out of Vietnam meant that "the U.S. no longer honors its commitments to halt the spread of Communism in the area." He insisted that the United States had an obligation to maintain the non-Communist regime in South Vietnam. A Wisconsin Evangelical Lutheran Synod (WELS) slide show made this same point, proclaiming that the United States needed to stop "the communist seizure of South Vietnam." Even after Saigon fell in 1975 to Communist forces, conservative Lutherans clung to these convictions. They declared that "lest we forget the screams in Southeast Asia as dominoes topple, we must make it lastingly clear that mature Americans will not again tolerate unchecked subversion of our responsibilities." They wanted the United States to protect every nation's ability to elect freely their government, so long as it was not Communist.[7]

Conservative demands that the United States assist the Vietnamese in fighting communism also contained paternalistic images of saving a weaker nation. Americans during the Cold War too often manifested a hubris that claimed that U.S. ideology about democracy and self-determination was what everyone wanted. They therefore assumed that, if democracy did not exist in a country, those people were too weak and afraid to obtain it for themselves. The language employed by prowar Lutherans demonstrates this all too well. For example, an LCA constituent admitted that the South Vietnamese "are not dedicated to overcoming the North Vietnamese" but that "is precisely why they are worthy of being defended." He asserted that the Vietnamese did not know enough to protect themselves and that the United States therefore had to fight for them. LCMS President J. A. O. Preus concurred that the United States had to train the South Vietnamese. He thought that South Vietnam had the capability but lacked the American knowledge and declared that all Asians "are going to be engulfed by the Communists if we pull out of this war before the South Vietnamese are able to defend themselves and their neighboring nations." These conservative opinions endured after the war. *Lutheran Sentinel*, published by the Evangelical Lutheran Synod, grieved about the fact that "the Vietnamese simply were not capable of self-government and the rigorous responsibilities of independence. The pity is that it is precisely among such primitive peoples that Communism scores its greatest successes." Conservatives saw the Vietnamese as ineffective fighters who needed the United States to teach them to combat communism. This paternalistic attitude took agency away from the Vietnamese and bequeathed it to the United States, an allegedly smarter nation because it chose democracy over communism.[8]

Indeed, this language of superiority became reason enough for conservative Lutherans to support the Vietnam War. They assumed that the Vietnamese were inferior, which led them to conclude that the United States had to defend them from communism. A reader of the LCA's *Lutheran* declared that the United States had to aid "underprivileged people" and was therefore "strongly behind the administration in the effort to help weak and helpless nations and peoples." Another person simply asked, "Is it wrong to help defend an otherwise defenseless country?" Because these Lutherans saw the Vietnamese as weaker than Americans, they concluded that the war was a just fight against deceitful Communists. One person asserted that by fighting for the South Vietnamese the United States was "giving hope to the small nations of Southeast Asia." In short, the strong United States protected "small" countries that were incapable of defending themselves from communism. None of the rhetoric took into account what the Vietnamese desired because it was assumed that they could not make such difficult decisions without U.S. assistance. Or, as another lay Lutheran put it, "The U.S. seeks no empire; our presence in Southeast Asia is defensive, to protect small people from utter oblivion by ruthless aggressors." It is important to note the language conservatives employed; the stereotype of Asians as smaller was regularly used to justify "protecting" them, presumably from the bigger aggressor of the Soviet Union. And when the allegedly strong United States failed to win, conservative thinkers utilized these typecasts to explain the loss: "We [the United States] attempted to help a weak, disorganized, divided and confused people beset with corruption and a dearth of national leadership in their feeble attempts to determine their own destiny." Vietnamese were described as weak, confused, and feeble, and the writer entirely dismissed Ho Chi Minh as a national leader, no doubt because of his Communist affiliation.[9]

THE NORTH VIETNAMESE "DEMON"

Conservative Lutheran portrayals of North Vietnam further buttressed prowar zeal. Similar to their accusations against the Soviet Union and China, prowar Lutherans insisted that North Vietnam's Communist government promoted atheism and was an evil force for Christians to combat. They claimed that the North Vietnamese used sinister tactics in fighting the war and that Ho Chi Minh's government relied upon torture to coerce innocent civilians. In truth, North Vietnam was at times an oppressive, Communist regime. But at other times it merely represented the will of the Vietnamese for self-determination. In other words, evidence suggests that the government oppressed those who questioned it, especially after it took over the entire nation in 1975, but it simultaneously enjoyed wide support from people tired of foreign domination. This conflicted legacy often buttressed prowar Lutheran opinion and, therefore, they claimed that North Vietnam was a "monster" that the United States fought in order to protect the innocent.

Conservative Lutherans also wanted to fight North Vietnam because of the Communists' atheistic agenda; this was as much a religious war as a political one to them. They linked North Vietnam directly to Soviet and Chinese expansionism and therefore assumed that it also wanted to purge the world of religion. In response to a National Council of Churches call for an end to the war, an LCA member asked if it therefore advocated "peace at the price of an atheistic (Godless) form of government." Another person asserted that Communist atheism doomed the Vietnamese to "a life of misery" without religion. Even after North Vietnam took over the entire country in 1975, conservative Lutherans lamented Communist atheism. A writer for the WELS's *Northwestern Lutheran* reminded readers that "as we turn to the Lord in prayer for ourselves, we also need to pray for that conquered and ravished country [Vietnam]. Whatever is left of the church there faces perilous times."[10]

Conservatives even depicted North Vietnam as a "diabolical" force because of its atheism. A Lutheran military chaplain proclaimed that the U.S. government "is 'bearing the sword to execute judgment upon evil-doers'" in Vietnam. Rightists further claimed that "the first thing they [the North Vietnamese] will do when they take over will be to put the men of the cloth against a stone wall and destroy all religions." In other words, they believed that North Vietnamese Communists murdered without provocation any religious leaders they encountered and insisted that a demonic force led this irreligious crusade. Some even demanded extreme measures to fight North Vietnam's allegedly evil designs: "If just one minister would ask President Nixon to use atomic bombs and wipe out the devil in North Vietnam, then I would believe that God is speaking through that minister." Conservative Lutherans mirrored their depiction of the Soviet Union and China as anti-Christian nations when they discussed North Vietnam. This atheistic Communist agenda therefore transformed conservative Lutheran support of the war from mere political or diplomatic opinions to the level of religious war.[11]

Conservative Lutherans also claimed that North Vietnamese Communists liked warfare and shunned the peace process. This contributed further to their demonizing of this U.S. enemy. Rather than fighting a foreign nation, they combated an evil entity that in no way wanted peace, which justified the fighting to them without having to use strict theological guidelines, such as the seven tenets of just war theory. An ALC *Lutheran Standard* writer insisted that the North Vietnamese killed "their fellow countrymen just because they would prefer a different form of government." He felt that rational people accepted their government without combating it and thought that the North Vietnamese never contemplated a peaceful settlement. An LCMS member asserted that "the enemy desires not peace, but conquest by murder, terrorism, and blatant armed attack." Rightist advocates therefore blamed the North Vietnamese alone for the failure of the Paris peace negotiations: "Hanoi never intended to negotiate except on the terms of a complete Communist takeover." Even LCMS President J. A. O. Preus described the North Vietnamese as "an extremely warlike people." Conservatives' fear of any form of communism took them to the point that they thought the North Vietnamese enjoyed combat.[12]

Conservative Lutherans also deplored North Vietnam's warfare tactics. An ALC convention resolution lamented that "we know too little of the cruelties and oppression inflicted" by the North Vietnamese armies. The resolution assumed that such "cruelties" existed. Conservative Lutheran pastors often made this same point. A Lutheran military chaplain stated that the Vietnamese Communists followed "the typical Communist terror-pattern of murdering in cold blood persons and their families" who defy their Communist agenda. Furthermore, an LCA pastor blamed Ho Chi Minh for these procedures: "Ho of North Vietnam butchered 40,000 perfectly innocent people and also liquidated quite a few of his own men to consolidate his despotic power." In short, conservatives believed that North Vietnam instituted "a military policy which is completely insane with the deliberate and wanton butchery of the poor innocent civilians." They even claimed that North Vietnam premeditated this indiscriminate murder. Thus, conservative charges about North Vietnam's tactics further convinced them of that nation's "demonic" capabilities.[13]

Right-leaning Lutherans also accused the North Vietnamese of using torture to enforce their will. A minister declared that the Vietcong used "civilians as human shields," punctured "a child's eardrums with chop-sticks if the child took candy from" an American, and "cut the genitals off living men and stuff[ed] them into their mouths to suffocate them." Each of these alleged acts frightened other people into obeying the North Vietnamese. Eyewitness accounts from soldiers in Vietnam who described the horrors of war fueled this depiction of all Vietnamese Communists as brutal. Although all factions in this war shared guilt in this regard, conservatives focused on what U.S. G.I.s claimed the Communists did to enemies because it supported their cause. For example, a returning Lutheran soldier explained that he saw "the bodies of women and children murdered by North Vietnam troops and their Vietcong allies." He speculated that this happened to everyone who challenged the Communists. Gruesome portrayals of North Vietnamese torture added to conservative advocacy for the Vietnam War.[14]

Ultra-conservative Lutheran periodicals also directly called the North Vietnamese barbaric. *Jesus to the Communist World* printed a returning Marine's claim that the Vietcong had brutally beheaded eleven nuns. Furthermore, the periodical asserted that "hundreds of *small South Vietnamese children have been mutilated, castrated or killed by the Communists." Through to Victory* mirrored this tone exactly. The periodical had dedicated itself solely to supporting all U.S. Cold War efforts, and this included a persistent prowar attitude about Vietnam. In explaining this position, it accused the North Vietnamese of wanton murder and stated that "it is declared policy on the part of the North Vietnamese and the Viet Cong, in a carefully documented program of terror and assassination, to teach the South Vietnamese who cooperate here with the government in Saigon that the price of such cooperation is death."[15]

Other conservatives used an even more volatile racial prejudice to depict the Vietnamese. Though a minority opinion, the following racist notions undermined the credibility of conservative prowar opinions. One writer claimed that "until recently this area of the world was content to remain relatively primitive." After the word primitive conjured the idea of a backward, prehistoric people, he continued that "it is only natural for Americans to believe that, as we help Asians help themselves, the same will be true for other nations as was true for Japan." His treatment of Asia is that of a parent to a child, as if the "adult" United States had to educate the "children" of Asia on how to behave maturely. Still another layperson referred to all of Vietnam as "a small Asian tribe." A laywoman further perpetuated harmful stereotypes when she described African and Southeast Asian nations, including Vietnam, as "*small countries* of uncivilized, uneducated, unable to govern themselves [and] *yes* even *cannibals*." This led others to compare the Vietnamese to animals, another common racial epitaph. An LCA woman blasted attempts to negotiate peace in Vietnam by asking, "How can a country deal with a bunch of wild animals, and that is what the Vietcong are?"[16]

Conservative Lutheran descriptions of the North Vietnamese paralleled their views of the Soviet Union, China, and alleged Communists in the United States. They justified their prowar attitude with this portrayal. To them, this planted the Vietnam War firmly within the Cold War framework of fighting monolithic communism. And the proof, both real and manufactured, that

North Vietnam was evil, enjoyed armed conflict, and used sinister tactics and torture fueled their convictions. These Lutherans believed that the United States protected the world from communism through its efforts to fight North Vietnam.

OBEYING THE U.S. GOVERNMENT

Conservative Lutherans' prowar attitudes also consistently defended the U.S. government. Studying this segment of Lutherans therefore contributes to understandings of how post-World War II conservatives came to support a strong state that Americans should not question. By placing their defense of U.S. government policy in Vietnam in the context of their Cold War stance, it makes sense that their fear of communism allowed them to back a strong central government that made decisions to protect American citizens from this force. In other words, Vietnam was an important cog in the global crusade against communism and the United States led this campaign. Loyalty to it therefore assisted this religious war against atheism.

Lutheran bodies and individuals made statements of support regarding their government. For example, ALC convention delegates proclaimed in 1966 that "we believe that the stated aims of our nation's government in assisting Vietnam are sound." Later ALC conventions would reverse this and pass resolutions that questioned the war. Thus, the ALC fits a pattern that historians have outlined regarding American views of the Vietnam War: during the first two to three years, many Americans supported the war as a necessary component of fighting the Cold War. Only after revelations of government deceit and the prolonging of the war did more and more Americans, including ALC delegates, change their opinion. Individual congregations also wanted to take public stances in this regard. An Alaskan congregation in 1970 declared that it "would support the President and the Congress of the United States in whatever decision they might make in connection with the war in Viet Nam and the Cambodian situation." President J. A. O. Preus also assumed that LCMS members upheld Nixon's Vietnam policy. Preus, a staunch conservative who publicly supported Nixon and had led White House church services, told a constituent that if the church denounced the war "about two-thirds of the church would probably be saying something they didn't believe." Prowar Lutheran patriotism proved that, despite the vocal antiwar movement, many Americans endorsed the government's Vietnam policies.[17]

This pro-government attitude led conservative Lutherans to accuse antiwar protestors of aiding the enemy. Because peace advocates questioned the U.S. government, conservatives assumed that they were Communist plants, sympathizers, or naive. They could not believe that anyone who truly cared about the United States could undermine its Cold War efforts to protect itself. In response to a World Council of Churches resolution against the war, an ALC member wrote that "it was so written to give aid and comfort and impetus" to those opposed to U.S. participation. Although it claimed to represent people around the world, he asserted that it only presented a pacifist opinion. An LCA minister concurred when he "join[ed] a host of others in feeling that many events and movements in our country give aid and support to the enemy." These people despised Americans who protested their government while it fought a war and assumed that "high powered left wing political propaganda" directed their actions.[18]

Prowar Lutherans also claimed that antiwar believers condemned the United States without censuring North Vietnam. An ALC representative to a National Council of Churches conference complained that "though very little criticism was ever directed at North Vietnam or the Viet Cong, the Johnson administration was vociferously damned night and day for its actions." An LCA constituent asked pastors to quit "meddling in worldly issues" when they condemned the United States. He asserted that North Vietnam deserved just as much blame for the war as did the United States. LCMS President J. A. O. Preus agreed. When a pastor questioned U.S. tactics after the My Lai massacre in which U.S. soldiers massacred a Vietnamese hamlet, Preus asserted that the trial of William L. Calley, Jr., who commanded the troops during this illegal act, showed how the United States was "at least trying to practice justice and righteousness in the handling of our enemies." In contrast, he frequently rebuked North Vietnam for injuring U.S. prisoners of war and refusing to enter peace negotiations. This conservative rhetoric shows that they trusted the state to protect them and make diplomatic decisions, which led them to condemn anyone as unpatriotic who did not display this same loyalty.[19]

Conservative Lutherans also asserted such faith in the state when they argued that the presidents possessed secret information that informed their handling of the Vietnam War. They assumed that both Johnson and Nixon fought based on confidential intelligence that revealed "evil" Communist designs, though no such evidence ever existed. A WELS writer stated that critics used "sanctimonious second-guessing of the government" in their antiwar diatribes even though he claimed that "Christians" knew the president worked for the best U.S. interests. A number of LCMS convention delegates tried to pass the following resolution: "*Resolved*, that the Lutheran Church–Missouri Synod refrain from giving advice to the government on how it should conduct the war in Vietnam." The resolution stated that critics formed their antiwar opinions on too little information while the government knew all of the facts. An ALC convention statement made this point more directly. It asserted that

Nixon "has the latest of [*sic*] best information on the status" of Vietnam and so commended him for his efforts to win the war while also removing U.S. troops.[20]

Conservative Lutherans thus frequently defended both Lyndon B. Johnson's and Richard M. Nixon's reasons for fighting the war. An LCA member simply stated that "three American presidents have decided that our presence in Viet Nam is necessary." After the Nixon administration bombed Cambodia in 1970, an ALC constituent declared that "I stand with our president. I believe he made the correct decision . . . and for the right reasons." But LCMS President J. A. O. Preus's personal relationship with Nixon best reveals how right-leaning Lutherans supported the president. He wrote the president that "I know from your personal remarks to me how anxious you are to bring this war to a close and I want to assure you of my personal confidence in you." His faith in Nixon continued after the U.S. pullout in 1973: "Let me add my congratulations to those I hope will come from millions of our fellow countrymen for bringing peace with honor."[21]

Patriotism shaped the prowar position of conservative Lutherans, who espoused a Cold War nationalism against all Communist nations and labeled criticism of the U.S. government Communist inspired. They called antiwar demonstrators naive because they condemned the United States but never denounced the North Vietnamese enemy. Trusting that presidents held secret knowledge that informed their decisions, they defended both Johnson's and Nixon's Vietnam policies. In short, right-leaning Lutherans believed that any U.S. military effort deserved their support because they insisted that only a strong U.S. state could defend the world from communism.

A JUST WAR

Prowar Lutherans also theologically justified their support for the Vietnam War. Christians had long lived with a contradiction between their faith and the reality of war. To explain this paradox, Augustine and numerous subsequent theologians constructed the "just war" theory. It held that certain circumstances necessitated war despite biblical admonitions against killing. Yet Christians seldom agreed about what "circumstances" allowed for combat. True, most agreed on the seven tenets that justified a war, but they disputed how to apply these principles to each particular war.[22] While a Christian antiwar movement vocally denounced the Vietnam War, rightist Christians justified the fighting. Few if any prowar Lutheran advocates went through the seven just war tenets and applied them to the Vietnam War, but this did not stop them from making a theological argument. Conservative Lutherans also

buttressed their prowar religious opinion with traditional Lutheran two kingdoms theology: the United States' decision to fight in Vietnam fell into the
category of obeying government authority within the kingdom on earth as
dictated by Luther.

A professor of theology at Concordia Seminary (LCMS) and former military chaplain, Arthur Carl Piepkorn, summarized this Lutheran position:

> He [a Lutheran] cannot himself withhold, or counsel and abet others in with-
> holding, from his government the obedience, the support, and the service that it
> has a right to expect and to exact from its citizens. He cannot deliberately and
> willfully give aid and comfort to the political enemies of his nation. He cannot
> allow his uncertainties, his disapproval of certain decisions that the government
> has taken, his frustrations, his impatience, or his partisan loyalties to deprive the
> leaders of the nation of the public and private respect to which their official ca-
> pacities entitle them. He cannot, without committing subversion and a species
> of treason, close his eyes to the barbarities of the enemy while he insists that the
> immoral acts of individual subordinate American leaders or the deplorable and
> irremediable consequences of imprudent decisions made at any level of author-
> ity are evidence of a calculated program of inhuman terror on the part of his own
> nation's leaders. He cannot exalt any specific course of political or military ac-
> tion in connection with the war to the level of a moral absolute.[23]

As Piepkorn suggested, conservative Lutheran theology argued that individual citizens did not have the right to question U.S. policy. Conservative Lutherans insisted that God commanded everyone to obey the government. This traditional Lutheran theology wedded itself nicely to the neo-conservative belief
in the protection of a strong state: in either case, Lutherans trusted the president
to make foreign policy decisions without question. They thus tacitly advocated
U.S. fighting when they gave U.S. officials autonomous authority to justify the
Vietnam War because they claimed that the church could not take a stand on the
issue. Piepkorn had help from other conservative leaders in making this point.
LCMS President J. A. O. Preus insisted that "I personally feel that the war in
Vietnam is a just war, in as far as any war can be just." He also publicly supported Richard M. Nixon and frequently defended the United States' official
policies regarding Vietnam. These public arguments created a paradox in conservative thinking. They claimed that God justified the war in so much as God
commanded people to obey the government without mixing politics and religion; but the very act of making such a statement combined their theological
views with U.S. politics.[24]

This theology contained emphatic pronouncements to trust the government. Preus's predecessor, who was otherwise more moderate theologically
and politically, LCMS President Oliver R. Harms, asked, "Who is going to

judge, or be able to judge, whether a war is just or not if we cannot trust the government to operate as it should under the Constitution of the United States [*sic*]?" J. A. O. Preus also insisted that the previous four American presidents "did what they thought was best in view of the facts that they had available to them at the time." Thus, he told people to trust their leaders and support the war. The *Lutheran Sentinel* of the small and conservative Evangelical Lutheran Synod more distinctly made this point. It informed readers that "unless we can prove beyond any doubt that our government is engaging in an unjust war, and who of us have all the facts in this present war to make such a judgment, then we ought to respect the judgment of our governmental leaders, and let the burden of the justice or injustice of the war rest upon them." Conservative Lutherans therefore blended their patriotism with a Lutheran theological justification of the Vietnam War.[25]

Conservative Lutherans' continued depiction of communism as "evil" added another theological argument to their cause. For example, a Far East Broadcasting Company (FEBC) film contained twenty minutes of battle scenes and stated that U.S. soldiers were "locked in mortal combat with [the] powers of darkness." In Christian theology, the term "darkness" refers to satanic forces; so the FEBC was essentially shaping the war into a holy crusade. An LCA pastor justified the combat because Communist tyranny was "written in the blood of the maimed, disemboweled, the tortured, persecuted peoples of both North and South Viet Nam." Or, as a constituent declared, "Sometimes it [war] is the only answer or mean [*sic*] to do God [*sic*] work." The periodical *Lutheran Spokesman* of the Church of the Lutheran Confession concurred when it asserted that "in saying that the government has the authority to exercise the power of the sword to execute wrath upon the evildoer we are saying that it has the right to take life." Conservatives not only obligated the United States to battle Communists, they proclaimed that God ordained this course of action.[26]

Such thinking led conservative Lutherans to assert that God wanted the United States to fight in Vietnam. A church newsletter compared the war to a parable. It stated that "Jesus said, 'when a strong man, fully armed, guards his own palace, his goods are in peace.'" This insinuated that Jesus sanctioned fighting if something threatened personal property; it then inferred that American power somehow gave it ownership of Vietnam, therefore concluding that even Jesus advocated the Vietnam conflict. Another minister contended that Christians had to combat sin. He assumed that all Communist governments embodied sin and thus defended the Vietnam War when he asked, "Has the Lord given us the option to pick and choose the brand of sin we'll oppose?" A reader of the Wisconsin Evangelical Lutheran Synod's *Northwestern Lutheran* summarized God's supposed endorsement of the war, a point of view with which many within this confessional and politically conservative church body agreed. He stated that "the Lord makes no mistakes. He doesn't deal haphazardly." This statement epitomized the thinking that God ordained all U.S. actions and protected the United States from making mistakes.[27]

This conservative just war theory construction ultimately led some conservative Lutherans to advocate an all-out war against North Vietnam. This minority point of view, even among those who advocated the war, manifested itself within every Lutheran denomination, regardless of theological or political norms within that body. A member of the usually moderate Lutheran Church in America explained that "when the money changers violated God's law in the temple, Jesus Christ resorted to violent war tactics by physically beating them until they were driven from the temple. The terroristic indiscriminate murdering of anyone who happens to be in the area that is carried out by the Viet Cong is a far greater violation of God's law." Based on this interpretation of Jesus' actions against the money lenders, this person sought to increase the fighting in Vietnam. Lutheran military personnel often agreed. An LCMS lieutenant colonel wanted to "use every means at our disposal to end this war quickly, even as Truman did in Japan," an apparent suggestion that nuclear weapons should be used in Vietnam. Simply stated, an ALC constituent thought that "Congress should officially declare war and get it over with in a hurry so our loved ones could come home."[28]

Lutherans believed that God justified certain wars. This theological premise allowed American Lutherans to religiously sanction any war they advocated. It took little effort for Lutherans to do so regarding the Vietnam conflict. They had long ago established in their minds that communism represented a "devilish" philosophy. Thus, any combat against the "red menace" warranted their support. Regarding the Vietnam War, they buttressed this idea with Lutheran two kingdoms theology, their trust in the U.S. government, and alleged proof that communism was evil.

HONORING U.S. SOLDIERS AND POWS

Prowar Lutherans also supported the Vietnam War because they wanted to honor U.S. soldiers. They claimed that antiwar activities dishonored the U.S. fighting men and instead comforted the enemy. And they explained in detail what they thought U.S. soldiers deserved from those on the homefront. To this end, they regularly supported the various Lutheran military chaplaincy programs. The Lutheran Council U.S.A., the Lutheran Church–Missouri Synod, and the Wisconsin Evangelical Lutheran Synod each had pastors who counseled the soldiers in combat. Like their just war theology, however, a close examination reveals that they molded their defense of the soldiers to fit their pro-Vietnam War mentalities. Conservative Lutheran rhetoric explained that soldiers' needs buttressed their support for the war even as it reinforced long-standing prejudices against communism.

Prowar Lutherans first declared that the war's constant reminder of a soldier's mortality created better Christians because the Lutheran church nurtured them through this turmoil.[29] The 1965 Lutheran Church–Missouri Synod delegates to their national convention called for the young men "to use their term of military service for a courageous witness of their faith with a consistent Christian life." According to this resolution, military service meant more than serving the government because obedience to the state honored their Lutheran background and because the disciplined life of a soldier made better citizens and more faithful men out of the soldiers. Prior to the creation of LCUSA, the National Lutheran Council provided the same function of bringing Lutherans together to serve important causes with which they all agreed. This included work to ensure that Lutherans in the Armed Forced received spiritual guidance. *A Mighty Fortress*, the National Lutheran Council periodical sent to servicemen, assisted with this function. Early during the U.S. involvement in Vietnam, therefore, it printed items that encouraged Lutheran soldiers to understand this point of view. For example, the periodical declared that "the serviceman is the child of God doing a necessary service to his family, to his country, and to himself." Propaganda from the WELS designed to encourage its laity to support the WELS chaplaincy made similar points. For example, a slide show presented to congregations trumpeted the WELS chaplains program because "there is no substitute for God's Word to sustain a good soldier of Jesus Christ when afraid . . . or tempted by the devil . . . through the oriental vices of immorality." None of these statements explicitly advocated the Vietnam War. But they implicitly did so by sanctioning the soldiers' actions, by placing God on their side, and by claiming that war led more young men to Lutheran churches.[30]

Four visits to Vietnam during the war by "Lutheran Hour" preacher Dr. Oswald C. J. Hoffmann solidified the notion that war cultivated young Christians. The "Lutheran Hour" was a weekly national radio program funded by the Lutheran Laymen's League. Hoffmann became a widely respected LCMS pastor through his service as the program's primary preacher. He traveled to Vietnam to lead Christmas services each year from 1969 to 1972 and there ministered to a vast number of people. Robert Garmatz's diary of the 1970 sojourn provides a good example. Garmatz traveled with Hoffmann, kept a meticulous diary, and stated that "the men in the military in Vietnam were great, brave people who knew their jobs and did them well." In relating soldiers' faith, Garmatz tells of one man who insisted that Hoffmann's visit was "simply great. They [servicemen] will go back to their 'hootches' and talk about it for weeks." In short, amid Vietnam's chaos, Garmatz found a true Christian witness among the soldiers. Prowar Lutherans therefore demanded full support for these soldier-believers. Other reports praised the men's attendance at each of Hoffmann's worship services. They especially noted the positive reaction to Suzanne Johnson, a former "Miss Illinois" in the Miss America pageant who sang for the soldiers. Hoffmann traveled to Vietnam to minister to U.S. soldiers, not to endorse the Vietnam War. But the rhetoric about the extreme faith everyone encountered among the soldiers inherently supported the idea that military service crafted good Christians. Hoffmann further affiliated himself with the Nixon administration policy by visiting the president to brief him on his Christmas 1970 trip to Vietnam. Thus, Hoffmann's trips became another tacit means of supporting the Vietnam War.[31]

Prowar Lutherans furthered this thinking in prayers for the soldiers' safety. Of course they first and foremost prayed quite honestly to protect those in harm's way. But even the wording that they used demonstrates a prowar bias. The American Lutheran Church's journal for women, *Scope*, prayed, "Hear our prayer, O Lord, for all Americans who serve the cause of freedom in Vietnam: Prosper their compassion for the suffering people whose future they seek to enhance; confirm their dedication to the principles of human dignity and self-determination; and strengthen their resolution that what is right will prevail. Be their Shield and their Shepherd in the shadow of death, their Fortress and the Anchor of their faith, for the sake of your Son, our Savior Jesus Christ. Amen." This prayer asked readers to champion the soldiers' cause when it not only called for their protection but also depicted their efforts patriotically. For example, it called them "Americans who serve the cause of freedom." But this was not a unique Lutheran prayer. Other denominations supported the same idea in the way that they prayed. A Wisconsin Evangelical Lutheran Synod resolution/prayer insisted that U.S. soldiers endangered themselves "because they are called to the colors by our nation's military needs." Conservative Lutherans again cloaked their prowar advocacy in an issue to which almost everyone agreed: they simply prayed for the soldiers' safety. But their rhetoric contained obvious patriotism that defended the U.S. actions. Thus, even praying for the servicemen became an opportunity to support the Vietnam War. In short, though not explicitly a theological justification for the fighting, their rhetoric firmly planted God on the American side. Images of soldiers in South Vietnam did the same thing. A picture of one man with "In God We Trust" on his helmet explained that the Marine "places his trust in God." Such religious propaganda by soldiers was not uncommon but when printed in Lutheran periodicals became another way of aligning the United States on the side of "righteousness."[32]

Such Lutherans also backed U.S. soldiers because they thought that they protected the world from tyranny. In other words, conservative Lutheran opinions about communism as a monolithic force encircling the globe contributed to their point of view regarding the soldiers. These young men not only served in the U.S. military but did God's work in combating this atheistic force. For example, an ALC pastor explained that everyone must venerate the servicemen because "it is important for the church to continue its efforts, together with our nation, in the war against Communism." LCMS President J. A. O. Preus seconded this position in a letter he wrote prior to becoming LCMS president. He condemned Christians who called for a bombing halt and stated that "we owe much more to our soldiers in Viet Nam than we do to irresponsible clergy and we have a far greater threat in communism than we do in the dangers of bombing North Viet Nam." Not only did he explain his position, but he condemned clergy with whom he disagreed as negligent. He also justified the U.S. bombing of North Vietnam as necessary in this global fight against Communist expansionism. Laypeople from all of the denominations who backed the war concurred with this position. An LCA mother asserted that "our oldest boy went overseas to be part of a *conflict* he feels is just." She demanded that the LCA's *Lutheran* support his fight against the North Vietnamese Communists, who she and her son thought threatened global security. And of course the periodical created to generate Lutheran support for the Cold War, *Through to Victory*, shared this idea. It printed a cartoon that combined a prowar statement with a condemnation of how the bombing halts affected soldiers and their families. The cartoon depicted two medics evacuating a dead U.S. soldier as bombs, with the Soviet hammer and sickle on them, drop from above. One of the men asks the other, "Who'll explain the bombing halt to Joe's widow?" The journal felt that the North Vietnamese, backed by Soviet and Chinese weapons, used the pauses to attack U.S. soldiers who were rendered helpless by their government.[33]

In a natural progression from this support for soldiers, prowar Lutherans also explained that U.S. troops fought and died for the Lord. Here, they shed their theological argument that Lutherans had to fight for the state regardless of whether or not they agreed with it and instead asserted quite plainly that they fought for God against the Communists. An LCA member maintained that antiwar statements made the soldiers' deaths "nothing more than fanatical suicides"; in contrast, he thought that these men died for a Godly cause. A Lutheran periodical that regularly supported conservative politics to its small constituency also made this point. *Lutheran Brotherhood* memorialized one soldier with a quotation from a letter he sent to his mother: "I do want you to know that no matter how this war ends or what the outcome of my stay over here, I shall never regret it. I am very much at peace with myself as a person. I will know that I did not idly stand by and talk as some are doing, but had it in my power to try to do something, or at least find out the truth." The accompanying article portrayed him as an American who sacrificed everything for his country and stated that he had come to a religious peace regarding his fate. The boy's statement emphasized that he had gone to Vietnam, investigated the situation, and concluded that the United States aided the Vietnamese. LCMS pastor and "Lutheran Hour" preacher Oswald Hoffmann seconded this opinion. A letter to a mother who lost her son stated that "greater love hath no man than to give his life for the brethren. Our Lord did that, as only he could. I am persuaded that everything Roger did was for the Lord Jesus Christ." This image suggested a parallel between Jesus's crucifixion and a U.S. soldier dying to fight communism in Vietnam. Hoffmann clearly meant that both instances represented the work of God. All of the above statements defended U.S. soldiers by portraying the Vietnam conflict as both a religious and a political war.[34]

The subject of prisoners of war solidified this connection between support for soldiers and prowar sentiments. Conservative Lutherans maintained that the North Vietnamese tortured captured U.S. servicemen and refused to guarantee their release even if the United States pulled out of the war. They further asserted that the large number of POWs/MIAs necessitated continued fighting and exploited this issue to garner more advocacy for their prowar attitudes. In other words, they claimed that the United States had to fight in Southeast Asia until the North Vietnamese guaranteed the release of all U.S. personnel. According to rightist attitudes, any withdrawal beforehand doomed these people to a life of captivity in the Democratic Republic of Vietnam. But the example of POWs does cloud conservative claims. The North Vietnamese did physically and psychologically torture U.S. POWs, which lends credence to prowar Lutheran assertions. Yet, simultaneously, the United States greatly inflated the number of POWs still alive in order to promote the Vietnam War. The government, for the first time during the Vietnam War, combined MIA and POW statistics and thereby amplified the number of men possibly held captive. While allegations about brutal treatment proved true, the insistence that large numbers of soldiers suffered this fate throughout the war tests false. Furthermore, North Vietnam never withheld prisoners after the United States exited the war, a fact that invalidates conservative claims that North Vietnam refused to release POWs.[35]

Despite this confusing reality, prowar Lutherans used the POW/MIA issue to denounce North Vietnam. A POW's wife mass mailed a letter to Lutherans and asserted that the North Vietnamese refused to release a list of U.S. prisoners. This Communist act left her and the couple's son in complete ignorance: "Each night my little boy kneels and prays, 'Please God, bring my daddy home soon.' Won't you help us please by sending your letters or telegrams" to President Nixon? Despite her assertion, throughout the conflict and after, North Vietnam insisted that it fully disclosed all POW names. An LCA member, nonetheless, complained that President Robert J. Marshall never mentioned "the enemy that has kept our sons [POWs] in dark silence." Still another LCA constituent pointed out that the North Vietnamese employed "barbaric treatment of Americans as well as Asians" to win the war. These sentiments persisted after the U.S. withdrawal from Vietnam. An LCMS laywoman censured the WCC for sending supplies to North Vietnam and wanted the shipments stopped until "an accounting is done for all of prisoners and missing men who have suffered in those cells and cages."[36]

Although countless laypeople and conservative Lutheran officials championed this point, none matched the zeal of LCMS President J. A. O. Preus. He spearheaded a national effort to learn more about the POWs, visited international leaders to try to free them, and even attempted to visit North Vietnam to inspect the conditions under which they lived. He declared "Sunday, March 14, 1971, as a Day of Prayer for the American POWs and MIAs" and asked churches across the United States, both Lutheran and non-Lutheran, to participate. He provoked sympathy for his cause when he stated that "it is a heart-rending experience to hear first hand of the unbelievable torture endured by these men." Such statements criticized North Vietnam without actually mentioning the Communist country: "I am convinced that the Lord of the church will hear and answer the prayers of His people in behalf of these suffering men and their sorrowing families." Furthermore, Preus expressed doubt that a U.S. withdrawal from the war would lead to the release of all prisoners. He distrusted the North Vietnamese, even after he met with Communist officials, and stated, "I wish I were as sure as you are that you are correct in saying that if we pull out they will return the POWs." He also chastised someone who questioned his efforts and declared that "I don't see how you can be so heartless as to deny these poor men who have served their country and are now suffering indescribable horrors the help which I was willing to give them." Preus worked to free the POWs because he worried about their plight; but his rhetoric revealed an anti-Communist bent when he constantly mentioned their horrible treatment and questioned the honesty of North Vietnamese officials.[37]

A number of Lutherans agreed with Preus's opinions. One LCMS member supported any church effort that ensured "humane treatment of all American prisoners of war." A couple wrote to Preus in 1971, stating that the army had listed their son-in-law as missing in action since January 1968. They appreciated that a leader of "our church" started a movement to demand answers from the North Vietnamese. But LCMS constituents endorsed their president's

actions with even more conviction in a 1971 convention resolution. It is noteworthy that such a resolution came after the conservatives had orchestrated a
takeover of the LCMS, put Preus in the presidency, and tried to expunge moderate and liberal faculty members from their St. Louis seminary. In other
words, this conservative resolution about POWs came in the midst of a conservative resurgence within the denomination. The resolution applauded his
efforts and also mirrored his denunciations of the North Vietnamese by criticizing their treatment of the POWs:

> Whereas, many servicemen and civilians are being held prisoners in Indochina;
> and
>   Whereas, many of them are suffering cruel and inhuman treatment in that spe-
> cific provisions of the Geneva Convention calling for letter-writing privileges,
> proper medical care, and identification of captives to their government appear to
> have been violated in some instances; and
>   Whereas, the continued suffering of these prisoners is inconsistent with
> Christian ideals of compassion and mercy; and
>   Whereas Dr. J. A. O. Preus, President of The Lutheran Church–Missouri
> Synod, has already sought to secure the release of American prisoners; therefore
> be it
>   Resolved that The Lutheran Church–Missouri Synod commend its President
> for his action; and be it further
>   Resolved that The Lutheran Church–Missouri Synod urge all the congrega-
> tions and individuals in its membership to remember these prisoners and their
> families in their prayers; and be it further
>   Resolved that the members of the Synod be encouraged to communicate their
> concerns to responsible officials on both sides, within the bounds of government
> policies.[38]

Beginning in 1964, many Lutherans wholeheartedly supported the Vietnam
War and its fight against communism. They therefore defended U.S. soldiers
and even saw them as special agents; not only did these men serve their country, prowar Lutherans insisted that they righteously fought the "demonic"
Communists. Thus, they consistently called for Americans to support the servicemen in Vietnam. The relationship to this attitude and their anti-Communist
sentiments especially appeared when they discussed prisoners of war. They
lamented the treatment of POWs and asked North Vietnam to release a list of
names. Although their calls for backing the soldiers and attempts to free the
POWs stemmed from genuine concern, they also manipulated these subjects
to further justify their prowar stance. Indeed, they bolstered pro-Vietnam War
convictions with the issue of soldiers because they insisted that these men
fought on God's side of the war.

CONCLUSION

Conservative Lutherans' Cold War fervor persisted when they discussed the Vietnam War. As they did with the Soviet Union, China, and alleged internal Communist threats, conservatives castigated Communist North Vietnam. This led them to defend U.S. actions in Southeast Asia as necessary. They viewed communism as a monolithic atheistic threat, such as the depiction one Lutheran used of a lion prowling around the globe. Because they so feared any form of communism, they naturally wanted to keep Vietnam from becoming a Communist nation. Thus, they constructed an elaborate defense of their position that went so far as to call the Communist North Vietnamese uniquely vicious. Patriotism further fueled their backing of U.S. warfare. Finally, they justified their position with a theological just war argument and claimed that U.S. servicemen deserved the homefront's universal support. Prowar Lutherans never analyzed the Vietnam War outside of its Cold War context; rather, they placed it into the international fight against communism and used the circumstances surrounding it to justify a preconceived conviction. Despite their adherence to this position, other Lutherans rose to challenge them.

NOTES

1. Little to no research exists to allow for comment on the overall American Christian context regarding prowar attitudes during the Vietnam War. As chapter 5 will demonstrate, religious historians have given the antiwar movement ample attention, but at the expense of outlining how conservatives and moderates within all of the churches supported the war and continued to trust the U.S. government; one good but brief overview that includes prowar Christian attitudes is Amanda Porterfield, *The Transformation of American Religion: The Story of a Late-Twentieth Century Awakening* (New York: Oxford University Press, 2001).

2. James D. Bales, "The Vietnam War in Context," *Christian News* 1 (29 January 1968): 7; Robert T. Smith to G. Elson Ruff, 6 April 1965, Evangelical Lutheran Church in America Archives, Chicago, Illinois (hereafter ELCA), G. Elson Ruff Papers, box 13, "Sk"; "Step-Up in Vietnam," *Lutheran Witness Reporter* 1 (8 August 1965): 4; Lutheran Church in America, 1966 Convention Minutes, 814, ELCA; Russell L. Stewart to Carl E. Thomas, 25 May 1970, ELCA, Robert J. Marshall Papers, box 106, "?"; Ralph Michaels, "A Case for Political Conservatism," *Lutheran Forum* 4 (November 1970): 12–13.

3. Thomas Basich, "The Confusion and the Commitment," *Dialog* 6 (Winter 1967): 34–43; Bruce W. Concord to G. Elson Ruff, 1 December 1967, ELCA, G. Elson Ruff Papers, box 2, "Ch-_"; Vincent M. Anderson, "Vietnam War," *Lutheran* 6 (31 January 1968): 49; Raynard Huglen, "General Chiang Kai-Shek," *Lutheran America* 13 (22 April 1975): 9.

4. Doris R. Vegelahn to G. Elson Ruff, 6 October 1966, ELCA, G. Elson Ruff Papers, box 15, "Ve"; Lieutenant Colonel George O. Taylor, "Chaplain Flays Beatniks," *Faith-Life* 39 (March/April 1966): 16–17; Morris F. Hovck, Jr., to Robert J. Marshall, 25 May 1970, ELCA,

Robert J. Marshall Papers, box 117, "War: Vietnam and Cambodia" (emphasis in original); L. O. Thompson to G. Elson Ruff, 29 November 1967, ELCA, G. Elson Ruff Papers, box 14, "Tho." Good examinations of the relationship between Hanoi, Moscow, and Beijing are Gordon H. Chang, *Friends and Enemies: The United States, China, and the Soviet Union, 1948–1972* (Stanford: Stanford University Press, 1990); William Bundy, *A Tangled Web: The Making of Foreign Policy in the Nixon Presidency* (New York: Hill and Wang, 1998); Keith L. Nelson, *The Making of Détente: Soviet-American Relations in the Shadow of Vietnam* (Baltimore: Johns Hopkins University Press, 1995); Ilya Gaiduk, *The Soviet Union and the Vietnam War* (Chicago: Ivan R. Dee, 1996); Qiang Zhai, *China and the Vietnam Wars, 1950–1975* (Chapel Hill: University of North Carolina Press, 2000); William J. Duiker, *The Communist Road to Power in Vietnam*, 2nd ed. (Boulder, CO: Westview Press, 1996).

5. R. C. Eckersley to G. Elson Ruff, March 1968, ELCA, G. Elson Ruff Papers, box 18, "E"; H. R. Heinz to J. A. O. Preus, June 1970, CHI, Executive Office, UPN box 79, "United States Government Offices, 1969–1971"; Alfred Staude to Albert P. Stauderman, 18 April 1973, ELCA, Albert P. Stauderman Papers, box 93, "Si-Sz 1973"; Charles H. Prutzman to Ove Nielsen, 4 August 1973, ELCA, Lutheran World Relief 4, Country Files, box 18, "North Vietnam, 1970."

6. Lowell B. Herlong to G. Elson Ruff, 10 March 1966, ELCA, G. Elson Ruff Papers, box 7, "Hem"; Joseph M. Barbat to Frederik A. Schiotz, 17 July 1970, ELCA, Frederik A. Schiotz Papers, box 63, "Cambodia/LWF Location" (emphasis in original). For the best discussions of the protest movement and its non-Communist inspiration, see Charles DeBenedetti and Charles Chatfield, *An American Ordeal: The Antiwar Movement of the Vietnam Era* (Syracuse, NY: Syracuse University Press, 1990); Terry H. Anderson, *The Movement and the Sixties: Protest in America from Greensboro to Wounded Knee* (New York: Oxford University Press, 1995); Melvin Small, *Johnson, Nixon, and the Doves* (New Brunswick, NJ: Rutgers University Press, 1988).

7. William B. Kyle to A. Henry Hetland, 17 April 1967, ELCA, Frederik A. Schiotz Papers, box 44, "National Lutheran Campus Ministry"; Charles J. Clark to Robert J. Marshall, 4 June 1970, ELCA, Robert J. Marshall Papers, box 117, "War in Vietnam and Cambodia"; Filmstrip, "Look How Thy Brethren Fare," 1968–1972, Wisconsin Evangelical Lutheran Synod Archives, Mequon, Wisconsin (hereafter WELS), "Military Chaplains in Vietnam"; Fred Neuhaus to Frank D. Starr, 4 February 1976, CHI, Lutheran Witness Letters, box 3, "N."

8. R. C. Eckersley to G. Elson Ruff, March 1968, ELCA, G. Elson Ruff Papers, box 18, "E"; J. A. O. Preus to Dan Kluse, 24 May 1971, CHI, Executive Office, UPN box 62, "POWs"; N. S. Tjernagel, "Editorial Briefs," *Lutheran Sentinel* 58 (26 June 1975): 178.

9. Lowell B. Herlong to G. Elson Ruff, 10 March 1966, ELCA, G. Elson Ruff Papers, box 7, "Hem"; L. O. Thompson to G. Elson Ruff, 29 November 1967, ELCA, G. Elson Ruff Papers, box 14, "Tha"; Samuel C. Elliot to G. Elson Ruff, 7 December 1967, ELCA, G. Elson Ruff Papers, box 4, "Ei"; Cynthia L. Stewart, "Opinions on Vietnam," *Lutheran* 6 (14 February 1968): 48–49; L. O. Simpson to Albert P. Stauderman, 24 January 1974, ELCA, Albert P. Stauderman Papers, box B-95, "Sa-Si 1974."

10. Sally Roik to G. Elson Ruff, April 1967, ELCA, G. Elson Ruff Papers, box 11, "Ro"; John Brantner to Albert P. Stauderman, 2 April 1974, ELCA, Albert P. Stauderman Papers, box 93, "B 1974"; Harold W. Wicke, "Briefs by the Editor," *Northwestern Lutheran* 62 (1 June 1975): 162.

11. Robert C. Fenning, "The Flag, Motherhood, and the United States Marine Corps," *Lutheran Chaplain* 27 (June 1966): 28–29; Robert E. Valgren to G. Elson Ruff, 24 February 1968, G. Elson Ruff Papers, box 22, "Tu-V"; Philip Kibena to Albert P. Stauderman, 4 January 1973, ELCA, Albert. P. Stauderman Papers, box 92, "K 1973."

12. Donald R. VanNatter, "Vietnam Is Troublesome," *Lutheran Standard* 7 (21 March 1967): 13; Scott D. Kelling to Martin W. Mueller, August 1967, CHI, Lutheran Witness Letters, box 2, "Ka-Ko"; Luther M. Schulze to Carl E. Thomas, 26 May 1970, ELCA, Robert J. Marshall Papers, box 106, "?"; J. A. O. Preus to Mr. and Mrs. Kenneth Kase, 10 May 1971, CHI, Executive Office, UPN box 62, "POWs."

13. American Lutheran Church, 1966 Convention Minutes, 35, ELCA; Martin H. Scharlemann, "NCC Stand on Vietnam: 'Somewhat Perverse,'" *Lutheran Chaplain* 27 (June 1966): 39; Donald M. Williams to Obed E. Lundeen, 21 January 1967, ELCA, Franklin Clark Fry Papers, box 95, "?"; Carl A. Zimmerman to Franklin Clark Fry, 16 April 1968, ELCA, G. Elson Ruff Papers, box 22, "Y-Z"; Marvin B. Lauver to G. Elson Ruff, 26 July 1968, ELCA, G. Elson Ruff Papers, box 20, "La-Ler"; Gilbert Sanchez to Albert P. Stauderman, 8 April 1975, ELCA, Albert P. Stauderman Papers, box 97, "S-Sh 1975."

14. Don Neiswender, "Missionary Raps Neuhaus on Vietnam," *Lutheran Forum* 1 (June 1967): 15; L. O. Simpson to Albert P. Stauderman, 24 January 1974, ELCA, Albert P. Stauderman Papers, box 95, "Sa-Si 1974."

15. Richard Wurmbrand, "Murder in Vietnam," *Jesus to the Communist World* (August 1969): 1–2; "Christians Crucified by the Vietcong," *Jesus to the Communist World* (August 1972): 3 (emphasis in original); William J. Caughlin, "A Massacre Nobody Talks About," *Through to Victory* 11 (June 1971): 11; "It Just Slipped Out of My Hand," *Through to Victory* 13 (October 1973): 2.

16. Wesley T. Sideen to G. Elson Ruff, 3 February 1968, ELCA, G. Elson Ruff Papers, box 21, "Si"; Alfred Staude to Albert P. Stauderman, 18 April 1973, ELCA, Albert P. Stauderman Papers, box 93, "Sj-Sz/1973"; Mrs. J. J. Klik to G. Elson Ruff, December 1964, ELCA, G. Elson Ruff Papers, box 8, "Kl" (emphasis in original); Mrs. L. B. Olson, "National Council and Vietnam," *Lutheran* 4 (16 February 1966): 49.

17. American Lutheran Church, 1966 Convention Minutes, 35, ELCA; Helen M. Donaldson to Frederik A. Schiotz, 1 July 1970, ELCA, Frederik A. Schiotz Papers, box 63, "Cambodia/LWF Location"; J. A. O. Preus to William Mayer, 26 December 1972, CHI, Executive Office, No box, "Vietnam Peace, 1972–1973."

18. Daryl M. Hanson to Frederik A. Schiotz, 27 September 1968, ELCA, Frederik A. Schiotz Papers, box 47, "WCC Reactions to 1968 Assembly I"; L. H. Steinhoff to Carl E. Thomas, 23 May 1970, ELCA, Robert J. Marshall Papers, box 106, "?"; C. E. Nelson to Frederik A. Schiotz, 7 July 1970, ELCA, Frederik A. Schiotz Papers, box 63, "Cambodia/LWF Location."

19. Thomas Basich to Frederik A. Schiotz, 22 December 1967, ELCA, Frederik A. Schiotz Papers, box 55, "NCC: Church and Society Conference, 1967"; H. J. Brede to Carl E. Thomas, 22 May 1970, ELCA, Robert J. Marshall Papers, box 106, "International Travel"; J. A. O. Preus to Frank Zeman, 24 March 1971, CHI, Executive Office, UPN box 62, "POW: Pastors."

20. Edward Fredrich, "The Churches and Vietnam," *Northwestern Lutheran* 53 (4 September 1966): 286; Paul C. Neipp, "To Refrain from Giving Advice to the Government on How to Conduct War in Vietnam," American Lutheran Church, 1967 Convention Minutes, 59, ELCA; American Lutheran Church, 1972 Convention Minutes, 944–45, ELCA. For a discussion of what the administrations knew, see Robert Buzzanco, *Masters of War: Military Dissent and Politics in the Vietnam Era* (Cambridge: Cambridge University Press, 1996); David L. Di Leo, *George Ball, Vietnam, and the Rethinking of Containment* (Chapel Hill: The University of North Carolina Press, 1991); Robert Dallek, *Flawed Giant: Lyndon Johnson and His Times, 1961–1973* (New York: Oxford University Press, 1993); Jeffrey Kimball, *Nixon's Vietnam War* (Lawrence: University Press of Kansas, 1998).

21. James M. Fillman, Sr., to G. Elson Ruff, 17 February 1966, ELCA, G. Elson Ruff Papers, box 4, "Fc"; A. G. Lewis to Frederik A. Schiotz, 14 July 1970, ELCA, Frederik A. Schiotz

Papers, box 63, "Cambodia/LWF Location"; J. A. O. Preus to Richard M. Nixon, 8 January 1973, CHI, Executive Office, No box, "Vietnam: Peace 1972–73"; J. A. O. Preus to Richard M. Nixon, 25 January 1973, CHI, Executive Office, No box, "Vietnam: Peace, 1972–73."

22. The seven just war tenets are as follows: the war has to have a just cause, be waged by a legitimate authority, be formally declared, be fought to restore a just peace, be a last resort, have a reasonable chance for success, and have means and ends that were proportional.

23. Arthur Piepkorn to Bertwin L. Frey, 9 June 1967, ELCA, Arthur Piepkorn Papers, box 106, "War." For one of the first tracts on Christian just war theory, see Saint Augustine, *Concerning the City of God against the Pagans* (New York: Penguin Books, 1984). Robert C. Clouse, "The Korean and Vietnam Wars," in Ronald A. Wells, ed., *The Wars of America: Christian Views* (Macon, GA: Mercer University Press, 1991), 256.

24. J. A. O. Preus to Herman A. Nelson, 8 July 1970, CHI, Executive Office, box 12, "Conscientious Objectors 1970–1971."

25. Oliver R. Harms to Jerry D. Ehrlich, 31 May 1966, CHI, Executive Office, box 12, "Conscientious Objectors, 1963–69"; J. A. O. Preus to Robert C. Spilman, 4 March 1971, CHI, Executive Office, UPN box 62, "POWs"; Norman A. Madson, Jr., "Can a Christian Go to War with a Good Conscience?" *Lutheran Sentinel* 55 (22 June 1972): 183–85.

26. Far East Broadcasting Company Board Minutes, 20 November 1965, BGCA, Bertermann Papers, FEBC, box 1, "File 5"; G. Thomas Weddington to G. Elson Ruff, 13 July 1968, ELCA, G. Elson Ruff Papers, box 22, "W"; Clifford E. James to Robert J. Marshall, 25 May 1970, ELCA, Robert J. Marshall Papers, box 117, "War in Vietnam and Cambodia"; G. Sydow, "Citizenship on Earth," *Lutheran Spokesman* 14 (July 1971): 2–5.

27. Harry H. Feistner, "Is Vietnam War Immoral," *Christ and Freedom Notes* (1970): 2; Paul J. Pfadenhauer to G. Elson Ruff, 12 November 1970, ELCA, G. Elson Ruff Papers, box 22, "1970–72 Last Letters"; Anonymous, "An Open Letter to a Soldier in Vietnam," *Northwestern Lutheran* 58 (25 April 1971): 144–45.

28. Donald W. Williams to Obed E. Lundeen, 21 January 1967, ELCA, Franklin Clark Fry Papers, box 95, "?"; Clarence A. Niemeyer to Martin W. Mueller, 19 April 1967, CHI, Lutheran Witness Letters, box 3, "N"; Joseph M. Barbat to Frederik A. Schiotz, 17 July 1970, ELCA, Frederik A. Schiotz Papers, box 63, "Cambodia/LWF Location."

29. When discussing U.S. servicemen, conservatives seldom distinguished between "Christianity" and "Lutheranism." On the one hand, they generalized their argument to celebrate any Christian faith, especially because they realized that many non-Lutherans attended services conducted by Lutheran ministers. On the other hand, however, they only used Lutheran chaplains, services, and soldiers in their stories, pictures, and advertisements. They thereby focused on the growth of Lutheranism in Vietnam.

30. Lutheran Church–Missouri Synod, 1965 Convention Minutes, "Resolution 14-14," 185, CHI; Virgil A. Ganze, "The Big Question: 'Who Am I?'" *A Mighty Fortress* 16 (June 1966): 3; Fred T. Eggert to Elmer Kraemer, 19 February 1968, CHI, Lutheran Witness Letters, box 1, "E"; Filmstrip, "Look How Thy Brethren Fare," 1968–1972, WELS, "Military Chaplains in Vietnam."

31. Fred and Edith Pankow, *75 Years of Blessings and the BEST Is Yet to Come! A History of the International Lutheran Laymen's League* (St. Louis: International Lutheran Laymen's League, 1992), 158–62; Robert Garmatz, "Christmas 1970," Lutheran Laymen's League Archives, St. Louis, Missouri (hereafter LLL); Oswald C. J. Hoffmann and Ronald J. Schlegel, *What More Is There to Say but Amen: The Autobiography of Oswald C.J. Hoffmann* (St. Louis: Concordia Publishing House, 1996), 283–300; LCUSA Photograph, May 1971, ELCA, NLC 3/1/3, Church and Government, box 3.

32. James W. Kelly, "Prayer for American Servicemen in Vietnam—1968," *Scope* 8 (July 1968): 9; Wisconsin Evangelical Lutheran Synod, 1972 Report to the Nine Districts, 47–48, WELS; "Pledging Allegiance to the Cross and Flag," *Christian News* 1 (22 January 1968): 5.

33. Walter G. McLeod to Frederik A. Schiotz, 9 August 1966, ELCA, Frederik A. Schiotz Papers, box 154, "Peterson, Adolf M."; J. A. O. Preus to Martin W. Mueller, 28 March 1967, CHI, Lutheran Witness Letters, box 3, "P"; Mrs. Bob Mickelson to Albert P. Stauderman, 19 February 1971, ELCA, Albert P. Stauderman Papers, box 87, "M"; "Our Apathy is Giving the Enemy the Victory," *Through to Victory* 9 (April 1969): 9.

34. Paul E. Sjogren to G. Elson Ruff, 19 March 1968, ELCA, G. Elson Ruff Papers, box 21, "Si"; "Winston Parker: War Hero," *Lutheran Brotherhood Bond* 45 (July 1968): cover, 4–5; Oswald Hoffmann to Mrs. Roger Anderson, 10 March 1971, LLL, Oswald Hoffmann Papers.

35. To examine the torture of POWs by the North Vietnamese, see Stuart I. Rochester and Frederick Kiley, *Honor Bound: American Prisoners of War in Southeast Asia, 1961–1973* (Annapolis: Naval Institute Press, 1999); a good explanation of the government's illegitimate use of POW statistics is H. Bruce Franklin, *M.I.A. or Mythmaking in America: How and Why Belief in Live POWs Has Possessed a Nation* (New York: Lawrence Hill Books, 1992).

36. Mrs. C. L. Hanson to Church Members, 29 March 1969, CHI, Executive Office, box 5, "AFC Correspondence, 1969"; Mrs. Gay Koonce to G. Elson Ruff, 28 August 1969, ELCA, G. Elson Ruff Papers, box 20, "Kn-Kz"; Walter Rowoldt to Carl E. Thomas, 25 May 1970, ELCA, Robert J. Marshall Papers, box 106, "?"; Walter Orton to Albert P. Stauderman, 15 February 1971, ELCA, Albert P. Stauderman Papers, box 87, "N-O"; Mr. and Mrs. Robert Van Bendigom to Albert P. Stauderman, 2 February 1973, ELCA, Albert P. Stauderman Papers, box 93, "T, U, V 1973." Franklin, *M.I.A.*

37. J. A. O. Preus to All LCMS Pastors, 29 January 1971, CHI, Executive Office, UPN box 62, "POW: Pastors"; Preus to Donald H. Ward, 3 March 1971, CHI, Executive Office, UPN box 62, "Prisoners of War: Laymen"; Preus to Herb Schmidt, 28 May 1971, CHI, Executive Office, box 12, "Conscientious Objection, 1970–1971"; Preus to Edward H. Wiese, 2 June 1971, CHI, Executive Office, UPN box 62, "Prisoners of War: Laymen."

38. Arthur J. Wuebben to J. A. O. Preus, 6 May 1971, CHI, Executive Office, UPN box 62, "Prisoners of War: Laymen"; Mr. and Mrs. Fred Avery to J. A. O. Preus, 17 May 1971, CHI, Executive Office, UPN box 62, "Prisoners of War: Laymen"; Lutheran Church–Missouri Synod, 1971 Convention Minutes, 197, CHI.

Chapter Five

The Mythology of Prowling Communists: Lutheran Antiwar Sentiments

While prowar Lutherans clung to traditional Cold War ideologies, their liberal to moderate counterparts questioned those who applied these concepts to the Vietnam War. Antiwar Lutherans discarded the United States' reliance on containment, as did a number of Americans. Numerous Christians belonged to this antiwar movement, in which they picketed, protested, wrote letters to the government, and generally fought against the war from the very beginning because they thought it unjust and immoral. They also created interdenominational organizations to lobby Americans, Congress, and the presidency to their point of view. The most extreme of these individuals became famous for their vocal opposition, none more so than the Catholic priests and brothers, Daniel and Philip Berrigan, who even broke into draft board offices and poured blood over files. Because these Christians did not believe the United States had a sound diplomatic or political reason for fighting, they seldom discussed just war theology. In order to contemplate this principle, one must think that at least a possibility exists for making a sound argument for war. Of course such a conversation went on among intellectuals and in some Christian circles, but for the most part antiwar Christians, including Lutherans, surmised that it was an immoral war based on their understanding of the situation in Vietnam without applying the seven just war tenets. Lutherans who protested the Vietnam War asserted that they represented prophetic Christian voices who realized that the war injured innocent people and did nothing to fortify U.S. interests.[1]

Much of the antiwar Christian argument stemmed from their knowledge about Vietnam and its history; they saw a complexity to the civil war taking place in that country. Where prowar advocates saw all Communists as one entity, antiwar Americans pointed out the many factions involved in the war. The National Liberation Front in South Vietnam was organized in the early

1960s as a cooperative venture between a number of South Vietnamese to fight against the dictatorial regimes in that country and included Communists and North Vietnamese spies but also middle-class South Vietnamese, religious protestors, such as the Buddhists, and assorted other groups that simply despised South Vietnam. These groups had plenty of reason to complain because the series of regimes backed by the United States, despite frequent changes in leadership, stole U.S. aid and put it on the black market for profit, arrested those who dared question the government, and forced people into the army, all of which outraged the Vietnamese. In addition, Vietnam had a long history of opposing foreign domination and not giving up, even when militarily overpowered. Antiwar Christians in America examined all of these realities and denounced the opinion that America fought for freedom against monolithic communism. They used churches and other organizations to make their point and brought many moderate Americans into their sway as more and more people came to question U.S. policy in Southeast Asia.[2]

Lutherans participated in this Christian opposition, both from within the Lutheran leadership and the laity. They challenged their government's diplomatic policies. Although the clergy of the ALC and LCA had more antiwar advocates within their ranks than did the laity, Lutheran church leaders *did* have a significant lay following when they denounced the war. While antiwar Christian leaders often isolated many of their constituents by becoming too radical, Lutheran antiwar protestors, in contrast, included individuals from both the laity and the leadership. Furthermore, most Lutherans disliked massive public demonstrations but readily contributed to opinion polls, correspondence campaigns, and peaceful debates within the church, defending themselves as patriotic Americans whose protest was against the war, not the nation. They were unwilling to allow conservatives to co-opt patriotism as something that belonged only to their side of the debate. To counter their conservative colleagues, liberal to moderate Lutherans denounced the domino theory, provided a more nuanced depiction of North Vietnam, called the war unjust, questioned its effect on humanity, and stated that it injured the U.S. soldiers who fought it.[3]

QUESTIONING THE DOMINO THEORY AND MONOLITHIC COMMUNISM

Antiwar Lutherans first denounced the Vietnam War by criticizing the domino theory. Rather than viewing communism as a monolithic demon, they saw variances within Communist ideology. Furthermore, they approached North Vietnam differently than their conservative colleagues. Instead of portraying the country as part of a worldwide conspiracy, they viewed it as a nation combating imperialism and insisted that it did not threaten U.S. security. In 1964 the Lutheran Church in America's periodical, the *Lutheran*, printed an article that responded positively to J. William Fulbright's March speech titled "Foreign Policy—Old Myths and New Realities." LCA leadership often manifested a liberal ideology and had from the beginning questioned U.S. involvement in Vietnam. Many of them therefore supported Fulbright, one of the first and most vocal senators to denounce the war. After this speech, Lutheran pastor Robert E. Van Deusen concurred with its challenge to the domino theory and called for a new foreign policy that incorporated a more complex diplomacy that allowed for disunity among the Communist nations. To demonstrate this position, the *Lutheran* included a cartoon in which a smiling globe kicks out "old myths" (the domino theory) and wears a banner proclaiming "new realities." Antiwar Lutherans easily related this belief to the Vietnam War. As Robert Jenson, a Lutheran commentator in the left-leaning intellectual journal *Dialog*, stated in 1966, "We are told by the sponsors of this war that it must be fought to 'stop Communism.' But there is no such thing as Communism. There are Communists, Communist governments and parties, and no doubt Communist plots; but this one great demon called 'Communism' prowling the world is a mythical being." In short, antiwar Lutherans thought that containment theory was "oversimplified," a point of view not necessarily left-leaning in nature. Rather, it demonstrated a nuanced approach to foreign policy that saw complexity where others saw one monolith. For example, the *Lutheran* editor G. Elson Ruff, who was generally moderate regarding politics and theology, explained that "the 'worldwide communist threat' has obviously fragmented into a variety of parts." Ruff disdained the Soviet Union and People's Republic of China but thought that Vietnam was unrelated. The LCA's sister journal for women, *Lutheran Women*, concurred that the "communist world is far from united." In other words, antiwar Lutherans insisted that Communists disagreed with one another and could not lead an international revolution. Antiwar Lutherans additionally worried about reducing international affairs "to a cosmic struggle between the children of Light and the children of Darkness" because such a simplified view led to "hysterical over-reaction." By 1973, these Lutherans asserted that "with the détente with both the USSR and the People's Republic of China, 'containment of Communism' is an altogether dead dogma."[4]

Because antiwar Lutherans shunned the belief in one Communist force, they declared that the Vietnamese in North Vietnam and their allies in the insurgent movements of the South fought for self-determination. Much of this argument came from liberal Lutheran intellectuals who studied the global situation and had a vast knowledge of Communist realities. *Lutheran Forum*, at the time a more liberal theological periodical, stated that Vietnamese "support for the National Liberation Front (the Vietcong) . . . is not so much outside [Soviet- or Chinese-inspired] aggression as it is an internal civil war." In other words, the Vietnamese promoted communism because they wanted to govern themselves, not because of Soviet or Chinese pressure. A writer to the Lutheran Laymen's League asserted that "most of us have concluded that we do not hold the answers for the Asians, that we cannot impose our interpretation of what their goals are as the reason for sacrificing our self respect and the wasting of human resources beyond possible measure." American Lutheran Church (ALC) President Kent S. Knutson also reminded people that "all Chinese and Vietnamese are not your enemies. And remember that *our* bombs have killed hundreds of thousands of innocent women, men and children in North Vietnam and South Vietnam who hate war as much as you do." These Lutherans asserted that the Vietnamese, including the Communists, did not represent a threat to global democracy.[5]

American Lutheranism's pacifist organization, Lutheran Peace Fellowship (LPF), especially called for Vietnamese self-determination. Although LPF represented a minority of Lutherans from a number of the Lutheran denominations (it had just over six hundred members in 1971), it ably articulated antiwar Lutheran ideals. Steven Schroeder has delineated that LPF gave Lutherans an opportunity to denounce the Vietnam War within a pacifist context. Furthermore, it allowed members to protest without publicly demonstrating. Vincent L. Hawkinson, the LPF secretary-treasurer, best illustrates their viewpoint. He wanted the United States to "let the people of Vietnam work out their own destiny without outside interference." He also called for the United States to cooperate with the North Vietnamese in a settlement. He believed that "we must recognize that the problem in Vietnam is to establish their national identity. It is a local revolution." Hawkinson articulated the LPF position that Vietnam represented a civil war and not part of an international Communist conspiracy.[6]

Importantly, antiwar Lutherans still disdained Soviet communism even as they castigated the domino theory. They maintained an American patriotism and declared that their antiwar sentiments served to strengthen the nation, not weaken it. Once again, the moderate editor of the *Lutheran* reveals this perspective. G. Elson Ruff stated that "if we were citizens of the Soviet Union we would realize we have nothing to say about the decisions made by the government. In a democracy, though, such as the U.S. surely all of us are responsible for careful study and thinking about such an urgent problem as our policy in Vietnam." Ruff blasted the USSR but simultaneously questioned U.S. actions in Vietnam by pointing out the importance of participatory democracy. Another Lutheran leader declared that U.S. conduct in Southeast

Asia hindered its fight against the Soviets. The Lutheran Council U.S.A.'s (LCUSA) Carl E. Thomas felt that the 1970 Cambodian bombings "apparently had had the effect of weakening the moral position of the United States vis-à-vis the Soviet Union." President Nixon had sanctioned the bombing of this Vietnam neighbor because North Vietnam used it to transport troops and war materials into South Vietnam. This illegal bombing on a non-combatant country outraged antiwar Americans when it was revealed in April 1970. Thomas represented the opinion that this decision angered other nations, called into question U.S. morality, and undermined its fight against communism in other parts of the globe. Lutheran Church in America (LCA) representatives to an Ecumenical Witness convention also criticized the Vietnam War while still combating the Soviet Union. They "approved a message which condemned U.S. involvement in Vietnam" but also "called on Russia, China, and other nations 'to cease supplying the Hanoi government with the materials of war.'" They therefore placed some blame for the war upon the USSR. Furthermore, as a Lutheran Church–Missouri Synod (LCMS) constituent proclaimed, "I believe that an essential part of [American] freedom is the allowing of nations to determine their own governments, even at the cost of their lives." Vietnam spurred antiwar Lutherans to question the domino theory, but they never stopped fighting the Cold War against the USSR or supporting the American system of government.[7]

Antiwar Lutherans also thought U.S. participation in the Vietnam War unnecessary. Pastor G. Elson Ruff stated that, "in as much as the U.S. is involved in this war unilaterally, and has almost no support or approval from any other country, our military venture can hardly be classified as essential." An LCMS pastor used harsher words: "We will not save the world by defeating or containing Communism. We may, we will, only bring the world from one degree of oppression and inequality into another." Like their counterpart Ruff did in the LCA's *Lutheran*, the ALC's *Lutheran Standard* editors criticized those who believed a military defeat harmed the United States; they wondered if "the historian's pen, dipped in the continued bloodletting, [will] write disaster on the pages of history." These Lutherans felt that Vietnam in no way threatened U.S. global security and declared that the war damaged the United States' international reputation.[8]

Discarding of the domino theory led antiwar Lutherans to call the Vietnam conflict a tragedy. G. Elson Ruff proclaimed in 1968 that "this war is a miserable, cruel, and pointless adventure." ALC President Frederik A. Schiotz, a moderate theologian who often took liberal political stances, suggested that ignoring Ho Chi Minh at Versailles in 1919 had led to catastrophe because "this becomes a good illustration of the sins of the fathers being visited upon their children." He referred to the fact that Ho Chi Minh had approached the victorious nations after World War I and asked for Vietnamese independence. The European powers, in no mood to weaken their colonial empires, refused to listen to him and returned control of Vietnam to France. Though not the United States' decision, Wilson and American delegates allowed Europe to retain their empiric holdings with minor protest. Schiotz had LCA colleagues who mirrored this sentiment. In 1971, *Lutheran* editor Albert P. Stauderman claimed that he had "a tormented and repentant feeling that we must end this involvement and prevent it from happening again." By the 1970s, a larger cross-section of Lutherans mirrored their liberal leaderships' opinions. The ALC continued to mirror Schiotz's point of view even after his death. The 1972 assembly, representing the nearly three-million-member church, declared that "we have come to the conviction that our military involvement in Southeast Asia, however well-intended, has proven to be a tragic mistake." As Schiotz's successor, Kent S. Knutson wrote, "I think the Viet Nam War is a tragedy of major proportions."[9]

Antiwar Lutherans denounced the Vietnam War in part because they no longer believed in containment. The Vietnam War taught them that no "monolithic Communist demon" haunted the globe, especially when they stated that most of the Vietnamese who fought did so for the right of self-determination. This viewpoint, however, failed to convince them that the Cold War had to end. They believed their stance was an attempt to redeem the United States, not a condemnation of it as their opponents charged, and persisted with their anti-Soviet sentiments even as they called for the United States to withdraw from Southeast Asia. But despite this continued antagonism, they asserted that Vietnam did not jeopardize American global security. Instead, they labeled the fighting a U.S. tragedy.

A CIVIL WAR IN VIETNAM

Antiwar Lutherans' rejection of the domino theory prompted them to assess the governments in Vietnam and the United States differently than their prowar colleagues. They saw North Vietnam in the context of suffering civilians, not as a dangerous Communist force, decried the corruption of the South Vietnamese government, and questioned the United States' true motives: did the United States seek a better government for the Vietnamese or merely another partner against communism? They also questioned U.S. leaders. Their brand of patriotism led them to denounce the Vietnam War in order to protect the United States' image. They highlighted the extreme suffering that the war inflicted upon the Vietnamese. An ALC pastor wrote, "More Vietnamese suffer from this war than Americans do" and therefore felt that the Vietnamese should decide the war's future without U.S. input. Independent Lutheran journals, which did not need to worry about constituent voting or wrath, often voiced these opinions forcefully. *Lutheran Forum* wondered how the persistent fighting helped the Vietnamese. It maintained that the warfare injured everyone in Vietnam and concluded that "we support urgently the calls upon America to stop its attempts to 'help' its friends by obliterating its 'enemies.'" Antiwar Lutherans thought that prowar Americans remained "oblivious or indifferent to the wanton murder and waste and cruelty inflicted by *this* country, daily, upon civilians and military alike, of the alleged enemy." According to these Lutherans, the people of Vietnam suffered because the United States continued the war.[10]

The fact that antiwar Lutherans did not depict the North Vietnamese as an evil Other, in contrast to their prowar counterparts, led them to despise the suffering inflicted upon these people as much as they disliked what it did to American soldiers and the South Vietnamese. Indeed, they included the North Vietnamese in their pleas to stop the suffering and felt that an appropriate Christian witness took into account all humans, not just U.S. allies. Early in the war, LCA President Franklin Clark Fry poignantly made this point to a constituent who worried that church funds went to North Vietnam: "No funds of the Lutheran Church in America are finding their way to North Vietnam to relieve the suffering there. We are not obeying the word of our Lord about loving our enemies that much." This inaction, however, changed as the war continued. Antiwar Lutherans wanted to assist North Vietnamese civilians, but the United States prohibited most humanitarian efforts, and the Hanoi government distrusted Americans who wished to assist in their country. Nonetheless, Fry's successor, Robert J. Marshall, revealed that "the only channel open to us is the World Council of Churches. On occasion that organization has been able to channel funds into North Vietnam." Regardless of denominational affiliation, antiwar Lutherans despised the war's effect on humanity and worried about the North Vietnamese "enemies."[11]

Antiwar Lutherans also questioned the United States' alliance with South Vietnam because of its dictatorial government. One LCA member explained that "though the leaders of the forces we face may be largely communists, a vast number of non-communists have had no choice but to join or support the N.L.F. and North Vietnamese because of the tyrannical Saigon government which has the support of the U.S." Other laity and clergy concurred. A 1972 memorial to the national convention resolved that "the Western North Dakota District of the American Lutheran Church in convention assembled encourage the total withdrawal of all United States force (including planes) from Southeast Asia and discourage support of the government of South Vietnam until reconstituted, out of real concern for all people involved." Antiwar

Lutherans questioned the domino theory, hoped for compassion toward the North Vietnamese, and called South Vietnam a praetorian government.[12]

Antiwar Lutherans also differed from their prowar colleagues in how they viewed the U.S. government. They persistently questioned the Johnson administration, but did so cautiously at first because they admired Johnson's liberal domestic policies and wanted to maintain cooperation with him in this regard. This was common among advocates of the president's domestic policy. Most famously, Martin Luther King, Jr., agonized about coming out against the war because he feared Johnson might turn against civil rights legislation in retaliation. But King's conscience finally drove him to protest the war, despite Johnson turning cold toward him and other black leaders denouncing this position. A writer to the *Lutheran* explained this point of view from a Lutheran perspective in 1965, when he simply hoped that Johnson was truthful when he said he was "seeking the way for negotiations." This sentiment persisted in 1966 when another reader stated that "I am sure President Johnson and his advisors realize this perfectly [the threat of a world war stemming from the Vietnam conflict] and are doing their best not to get involved in a hopeless and endless land war in Asia." But their conciliatory tone changed entirely by 1968, when antiwar Lutherans censured Johnson for not ending the war and thanked "God that men of the Church of Jesus Christ are willing to be publicly lacerated for unpopular positions" when they "stand against one's President, Government, and many friends."[13]

After criticizing a Democratic president, antiwar Lutherans easily denounced the Republican Nixon's Vietnam policies. LCA President Robert J. Marshall was "very pessimistic" about the chances of Nixon withdrawing quickly from the war. These sentiments magnified as the war persisted. In 1970, twenty-six students from the Lutheran Theological Seminary in Gettysburg, Pennsylvania, wrote Nixon that they "deplore your recent decision to extend the war in southeast Asia by sending United States troops into Cambodia. Such increased entanglements can only prolong this already fruitless and disastrous conflict, and they can only further undermine our confidence in your professed desire for peace." ALC President Frederik A. Schiotz concurred, telling Nixon that "there is no extricating ourselves from Vietnam involvement without compromise—God has not ordained that the U.S. shall always 'win.'" He then asked the president to respond positively to UN General Secretary U Thant's call for a peace conference. By 1971, some antiwar Lutherans escalated the rhetoric and demonstrated their exasperation with the continued conflict. An LCA laywoman who wrote regularly to the *Lutheran* about her antiwar views, complained that "we are being governed by a group of Blood Thirsty War Mongers," and wanted "to see support for Senator George McGovern [the eventual 1972

Democratic nominee for president] from all sources." Liberal to moderate Lutherans held Nixon responsible for the war's continuation and urged him to stop it.[14]

But other antiwar Lutherans condemned the U.S. government more generally without blaming only one person. As an ALC constituent stated, "I am sorry I cannot obey the government, but sorrier still because the government insists on pursuing a course of action that is wrong." The LCA often voiced this opinion, especially within its leadership. *Lutheran* editor Albert P. Stauderman asserted that the 1972 bombing was "an additional waste of human life and resources and means more devastation for that poor country." LCA President Robert J. Marshall became more forceful in his antiwar stance as the fighting persisted. In 1973, he applauded a Lutheran Theological Seminary fast against the war because "your action probably would have fit my own feelings best. While I wanted to cry from the housetops about the atrocity of the bombing, I was filled with a tremendous sense of frustration and cynicism at the ineffectiveness of all the channels by which the church's opposition to the war had been proclaimed." Yet the LCA was not alone. An ALC member voiced similar disgust in regard to paying federal taxes because the money went toward "the senseless and indiscriminate slaughter from the air of men, women, and babies in Cambodia." These Lutherans expressed frustration that the war continued, helplessness in trying to stop it, and outrage as the government continued to fight.[15]

Despite their criticisms, these protestors' anticommunism and patriotism never wavered, their anti-Vietnam stance indicating neither anti-Cold War hostilities nor denunciations of the United States apart from its Vietnam involvement. The moderate editor of the LCA's *Lutheran* exemplifies this fact. G. Elson Ruff assured everyone that "there won't ever be any support in The Lutheran for the Communist movement in Vietnam." Although he spoke against the war, he never stopped advocating democracy over communism. Similarly, the American Lutheran Church in convention called for an end to the war when it "resolved, That we request the President of the United States to negotiate a complete end of armed conflict in Southeast Asia." But the resolution went on to insist that the peace settlement "maintain the honor of our country." In other words, the delegates wanted the war to end but not at the expense of U.S. prestige.[16]

Antiwar Lutherans, lamenting the Vietnamese suffering and insisting that the United States gained nothing from its backing of a corrupt regime, concluded that losing Vietnam to communism did not threaten U.S. security. Throughout the war, this assessment of the Southeast Asian situation led them to criticize the president and U.S. government. Antiwar Lutherans demanded peace and asserted that this stance represented the greatest form of Christian patriotism. Embarrassed by the war, liberal to moderate Lutherans wanted to end it immediately.

AN UNJUST WAR

Like their prowar counterparts, antiwar Lutherans constructed a theological justification for their antiwar stance. In contrast to the argument that God ordained the war, they lamented the human cost of fighting and called U.S. participation in Vietnam immoral. Much of this rhetoric centered on the human casualties of war; these Lutherans decried the loss of life, the displacement of innocent people, and the domestic turmoil. Interestingly, like their conservative colleagues, there is little evidence that a widespread and deliberate effort took place to denounce the war by applying the seven just war tenets. Rather than a formal process, antiwar Lutherans simply stated that the conflict was unjust because of what it did to humanity. These humanistic elements led them to demand action by the church when they mourned the war's international implications and demanded an end to U.S. involvement. This mirrored their Christian colleagues around the nation; while a vibrant part of the antiwar movement included Christians, they seldom articulated a formal theological justification for their position, instead outlining reasons to call the Vietnam War immoral based on examples of atrocities from that country. This general sense of immorality outraged their Christian conscience.

Antiwar Lutherans first reminded people that God punished humanity with war, regardless of whether or not it was just. An ALC convention resolution proclaimed that war occurred because of a "world estranged from God." Later ALC delegates asserted that "war, injustice, and the denial of human rights profane God's creation." Others lamented war by questioning soldiers who wrote Christian messages on their helmets. A layman stated that "what I object to is the implication that this in any sense represents the position of the Christian church with respect to war." He feared that this image led people to believe that God supported the soldiers', or the United States', position. A 1970 memorial sent to the Lutheran Church in America's convention shared these sentiments, stating that "war is always wrong in the context of Christ's command to love and can only be justified under extreme conditions" that were not met by the Vietnam conflict. Furthermore, the LCA's *Lutheran* editor, Albert P. Stauderman, worried that modern technology eliminated the just war theory. He declared that "to say that war has become 'uncivilized' sounds odd, but I think it impossible to regard today's kind of war as 'just.'"[17]

This belief that war went against God's will led antiwar Lutherans to call the Vietnam War sinful. As three students from the Lutheran-affiliated Wittenberg University asserted, "The war in Vietnam is immoral. The goal of eliminating poverty, disease, and hunger which both sides hope to achieve cannot be won by a military victory." An LCA layman lamented that the church never spoke forcefully against the war's vices and grieved "over the chance for moral vitality lost to our church." By not issuing a prophetic statement against Vietnam, he felt the LCA neglected to condemn a tragic situation. But it was not only the mainline LCA that held these opinions within its constituency. An ALC pastor also tried to spur his congregation to action when he demanded that President Kent S. Knutson condemn the war: "As *pastor pastorum* you have a responsibility to lead the people and clergy of the ALC in directions you feel they should go. That goes quite a ways beyond the mere reflection of consensus. The war is a moral issue."[18]

Antiwar Lutherans also stated that the war destroyed the United States; they crafted a patriotism that reflected their point of view in order to counter conservative charges that they were "un-American." An LCA member asserted, "I love America. We see America destroying herself. We say: Let us stop and reconsider." According to him, the war's turmoil injured U.S. prestige and therefore necessitated an immediate end. The editor of his church's periodical, Albert P. Stauderman, also concluded that the war harmed the United States: "I do agree that the Vietnam War is illegal, since it has never been declared by Congress, and that it is a degrading and divisive force which must be halted." Even after the U.S. withdrawal of military forces from Vietnam in 1973, antiwar Lutherans concluded that "the war was wasteful and probably useless." These Lutherans deduced that no monolithic Communist demon threatened Christianity and therefore questioned the Vietnam War's importance. This especially held true when they discussed its negative effect upon U.S. society and its image abroad.[19]

Once again, the few but passionate and interdenominational members of Lutheran Peace Fellowship best illustrate antiwar Lutheran theological convictions. Indeed, they represented a rare attempt to deliberately assess the just war theory and summarized these antiwar points in an argument that called the conflict unjust. The 1965 LPF Secretary-Treasurer Lloyd A. Berg questioned the war's justifiability after the United States began using chemical weapons in Vietnam. He stated that "we believe this is a moral and religious question of highest priority" because it was a "significant and shameful hour in human adventure." He insisted that no Christian should sanction such wanton disregard for human suffering. His successor, Vincent L. Hawkinson, asserted that "there is a growing discontent with the whole philosophy of might making right." Rather, he hoped that people saw the wrongness of U.S. actions in Southeast Asia. But a layman's letter best linked these thoughts directly to just war theology: "I am opposed to our nation's military intervention in Viet Nam partly because I feel that it very flagrantly violates the conditions which must be fulfilled according to traditional just war doctrine before a Christian can in good conscience participate in war."[20]

LCA and ALC presidents also theologically denounced the Vietnam War, unlike their LCMS counterpart J. A. O. Preus who consistently supported U.S. involvement. Disagreement with their colleague over the war squared with their opinions regarding other matters that they sometimes disagreed with him about, including support for conservative political candidates and welfare programs, as well as theological issues such as biblical inerrancy, the ordination of women, and unionism. Careful study convinced them that no viable reason existed for the United States to fight. As LCA President Franklin Clark Fry wrote, "I have . . . anxiously analyz[ed] the Vietnam situation and I have always ended by confessing that it has created a great ache in my own life, driving me to my knees." In his column to ALC pastors, Frederik A. Schiotz printed an antiwar letter he had received. He instructed the pastors to see it "as a 'cry in the wilderness,' spoken in the language of John Q. Public and representing the ache in millions of hearts." Schiotz thereby labeled the dissenters prophetic voices. He later added his own voice to the prophesy, stating that the Vietnam War "rocked" the American economy and asked, "Are not these signs through which God is speaking to us?" He also told pastors to listen to the youthful antiwar protestors' message: "The Lord indeed may be using our youth to open our eyes to our present predicament. He may be showing us anew how 'our young men shall see visions and your old men shall dream dreams.'" Fry and Schiotz contributed their leadership voices to antiwar admonitions by describing how they felt a divine force calling them to oppose the war.[21]

Published *Lutheran* and *Lutheran Standard* letters to the editor demonstrate that many laypeople's convictions also drove them to religiously oppose the Vietnam War. An LCA member wrote, "It is a magnificent absurdity that at this late date we are able to convince ourselves that we can worship and profess to follow the teachings of the greatest pacifist of all time while we at the same time take up arms against our fellowman." Another reader stated that "anyone who calls himself a Christian should be greatly shocked by the wholesale slaughter in Vietnam." These laypeople claimed that the United States murdered by fighting in Southeast Asia and lamented the loss of lives. This sparked their conscience, which turned them to their faith for answers. Because they saw war's inhuman destruction, they finally asked, "How could Americans' role in Vietnam ever, in any manner, be interpreted as God's will?" An ALC constituent concluded that "America must repent of this unjust, immoral war." These letters illustrate that members of the two moderate Lutheran denominations formed religious convictions against the Vietnam War based on its massive loss of human life.[22]

The war's human suffering also led an LCA congregation to fire its pastor. Carl Danielson, pastor at Zion Lutheran Church in Galveston, Texas, protested the war after his daughter returned from serving in Vietnam as a physical therapist. She described to him the turmoil caused by the U.S. bombings and insisted that the Vietcong fled to avoid the damage and left peasants and children behind to die. He subsequently joined public protests and denounced the war on television. His congregation responded by forcing him to resign because they disliked the notoriety that his activism generated. But their action led to even more publicity when both the *Houston Chronicle* and the *Washington Post* carried the story of his coerced resignation on their front pages. They described a "tall, gray-haired, distinguished-looking man" who "said it was time to be Christian and love our enemies." Danielson's case demonstrates that Christian convictions led some Lutherans to denounce the war when their conscience encountered its devastation.[23]

Antiwar Lutherans also accused the United States of destroying Vietnam and acting in an un-Christian way toward other people, in this case the Vietnamese. Using the biblical admonition that Christians should assist others in need, an LCA laywoman complained that "total destruction of a land, its people, its homes, its food supply is not being my brother's keeper." An LCMS pastor made the same argument: "What possible justification can there be before God, for the death and devastation we have rained upon countless civilians, to say nothing of soldiers whose major objective has been national liberation from (our) foreign control? A prayer goes up today from Indochina; 'They crush Thy People, O Lord, and afflict the heritage. They slay the widow and sojourner, and murder the fatherless; and they say, "The Lord does not see . . ."' (Psalm 94)." This same antiwar sentiment also proclaimed that "our nation is involved in unprecedented mass murder. Thousands of people are dying from our bombs."[24]

The war's injury to Vietnamese children especially incensed antiwar Lutherans. An LCA member stated that "it is heartbreaking to see on TV what women and children are going through" in Vietnam. Another constituent wondered how Christians could support a war that harmed innocent children when she asked, "Can you see Jesus Christ burning children alive with napalm in Vietnam?" Other Lutherans more subtly used children, as when an antiwar article by Lutheran pastor Ralph Moellering simply included the picture of a young Vietnamese boy crying. Antiwar Lutherans emphasized the war's ill-effect on children to convince others to denounce the war.[25]

Lutheran relief agencies also used the images of children to gain support. Inter-Lutheran agencies such as Lutheran World Action (LWA) provided food, medicine, and clothing to those ravaged by natural disasters, war, and other catastrophes. They naturally participated in efforts to assist those affected by the war in Vietnam throughout the conflict and solicited American Lutherans for funds to support these endeavors. To do so, they commonly used Vietnamese children to promote their work and encourage contributions. One LWA advertisement included a Vietnamese girl and the words "with love" prominently displayed to indicate the care the child might receive from LWA efforts even while living in the midst of war. Another poster depicted three children to demonstrate LWA's global reach and to indicate the need for funding around the world, but contained a hint of U.S. paternalism in its pictures by having children represent other countries (one of the pictures is of a Vietnamese boy) while the United States is embodied in a white U.S. soldier. The ad also contains the words "my brothers," which told people that they could not ignore suffering people, while a white hand holding a cross symbolized how the church aided the less fortunate. LWA also produced a filmstrip to promote its work. In one scene, a white father reads a newspaper while glancing at his son, but a bubble over his head indicates that he is thinking of a starving foreign boy; the slide's explanation said that "this visual aid presents a clear answer to the question, 'What can I do?' in relation to church relief and rehabilitation projects overseas." Again, children are used to represent the world because they elicit sympathy while Americans are depicted as well fed and strong. The man's son is clothed, playing with a toy, and happy while the darker skinned boy in his mind is skinny, frowning, and holding out an empty hand for food. Paternalism notwithstanding, LWA officials and their activities often aligned the organization with the antiwar platform; thus, advertisements for money implicitly fought against the war's effect on children by using Vietnamese boys and girls to gain empathy.[26]

Because antiwar Lutherans claimed that the Vietnam War went against God's will, they wondered why their Lutheran denominations failed to act. This questioning came from members of all three of the largest Lutheran denominations: the LCA, ALC, and LCMS. Lutheran churches were relatively quiet during this period because they feared that open debate would factionalize their membership. Some leaders criticized the war but always emphasized that they spoke as individuals, not for the church, and the denominational organizations that did act remained quiet about their assistance. The churches as a whole, therefore, said almost nothing. None of the churches passed a resolution during the war that opposed it. When their denominations failed to act, antiwar Lutherans complained. An LCMS laywoman protested that she found "it deeply disturbing that American Christians go halfway around the world to kill people because of political differences while 'my' church remains carefully neutral." Another member questioned how "churches proclaim the Christmas message without a concurrent protest against this outrage against humanity, the earth, our children and grandchildren." More pointedly, a layman asserted that "I am asking why the Lutheran leaders have not taken a stand against this wholesale murder." This lack of denominational action also caused grief for Lutherans after the U.S. withdrawal in 1973. A group of seminary professors stated that "it is our shame that the Church did not speak openly and often during this insidious conflict with words of utter condemnation."[27]

Antiwar Lutherans saw little need to construct an elaborate religious defense for their position; it seemed obvious to them that war went against Christian teachings and therefore God's will. Vietnam horrified them in particular because they saw no justifiable reason for the fighting: in their eyes this was not a just war. They no longer feared a monolithic Communist demon and instead focused on the suffering that the combat caused the North Vietnamese, the South Vietnamese, individual Americans, and U.S. society as a whole. Indeed, their viewing of the human costs of the war enabled them to move beyond a view of communism as entirely bad and to instead analyze each situation individually. The war's horrific effect on the Vietnamese outraged them, and they accused the United States of terrorism. Because antiwar Lutherans saw no reason for the U.S. fighting, they saw the war as an immoral campaign.

LUTHERAN WORLD RELIEF AND
VIETNAM CHRISTIAN SERVICE

Antiwar Lutherans also shaped their opinions based on the evidence acquired by Lutheran World Relief and Vietnam Christian Service. Lutheran World Relief (LWR) was a joint LCA and ALC effort that provided food, shelter, and economic assistance to war refugees and natural disaster victims. To better facilitate its efforts in Vietnam, LWR joined with Christian World Services, the relief agency of the National Council of Churches, and the Mennonite Central Committee to form Vietnam Christian Service (VCS). This cooperative venture assisted Vietnamese refugees, provided medical assistance, located homes for orphaned children, and orchestrated other humanitarian endeavors. Although the organization officially remained neutral, antiwar Lutherans gave it the most support. This especially held true because the LCMS, where many of the prowar Lutheran leaders belonged, refused to participate in LWR because of theological differences with the ALC and LCA. In addition, VCS *created* protestors because of the information it reported from Vietnam. Lutheran philanthropic efforts in Vietnam solidified antiwar sentiments and turned more people against the war because its firsthand accounts passionately revealed the devastation wrought by U.S. involvement.

Vietnam Christian Service strove to remain officially neutral in order to assist people from both sides. An LWR supporter explained this by stating that Christians must remember God's command that "if your enemy is hungry, feed him." Few VCS relief efforts, however, made it to North Vietnam because the Communist government distrusted any form of U.S. aid. But the VCS still wanted to "rise above political considerations and boundaries." To this end, VCS avoided giving aid to South Vietnamese political entities such as the National Liberation Front that was allied with North Vietnam or the U.S. backed South Vietnamese government. VCS even maintained that "association with U.S. government and U.S. military personnel should be limited to work-related requirements." Furthermore, it declared neutrality in order to protect its postwar position because it feared that any close association with the U.S. government would doom efforts to remain in Vietnam after the war ended. This became especially important after 1970, when LWR leaders concluded that "the war is already lost for the United States." VCS persisted with relief efforts in South Vietnam until the 1975 fall of Saigon to Communist forces, and in June 1973 LWR also filtered funds through the Lutheran World Federation that helped rebuild a maternity hospital in Haiphong, North Vietnam. LWR officials claimed that these were the first funds from a North American church to assist the Communist country. Vietnam Christian Service officially maintained a neutral policy because it wanted to provide humanitarian relief to anyone in need.[28]

The mere fact that the fighting created a need for humanitarian relief turned Lutherans against the war. An announcement about VCS's creation stated that "neither a man's politics nor his theological stance can make him oblivious to the flood of need that widens daily in the war-rocked country of Vietnam." The LWR board of directors highlighted the connection between seeing this urgency and opposing the war. The 1966 board minutes stated that LWR joined VCS "to help the people of Viet Nam who suffer as a result of decades of military action, action which has been vastly intensified during the last few years and has made the people of Viet Nam a people in agony." The statement therefore asserted that the "greatest need is an end to the war."[29]

Vietnam Christian Service proponents also opposed the war after they witnessed its negative effect on the Vietnamese. As early as 1965, VCS workers asserted that "many villages . . . have special needs resulting from the disruption of normal life and the spread of disease" caused by U.S. bombings. VCS also described how U.S. programs failed to assist the Vietnamese. For example, the South Vietnamese had instituted a U.S.-designed program to force peasant farmers into fortified villages at night in order to separate them from the revolutionary NLF fighters who often attacked in the dark. But rather than assist the war effort, the Strategic Hamlets Program angered many neutral farmers who resented being forced off of their land. A VCS account of this program asserted that "in camps the traditional structure of hamlet life tends to fall apart. Frequently adolescent girls become prostitutes and boys become petty criminals." The war also caused children to die from "years of malnutrition, intestinal infections, and malaria." A 1971 LWR report linked this wish to provide humanitarian aid with antiwar feelings. It maintained that the "chief needs of the people of Viet Nam are for social and political stability, a sense of the worth of the individual person, a place for human dignity instead of human degradation . . . and the need for assurance that someone cares about Viet Nam for reasons other than lie beyond international policies." VCS used the same mantra in 1973 when it proclaimed that "hardly a family in South Vietnam has escaped the dislocations and horrors of war. Loved ones have gone off to fight and die. Parents and children have been killed at home. Others have suffered from debilitating injuries like burns or the loss of limbs." VCS officials and volunteers saw firsthand evidence of war's devastation, which led them to want it to end as quickly as possible.[30]

The first death of a VCS Lutheran volunteer embedded antiwar sentiments within LWR circles. Gloria Redlin, a Lutheran nurse, died after a bullet pierced her spine on 13 October 1970. She and a U.S. sergeant were driving a motorcycle shortly after midnight when a People's Self-Defense Forces unit—a South Vietnamese organization that regulated the movement of people during the night in order to protect against NLF attacks—ordered them to halt. They failed to stop and the guards opened fire. The sergeant died instantly while medical personnel evacuated Redlin to a Pleiku hospital where she later died. The Vietnamese placed the PSDF soldiers in custody and VCS officials concluded that her death resulted from a "tragic accident." An LWR leader reminded "Christians in this country of the special risks taken voluntarily by dedicated men and women working in mission and service projects around the world." Confidential reports admitted that "Gloria violated the official curfew." Nonetheless, her death became yet another symbol of Vietnam's catastrophic circumstances; VCS advocates saw that even attempts to alleviate suffering risked human lives.[31]

These general statements against the war's impact turned directly against the United States when VCS volunteers described U.S. atrocities. A 1966 report illustrated this point:

Two nights before there had been a mortar attack on the Chieu Hoi resettlement village 10 kilometers South of Pleiku. We went out to look. One house was destroyed made [*sic*] and several fields of veggies were ripped up. Shell fragments made possible tracing the shots to a newly-arrived U.S. Army unit over the hill which hadn't bothered to check to see if there was a village in the way. This is bad enough in itself, but Chieu Hoi is [in] the "open arms" program. All the people in it are returned from active service as Vietcong in one capacity or another. They have returned to the safety of government protection—and then they are shelled by us. Fortunately, no one was injured, but we didn't win any friends.

LWR also disseminated such information to Lutheran constituents. In 1969, the ALC's women's magazine, *Scope*, printed an article that contained an interview with a VCS volunteer who explained that the Vietnamese "see American bombers destroy their homes, American trucks clogging and endangering their highways, their women violated. It is estimated that ten civilians are killed for every soldier." Proof that the U.S. effort harmed innocent victims solidified VCS opinions against U.S. involvement in Vietnam.[32]

Vietnam Christian Service became another source of negative information for antiwar Lutherans. The organization remained neutral in order to protect its efforts; it cooperated with the U.S. government out of necessity and assisted North Vietnamese civilians whenever possible. But this official stance masked a general attitude against war, and the Vietnam War specifically. VCS reports demonstrated how the war destroyed the lives of innocent people, and some of the correspondence blamed the United States for these problems. Regardless of where VCS leaders and volunteers stood prior to the war, their experiences during the conflict led them to oppose it almost without exception.

PROTECTING THE SOLDIERS, SAVING THE POWS

Antiwar Lutherans who opposed the war also addressed the subject of U.S. soldiers and prisoners of war. But unlike their conservative counterparts who used this topic to buttress prowar arguments, antiwar Lutherans saw it as another reason for the United States to withdraw from Vietnam. Here again, they articulated a counter-patriotism: they were not willing to allow conservative support of the war to make them look un-American or as if they did not care about the U.S. soldiers in Vietnam. Instead, they insisted that the war negatively affected soldiers and their families and worried about how the fighting affected young men's spirituality. Furthermore, they declared that North Vietnam would not free the POWs until the U.S. military vacated their country. They disagreed with LCMS President J. A. O. Preus and his supporters who maintained that a withdrawal doomed the POWs. Indeed, antiwar Lutherans maintained that a U.S. pullout was the only hope for POWs and U.S. soldiers.

Antiwar Lutherans first focused on the angst that the war caused soldiers' families. A mother and member of the Lutheran Church in America felt extreme joy when her son returned home safely from Vietnam, but she still explained that the war had caused her months of unease: "Knowing that the war is still in effect is the one heart-breaking thought that is still with us." Another mother fretted over her son's future: "Many of us have someone dear to us in Viet Nam, or soon on there [*sic*] way. In a recent editorial I read: 'the staff and the White House have been busy preparing all this week for our President's trip abroad. Leaving little time for thought to the Viet Nam War.' Dear God, my son will soon be going there, I wish someone wasn't too busy to care." And still another mom felt "sick" as she watched her son leave for combat but thought "somehow I must weather this traumatic experience and help my son get through it too." For antiwar Lutherans, the Vietnam War caused unnecessary anguish for the soldiers' mothers. The trauma of sending their children to war rallied them to the antiwar position, and they used their stories to gain further support from friends, family, and their churches.[33]

Antiwar Lutherans also deplored the war's effect on the soldiers themselves. A reader wrote to the LCA's *Lutheran*, wondering whether hawks ever "talked to a young man who has spent time at Khi Sahn where a shell falls every 63 seconds and young men's nervous systems are so shattered that the body no longer retains or desires food." In other words, many who opposed the war refused to ignore the realities of combat and what it did to the psyche of those who fought. Unlike prowar Lutherans who never addressed this topic because they thought the war a necessary evil, antiwar Lutherans pointed out the damage war did to these young men because they saw no reason for fighting in Southeast Asia. Other antiwar Lutherans questioned how soldiers were chosen to fight, especially in the early part of the war when wealthier citizens avoided the draft by going to college. This meant that African Americans disproportionately went to combat. Indeed, an LCMS African-American congregation mirrored the sentiments of many civil rights leaders when they asserted that "a greater percentage of black young men in proportion to their representation in the population have had to fight, have been maimed, and have lost their lives because of this undeclared war." They therefore refused to support it and told President J. A. O. Preus that his prowar stance demonstrated an "inadequate interpretation of the realities of the war." Aside from the trauma of combat, high drug use among soldiers concerned many citizens. Those who opposed the war understood that much of this addiction stemmed from the soldiers' inability to otherwise cope with the fighting. Thus, antiwar Lutherans worried about the high amount of drug use and indicated that "an average of two deaths a day [occurred] in Southeast Asia from heroin overdose." LCA President Robert J. Marshall lamented that drug use "is a temporary kind of pastime." As opposed to prowar Lutherans who argued that soldiers matured because of their service, antiwar

Lutherans maintained that the war merely risked the soldiers' health, well-being, and lives.[34]

Even while addressing the harsh realities that war presented to the soldiers, antiwar Lutherans also showed concern for the soldiers' spirituality. And once again, their arguments diametrically opposed those of Lutheran hawks who claimed that the war led young men to God. Antiwar Lutherans insisted that the actual circumstances were much less certain. The ALC's *Commentator* asked Lutherans to pray for the soldiers because "how well these young men, many barely out of High School, will adjust to the rigors, shocks, and loneliness of military life where they will face suffering and possible death will depend upon the spiritual resources provided by home and church." This statement depicted a bleak future for the soldiers, not an opportunity for growth. Magnus P. Lutness, writing in LCUSA's *Focus* about the importance of ministry to service personnel, explained that "those who know the horrors of war fervently seek the time of peace. They also share the conviction that those who are in the throes of battle need the strength of God to sustain faith and life. With this in mind, the church serves her members" with military chaplains. This underscored an important point; most antiwar Lutherans supported the chaplaincy program. But they simultaneously wondered how many would use it and feared that the war hurt many more boys than it helped. A former chaplain's assistant stressed this point when he told the LCMS's *Lutheran Witness* that "attendance at religious services in Vietnam is negligible." In short, many of the war's opponents felt confusion about how to handle the soldiers' faith-life. They questioned "how we minister to people such as 18-year old Army privates who have not yet reached the degree of maturity to grapple with the esoteric fine points of the Just War Theory; who haven't yet questioned their participation in this war; who have never been away from home and now find themselves in a foreign country, where everyone looks alike and the enemy is invisible. How do we help these young men?"[35]

The LCA's *Lutheran* provides a good example for how antiwar Lutherans worked to support the soldiers at the same time that they opposed the war. In 1969, the editors printed an article about a returning soldier, consistently emphasizing the danger he faced in Vietnam and his displeasure with U.S. participation. The author first quoted him as saying that "over there, you're not sure you'll live." The soldier also asserted that he had "thought of going AWOL. But I decided to take my year . . . and hope." His Vietnam experience led to antiwar sentiments: "Everything was so paradoxical. Good Sunday school kids would catch a booby trap. We were told to love our neighbor and then we had to go shoot people we had never seen before." Finally, the soldier indicated that he "might even take part in a 'Bring the boys home' protest." *Lutheran* editors used this story of a man who had served in the military to demonstrate how even responsible citizens spent months of uncertainty in Vietnam and returned home opposed to the U.S.-backed conflict.[36]

Again in contrast to their prowar counterparts, antiwar Lutherans addressed the POW topic by asserting that the United States first needed to withdraw in order for North Vietnam to release U.S. prisoners. They approached this topic from the perspective that the POWs gave the North Vietnamese leverage against the United States in any negotiations. Against the world's largest super power, North Vietnam held all of the cards in this debate. But where prowar advocates used this to continue the combat, antiwar Lutherans felt that only a U.S. withdrawal would force their release. *Lutheran* editor G. Elson Ruff stated that "I . . . suspect nothing can be done for them [POWs] until we bring the war to an end." Or, as a reader later wrote, "The government policy of perpetuating our presence indefinitely through puppet regimes in Saigon and elsewhere means that these men are sentenced for life." Furthermore, Ruff's successor, Albert P. Stauderman, stated, "It seems that only the end of the war or the overthrow of the North Vietnamese government will bring about their release." One of the ALC's North Dakota Districts mirrored these sentiments in a memorial it sent to the 1972 national convention. In a list of reasons for opposing U.S. involvement in the Vietnam War, it stated that "the fate of our prisoners of war and persons missing in action appears to hinge on total withdrawal and the nonsupport of the present government in South Vietnam." Antiwar Lutherans insisted that the best means of saving the POWs was for the United States to end its active interest in the war.[37]

Antiwar Lutherans further wondered why conservatives only discussed *U.S.* prisoners. An LCA member stated that someone needed to protest "the pictures of Americans standing by and giving tacit approval to the torture of [North Vietnamese] prisoners" by the dictatorial and oppressive government in South Vietnam. Another LCA constituent questioned why "no mention [was] made of the thousands of prisoners held by the government of South Vietnam." Again, antiwar Lutherans viewed both sides of the debate; they understood that any negotiations regarding the POWs must also account for those held by South Vietnam. In other words, antiwar Lutherans saw a complexity to the Vietnam War. They viewed it as a civil war, despised U.S. involvement, and criticized those who concerned themselves with American POWs without placing them into the war's larger context.[38]

In addition to general criticisms of prowar POW opinions, many antiwar Lutherans lashed out against J. A. O. Preus's efforts to free U.S. prisoners. This included people from within his own church body. A letter sent to Preus

with ninety-six signatures from Concordia Lutheran Seminary best summa-
rizes this position:

> Your statement implies that the mistreatment of American prisoners in North
> Vietnam has to do with "basic moral values" and "humanitarian concerns." It
> seems to us that many other aspects of the war also violate these same basic
> moral values and are therefore cause for the same humanitarian concern. We
> find it nothing short of incredible that a major church leader should choose to
> speak out on this particular issue while at the same time failing to speak out on
> other distressing aspects of the war: the well-documented, continued mistreat-
> ment of enemy prisoners by American and South Vietnamese authorities, the
> great loss of human life on both sides, the use of defoliation and herbicides as
> weapons of war on a massive scale, and the forced displacement of large num-
> bers of civilians. Furthermore, we cannot accept the suggestion that the treat-
> ment of prisoners is a moral issue which demands the churches' comment but
> that the whole issue of American involvement in Indo-China is merely a politi-
> cal and ideological matter about which churches are neither required nor enti-
> tled to speak.

This blast against the president came during a battle between Preus and the
seminary over biblical criticism. This friction eventually led students to walk
out of the seminary and Preus and his backers to fire the seminary president
and other faculty members. This letter came in the midst of a major theological quarrel that later splintered the denomination; it is noteworthy that they
disagreed on the Vietnam War as well and saw it as another battleground. But
the seminary students were not the only LCMS constituents who opposed the
war. A laywoman wrote Preus that "the quickest and most humane way to free
all prisoners—on both sides—and at the same time save the lives of future innocent victims of war—is to withdraw all U.S. troops from Indo-China." A
layman simply told Preus that the "key to the [POWs'] jail is in Washington.
By continuing to interfere in their civil war, by keeping the blood bath alive,
[Nixon is] keeping the POWs in jail." Some LCMS constituents took aim at
their president's prowar actions. They exposed the hypocrisy of his instruct-
ing them to separate religion and politics while he campaigned against North
Vietnam and wondered how he labeled his actions altruistic but their antiwar
positions inappropriate.[39]

The most liberal Lutheran periodicals especially castigated Preus's actions.
These journals represented left-leaning Lutheran theologians and intellectuals, primarily from the LCA and ALC but including some supporters in the
LCMS. The theological journal *Dialog*, an independent publication, asserted
that Preus's conduct was purely political because "the Nixon administration
began this business of turning the prisoner issue into a trick to arouse world
opinion against Hanoi." Indeed, the U.S. president did use POWs to garner

American support for his Vietnam War position, often channeling this strategy through other people and institutions to make it a stronger case. Having a church leader legitimized this position in the administration's eyes, but *Dialog* called this bluff. The editors sarcastically continued that "within a week of this news-release he [Preus] becomes the guest preacher at the White House." An independent journal devoted to "radical Lutheranism" agreed. *Metanoia* asserted that "motives do not have to be called into question to see Dr. J. A. O. Preus's spring junket to Sweden, the Vatican, and Vietnam as strange and somewhat pathetic. Poor judgment of what our times require seems patently obvious." Both periodicals sounded the familiar refrain that the United States must exit Vietnam before the prisoners would be released. *Dialog* contended that "if Preus' motives are so altruistic, why did he not think of the simplest and the only way of getting our prisoners free? That is not by escalating the war into Laos and intensifying the bombing, but by getting all Americans out." *Metanoia* had harsher words: "For high leadership among Christians to [campaign against North Vietnam] with the implication that American participation in the war is right and noble and without addressing the plight and devastation of the Vietnamese people as human beings reduces that cry to a myopic self-concern and self-interest." In each case, these journals debunked Preus's assertion that he only wanted to assist a humanitarian effort. Rather, they stated that a combination of altruistic concerns, personal gain, and conservative politics guided the LCMS president.[40]

Antiwar Lutherans rarely related their position on soldiers and prisoners of war to their opinion of world communism because they saw few links between the two concepts. They took great care in other areas to construct their denunciations of the Vietnam War and often reprimanded Americans who clung to the domino theory. Having thoroughly disregarded the need for fighting in Southeast Asia, they discussed soldiers and POWs with a view toward the war's effect upon these "governmental pawns." Here, they spoke clearly. They despised the combat's impact on families, soldiers, and POWs, and proclaimed that the only solution to each of these concerns was for the United States to immediately withdraw from the civil war in Vietnam.

CONCLUSION

Lutherans who opposed the Vietnam War did so because they dismissed the domino theory as an outmoded relic of the past and saw no just cause that mandated the U.S. fighting. They asserted that Vietnamese communism differed from Soviet or Chinese communism; they viewed the Vietnam conflict as both civil war and autonomous fight to throw out imperialist nations. They thought that the fall of Vietnam represented no national or global security threat. They even considered positive aspects to North Vietnam's government and highlighted the defective thinking of both the Johnson and Nixon administrations. With no political or diplomatic justification for the fighting, antiwar Lutherans instead focused on the human suffering that the war caused. Through news reports, returning soldiers, international contacts, Vietnam Christian Service, and a variety of other sources, they learned about the war's negative effect on the people of Vietnam. Furthermore, they saw firsthand the fighting's terrible influence on Americans, including those who fought. Their patriotism demanded that they denounce the war publicly and fight for a U.S. withdrawal; indeed, they refuted claims that they were un-American by describing how an antiwar platform was patriotic. U.S. atrocities embarrassed them, the refugee problem worried them, the loss of life sickened them, and the influence on soldiers and prisoners of war troubled their minds. Antiwar Lutherans came to understand the global situation on a more sophisticated level than did their prowar counterparts. Where prowar Lutherans saw a demonic Other, antiwar Lutherans saw varying Communist ideologies. And when rightist Lutherans needed the United States to take a stand against communism in Vietnam, leftist Lutherans sensed the war's futility and its waste of life. In the end, they seldom discussed the just war theory because to even enter a debate about it required that the person see some political or diplomatic reason for fighting. Antiwar Lutherans saw no political justification, so arguing about just war theology was futile to them.

NOTES

1. A myriad of studies examine Christians who opposed the Vietnam War. The best overview of antiwar opinions is Charles DeBenedetti and Charles Chatfield, *An American Ordeal: The Antiwar Movement of the Vietnam Era* (Syracuse, NY: Syracuse University Press, 1990). Other examinations include Michael Brooks Friedland, *Lift Up Your Voice Like a Trumpet: White Clergy and the Civil Rights and Antiwar Movements, 1954–1973* (Chapel Hill: University of North Carolina Press, 1998); Mark David Hulsether, *Building a Protestant Left: Christianity and Crisis Magazine, 1941–1993* (Knoxville: University of Tennessee Press, 1999); Mitchell K. Hall, *Because of Their Faith: CALCAV and Religious Opposition to the Vietnam War* (New York: Columbia University Press, 1990); Jill Kristine Gill, "'Peace Is Not the Absence of War but the Presence of Justice': The National Council of Churches' Reaction and Response to the Vietnam War, 1965–1972" (Ph.D. diss., University of Pennsylvania, 1996).

2. For the best study of the NLF, see Robert K. Brigham's *Guerilla Diplomacy: The NLF's Foreign Relations and the Viet Nam War* (Ithaca, NY: Cornell University Press, 1999).

3. Hall, *Because*, and Gill, "Peace," offer the best examinations of how liberal Protestant clergy alienated the moderate laity with antiwar protesting.

4. Robert E. Van Deusen, "Wanted: Some Fresh Thinking," *Lutheran* 2 (15 July 1964): 16; Robert Jenson, "Viet Nam: A Comment," *Dialog* 5 (Spring 1966): 84–85; Ralph Moellering, "I

Stand Opposed," *Lutheran Witness* 85 (June 1966): 18–19; G. Elson Ruff to Donald E. Barrick, 24 July 1968, Evangelical Lutheran Church in America Archives, Chicago, Illinois (hereafter ELCA), G. Elson Ruff Papers, box 17, "B"; Susan Thompson, "May Christians Choose Their Wars?" *Lutheran Women* 7 (November 1969): 18–21; Richard J. Niebanck, "Conscience, War, and the Selective Objector," in Cedric Tilberg, ed., *Religious Liberty* (New York: Lutheran Church in America Board of Social Ministry, 1968), 25; Richard J. Niebanck, "On Present Context: A Precis," 1 October 1973, ELCA, Lutheran Council U.S.A., Office of Government Affairs, Administration Files, box 8, "Indo-China, 1971–73." Secondary literature that explains the Communist fragmentation includes Gordon H. Chang, *Friends and Enemies: The United States, China, and the Soviet Union, 1948–1972* (Stanford: Stanford University Press, 1990); Qiang Zhai, *China and the Vietnam Wars, 1950–1975* (Chapel Hill: University of North Carolina Press, 2000); Ilya Gaiduk, *The Soviet Union and the Vietnam War* (Chicago: Ivan R. Dee, 1996); William J. Duiker, *The Communist Road to Power in Vietnam*, 2nd ed. (Boulder, CO: Westview Press, 1996).

5. James A. Looken, "Why Are We in Vietnam?" *Lutheran Forum* 2 (January 1968): 6–7; Henrietta K. Maddox to Oswald C. J. Hoffmann, 11 March 1971, Lutheran Laymen's League Archives, St. Louis, Missouri (hereafter LLL), Oswald C. J. Hoffmann Papers; Kent S. Knutson to Russell Thompson, 7 February 1972, ELCA, Kent S. Knutson Papers, box 2, "T."

6. "Membership List," 1971, Swarthmore College Peace Collection, Swarthmore, Pennsylvania (hereafter SCPC), Lutheran Peace Fellowship, DG 171, box 1, "Membership Lists"; Vincent L. Hawkinson to William E. Gramley, 29 June 1967, SCPC, Lutheran Peace Fellowship, DG 171, box 1, "1967"; Hawkinson to John W. Olson, 3 April 1969, SCPC, Lutheran Peace Fellowship, DG 171, box 1, "1969." Steven Schroeder, *A Community and a Perspective: Lutheran Peace Fellowship and the Edge of the Church, 1941–1991* (Lanham, MD: University Press of America, 1993), 61–73.

7. G. Elson Ruff to Ernest Clay, 25 May 1967, ELCA, G. Elson Ruff Papers, box 2, "C"; Carl E. Thomas to Luther M. Schulze, 26 May 1970, ELCA, Robert J. Marshall Papers, box 106, "?"; "Lutherans Urged to 'Reflect and Act' on U.S. War Policy," *Lutheran* 16 (February 1972): 29; William Meyer to J. A. O. Preus, December 1972, Concordia Historical Institute, St. Louis, Missouri (hereafter CHI), Executive Office, n.d., "Vietnam Peace, 1972–73."

8. G. Elson Ruff to Charles R. Greene, 7 December 1965, ELCA, G. Elson Ruff Papers, box 5, "Gi"; Robert Hoyer, "Sad Self-Justification," *Dialog* 6 (Spring 1967): 142–44; "America's Agony," *Lutheran Standard* 10 (28 May 1970): 20.

9. G. Elson Ruff, "Editor's Opinion," *Lutheran* 16 (17 January 1968): 50; Frederik A. Schiotz to Andrew H. Henrich, 2 July 1970, ELCA, Frederik A. Schiotz Papers, box 63, "Cambodia/LWF location"; Albert P. Stauderman to Warren Strickler, 30 April 1971, ELCA, Albert P. Stauderman Papers, box 88, "Si-Sz 1971"; American Lutheran Church, 1972 Convention Minutes, 1114–15, ELCA; Kent S. Knutson to James A. Lokken, 4 May 1971, ELCA, Kent S. Knutson Papers, box 1, "Li."

10. William Weinerth to George Glaser, 20 January 1967, ELCA, Frederik A. Schiotz Papers, box 35, "Luther League Dallas/Seattle Convention 1967"; "Action for Peace," *Lutheran Forum* 3 (November 1969): 14; Dan Kluge to J. A. O. Preus, 11 May 1971, CHI, Executive Office, UPN box 62, "POWs."

11. Franklin Clark Fry to Mrs. George L. Dodson, 9 January 1967, ELCA, Franklin Clark Fry Papers, box 95, "?"; Robert J. Marshall to Richard E. Olson, 4 January 1973, ELCA, Robert J. Marshall Papers, box 1, "Special Ministries in Vietnam."

12. Ruth H. Pool to Albert P. Stauderman, 30 March 1971, ELCA, Albert P. Stauderman Papers, box 87, "P"; American Lutheran Church, 1972 Convention Minutes, 674–75, ELCA. The following studies demonstrate the dictatorial realities of South Vietnam's various regimes

throughout the war: George C. Herring, *America's Longest War: The United States and Vietnam, 1950–1975* (New York: Wiley, 1979); David F. Schmitz, *Thank God They're on Our Side: The United States and Right-Wing Dictatorships, 1921–1965* (Chapel Hill: University of North Carolina Press, 1999). See also Frances Fitzgerald, *Fire in the Lake: The Vietnamese and the Americans in Vietnam* (New York: Vintage Books, 1972), and Marilyn B. Young, *The Vietnam Wars, 1945–1990* (New York: HarperPerennial, 1991).

13. Michael Eric Dyson, *I May Not Get There with You: The True Martin Luther King, Jr.* (New York: Simon and Schuster, 2000). Clifford L. Schreck to G. Elson Ruff, 10 June 1965, ELCA, G. Elson Ruff Papers, box 12, "Scho"; G. Elson Ruff to Courtney W. Anderson, 23 February 1966, ELCA, G. Elson Ruff Papers, box 1, "A-An"; Norman J. Thalman to G. Elson Ruff, 23 January 1968, ELCA, G. Elson Ruff Papers, box 22, "Ta."

14. Robert J. Marshall to Richard E. Olson, 4 January 1973, ELCA, Robert J. Marshall Papers, box 1, "Special Ministries in Vietnam," 26; Lutheran Theological Seminary Students to Richard M. Nixon, 7 May 1970, ELCA, Lutheran Council U.S.A. 12/1/4, Division of Educational Services, Administrative Files, box 1, "Campus Strife"; Frederik A. Schiotz to Richard M. Nixon, 22 June 1970, ELCA, Frederik A. Schiotz Papers, box 63, "Cambodia/LWF Location"; Robert J. Marshall to John Arthur, 14 September 1971, ELCA, Robert J. Marshall Papers, box 110, "?"; Virginia Toth to Albert P. Stauderman, 3 June 1972, ELCA, Albert P. Stauderman Papers, box 90, "T, U, V 1972."

15. John F. Backe to Frederik A. Schiotz, 29 May 1969, ELCA, Frederik A. Schiotz Papers, box 143, "C.O."; Albert P. Stauderman to W. Martin Peterhaensel, 14 February 1972, ELCA, box 90, "P, 1972"; Robert J. Marshall to Franklin Sherman, 9 February 1973, ELCA, Robert J. Marshall Papers, box 1, "Special Ministry to Vietnam"; Dale Elizabeth Ellison to David W. Preus, 7 May 1973, ELCA, David W. Preus Papers, box 13, "Draft Counseling."

16. G. Elson Ruff to Dole E. Everson, 12 January 1966, ELCA, G. Elson Ruff Papers, box 4, "En"; American Lutheran Church, 1972 Convention Minutes, 944–45, ELCA.

17. American Lutheran Church, 1966 Convention Minutes, 492–501, ELCA; American Lutheran Church, 1972 Convention Minutes, 244–46, ELCA; Stewart W. Herman to William J. Reiss, 20 June 1967, ELCA, Lutheran Counsel U.S.A. 2/6, General Secretary, Division of Service to Military Personnel, box 1, "1966–72"; Lutheran Church in America, 1970 Convention Minutes, 61, ELCA; Albert P. Stauderman to L. W. Newcomer, 6 May 1971, ELCA, Albert P. Stauderman Papers, box 87, "N-O."

18. Dorothy Blank, Sigrid Beier, and Laura Christian to G. Elson Ruff, 29 March 1968, ELCA, G. Elson Ruff Papers, box 17, "B"; Warren Strickler to G. Elson Ruff, 27 April 1971, ELCA, Albert P. Stauderman Papers, box 88, "Sj-Sz, 1971"; James A. Lokken to Kent S. Knutson, 7 May 1971, ELCA, box 1, File "Li."

19. Stephan H. Hornberger to G. Elson Ruff, 6 December 1967, ELCA, G. Elson Ruff Papers, box 7, "Ho"; Albert P. Stauderman to Abner T. Cunningham, 21 June 1972, ELCA, Albert P. Stauderman Papers, box 88, "C-D 1972"; Edgar Trexler to Derwood M. Dudley, 2 April 1973, ELCA, Albert P. Stauderman Papers, box 91, "C-D 1973."

20. Lloyd A. Berg to Lutheran Peace Fellowship Members, 23 March 1965, SCPC, Lutheran Peace Fellowship, DG 171, box 1, "LPF, From GDGA"; Vincent L. Hawkinson to G. D. Owen, 4 May 1966, SCPC, Lutheran Peace Fellowship, DG 171, box 1, "1966"; Gerald Krom to Vincent L. Hawkinson, 20 September 1966, SCPC, Lutheran Peace Fellowship, DG 171, box 1, "1966."

21. Franklin Clark Fry to Jacob A. Longacre, 31 May 1967, ELCA, Franklin Clark Fry Papers, box 96, "?"; Frederik A. Schiotz, "Dear Fellow Workmen in the King's Business," *Commentator* 9 (November 1969): 5; Frederik A. Schiotz to ALC Pastors, 19 June 1970, ELCA, Frederik A. Schiotz Papers, box 63, "Cambodia/LWF Location."

22. Constance Moore, "War in Vietnam," *Lutheran* 4 (12 October 1966): 49; J. Louise Owens, "Vietnam Opinion," *Lutheran* 5 (11 October 1967): 49; Mrs. L. Bennett, "About Vietnam War," *Lutheran* 6 (17 January 1968): 49; Ole Stalheim, "War Guilt," *Lutheran Standard* 13 (16 January 1973): 14.

23. Lambert Brose to Erik W. Modean, 9 September 1970, ELCA, Pastor Files, "Danielson, Carl."

24. Mildred Reeser to G. Elson Ruff, 21 March 1966, ELCA, G. Elson Ruff Papers, box 21, "R-Rie"; Arnold M. Hilper to J. A. O. Preus, 18 May 1971, CHI, Executive Office, UPN box 62, "POWs: Pastors"; H. Eberhard Von Waldow to Robert J. Marshall, 9 January 1973, ELCA, Robert J. Marshall Papers, box 1, "Special Ministries in Vietnam."

25. Gustav Peterson to G. Elson Ruff, 4 February 1968, ELCA, G. Elson Ruff Papers, box 21, "P-Pil"; Priscilla J. Stensaas to G. Elson Ruff, 21 February 1971, ELCA, Albert P. Stauderman Papers, box 88, "Sj-Sz 1971"; Ralph Moellering, "Vietnam," *Arena* 74 (December 1965): 4.

26. Lutheran World Action, 1967, ELCA, NLC, 3/1/3, box 16, "LWA Posters"; Lutheran World Action, n.d., ELCA, NLC 3/1/3, box 16, LWA Posters"; "One Traveler," LWA Filmstrip, May 1963, ELCA, NLC 3/1/3, box 16, "LWA General."

27. Mrs. Ray Jacobs to J. A. O. Preus, 24 May 1971, CHI, Executive Office, UPN box 62, "POWs"; Mrs. L. D. T. Cox, Jr., to J. A. O. Preus, 22 December 1972, CHI, Executive Office, No box, "Vietnam: Peace, 1972–73"; J. Sauers to J. A. O. Preus, 28 December 1972, CHI, Executive Office, No box, "Vietnam: Peace, 1972–73"; Lutheran School of Theology in Chicago Seminary Professors to Robert J. Marshall, 22 January 1973, ELCA, Robert J. Marshall Papers, box 1, "Special Ministries to Vietnam."

28. Arthur Simon to Bernard A. Confer, 1 February 1967, ELCA, Lutheran World Relief 3, Administrative Files, box 1, "Correspondence, 1966–67"; Paul Longacre, "Vietnam Christian Service Guidelines," 23 May 1968, ELCA, Lutheran World Relief 2, Administrative Files, box 33, "South Vietnam: Consultative Committee"; Ove Nielsen to Robert J. Marshall, 22 December 1970, ELCA, Robert J. Marshall Papers, box 108, "Lutheran World Relief"; "Lutheran World Relief Votes $35,000 Aid to North Vietnam," 26 June 1973, ELCA, Lutheran Council U.S.A. 16/6/6, Office of Communication and Interpretation, News Bureau, Country Topical Files, box 18, "Vietnam, 1971–86."

29. "LWR: Big Weapon in a Bigger Battle," *Commentator* 6 (Ascension 1966): 3; Board of Directors Minutes, Lutheran World Relief, 24 November 1969, ELCA, LWR 1, box 6, "1969."

30. Lutheran World Relief Board of Directors Minutes, 2 December 1968, ELCA, Lutheran World Relief 1, box 6, "1968"; Ove R. Nielsen to Livonia Alehouse, 28 April 1971, ELCA, Lutheran World Relief 3, Administrative Files, box 5; LCA Lutheran World Relief Board of Directors Minutes, 15 September 1965, ELCA, Lutheran World Relief 1, box 5, "1965"; Lutheran World Relief, "Vietnam Program, 1971," May 1971, ELCA, Robert J. Marshall Papers, box 108, "Lutheran World Relief"; Lutheran World Relief Board of Directors Minutes, 20 November 1973, ELCA, Lutheran World Relief 1, box 7, "1973."

31. Barnard A. Confer to Lutheran World Relief Staff, 23 October 1970, ELCA, Lutheran World Federation, LWM 3/4, General Secretary, Country Files, box 57, "Vietnam"; Robert W. Miller to VCS Staff, 19 October 1970, ELCA, Lutheran World Federation, LWM 3/4, General Secretary, Country Files, box 57, "Vietnam"; Paul C. Empie to Bernard A. Confer, 16 October 1970, ELCA, Lutheran World Federation, LWM 3/4, General Secretary, Country Files, "Vietnam."

32. Lance R. Worded, "Report on Vietnam," 11 August 1966, ELCA, Lutheran World Relief 4, Country Files, box 21, "South Vietnam, 1966–67"; Naomi Frost, "Where There Is Need," *Scope* 9 (November 1969): 6–8.

33. Alverda Shagg to G. Elson Ruff, June 1968, ELCA, G. Elson Ruff Papers, box 21, "Rig-Rz"; Mrs. Harold Turner to G. Elson Ruff, March 1969, ELCA, Albert P. Stauderman Papers, box 86, "T, U, V"; Jane Pitcairn Jobson, "Departures," *Scope* 13 (February 1973): 10–11.

34. Mildred Resser to G. Elson Ruff, 21 March 1968, ELCA, G. Elson Ruff Papers, box 21, "R-Rie"; Alanzo Chamblis to J. A. O. Preus, 15 March 1971, CHI, Executive Office, UPN box 62, "POWs"; "An Editorial: Pass the Word," *In Step* 2 (March/April 1971): 6; "Churchmen Report on Visit to U.S. Troops in Vietnam," *Lutheran* 9 (3 March 1971): 25. For examinations of soldiers' lives in Vietnam, including the inequitable drafting system and drug use, see Christian G. Appy, *Working-Class War: American Combat Soldiers in Vietnam* (Chapel Hill: University of North Carolina Press, 1993); William M. Hammond, *Reporting Vietnam: Media and Military at War* (Lawrence: University of Kansas Press, 1998); Richard Moser, *The New Winter Soldiers: GI and Veteran Dissent during the Vietnam Era* (New Brunswick, NJ: Rutgers University Press, 1996).

35. V. T. Jordahl, "Remember Our Defenders during Advent Season," *Commentator* 5 (November 1965): 4; Magnus P. Lutness, "Ministry to the Military," *Focus* 1 (1 October 1967): 1–2; Jerry L. Lembcke to *Lutheran Witness* editors, 11 May 1971, CHI, Executive Office, box 5, "AFC: Correspondence, 1971"; Carolyn M. Wittack to Wayne W. Landgrebe, 7 August 1972, ELCA, LCUSA 16/2, Office of Communication and Interpretation, Administrative Files, box 6, "Publications: Military Personnel—*In Step*, Reader's Reactions."

36. Edgar R. Trexler, "Coming Home Is Living Again: Bill Rakita Returns from Vietnam," *Lutheran* 7 (5 November 1969): 6–10.

37. G. Elson Ruff to Mrs. Gay Koonce, 10 October 1969, ELCA, G. Elson Ruff Papers, box 20, "Kn-Kz"; Lois Stierhout to Albert P. Stauderman, 3 February 1971, ELCA, Albert P. Stauderman Papers, box 88, "Sj-Sz, 1971"; Albert P. Stauderman to Margaret Focht, 15 May 1972, ELCA, Albert P. Stauderman Papers, box 89, "E-F 1972"; American Lutheran Church, 1972 Convention Minutes, 674–75, ELCA.

38. Mrs. Ludwig Fiedler to G. Elson Ruff, 7 August 1965, ELCA, G. Elson Ruff Papers, box 4, "F"; Steve Hornberger to Albert P. Stauderman, 10 March 1971, ELCA, Albert P. Stauderman Papers, box 87, "H."

39. 96 Concordia Lutheran Seminary Students to J. A. O. Preus, 5 February 1971, CHI, Executive Office, UPN box 62, "POWs"; Mrs. Adalin B. Malinoff to J. A. O. Preus, 15 February 1971, CHI, Executive Office, UPN box 62, "POWs"; Frank Zeman to J. A. O. Preus, 16 March 1971, CHI, Executive Office, UPN box 62, "POWs: Pastors"; W. M. Buescher to J. A. O. Preus, 11 May 1971, CHI, Executive Office, UPN box 62, "POWs."

40. Carl E. Braaten, "The Hanoi Ploy," *Dialog* 10 (Winter 1971): 89; Omar Stuenkel, "Preus at the Precipe," *Metanoia* 3 (June 1971): 2. For an excellent explanation of how the Nixon administration misused the POW issue, see H. Bruce Franklin, *M.I.A. or Mythmaking in America: How and Why Belief in Live POWs Has Possessed a Nation* (New York: Lawrence Hill Books, 1992).

Chapter Six

Adrift on a Sea of Doubt: Lutheran Debates about Domestic Vietnam Concerns

Although the conflict in Southeast Asia brought into focus how Lutherans viewed foreign policy in the middle of the Cold War and in the midst of the Vietnam War, the discord over the war's domestic concerns threatened to divide Lutherans permanently. The argument over "homefront" issues underscores the differences between those who continued to believe in containment and those who discarded it. Lutherans from the right and left became more passionate in their rhetoric and more sardonic in their condemnations of each other because they witnessed firsthand the war's direct impact on U.S. society. Lutherans confronted massive antiwar protests that highlighted young adults' dissatisfaction with their current government, but right-leaning Lutherans labeled the demonstrations treasonous while their opponents defended them as necessary. The draft accentuated the tension. Conservative Lutherans backed it because it protected U.S. global interests against communism while their counterparts called it unfair. Furthermore, implementation of the draft created disputes about conscientious objection because U.S. law did not clearly define who could claim this status. Domestic matters also sparked a dispute over amnesty for those who avoided the draft. Conservatives wanted to give the "draft-dodgers" no leniency while their antiwar colleagues advocated forgiveness. Despite the potential for these issues to divide Lutherans, an uneasy accord prevailed by the end of the war when Lutherans called for reconciliation in order to put the war behind them.[1]

DEBATING ANTIWAR PROTESTS

All America debated the Vietnam War beginning in 1964 and continuing until the U.S. withdrawal in January 1973. Though much of American memory

147

about the decade now focuses on the antiwar movement, especially in its most radical forms, the truth is much different. Prowar advocates supported the government and even argued for stepped-up U.S. involvement in Southeast Asia in order to combat the Communists, while many moderates felt conflicted about the war. They still trusted their government and disdained communism but also questioned the need for fighting in Vietnam. Still others protested the war, but not all did so in public demonstrations. Rather, they voiced their opposition by writing to congressional representatives and by voting. Because this controversy so enveloped the nation, Lutherans naturally participated in the dialogue within their institutions and periodicals.

Not surprisingly, far-right periodicals led the Lutheran condemnations of the antiwar protests, linking the demonstrations to Communist front groups and calling the participants lawless Americans. *Christian News* lamented that "the majority of [protestors] are either duped or misinformed or merely follow." The journal claimed that these people unknowingly supported communism, assuming as fact that Communists instigated the antiwar protests to undermine U.S. efforts in Vietnam and accusing all participants of therefore either treason against the nation or of blindly and ignorantly following Communist forces. *Lutherans Alert* mirrored this philosophy and complained about people who defended the "lawless" demonstrators, charging all who opposed the war with criminal behavior. To this end, *Lutherans Alert* supported the Ohio National Guard after it shot and killed four people at Kent State University in May 1970. After Richard Nixon admitted publicly in April that the United States was bombing Cambodia, the antiwar movement erupted anew across the nation at this escalation of the war. The Kent State shootings took place during one such demonstration. Rather than voice sympathy for the fallen students, however, the editor asserted that the Guard "fired into rioters who were hurling rocks and bottles at them." He concluded that "killing by soldiers in the line of duty in countering aggression is not murder" and dismissed the biblical commandment against killing because these deaths were not "the deliberate, malicious taking of human life."[2]

Conservatives also criticized the protests because they despised anything that questioned the U.S. government. In the post-World War II United States, the neo-conservative movement to which some Lutherans belonged insisted that Americans support a strong central government that protected them from foreign influences that they claimed might undermine American democracy. Any criticism of the government opened people up to attack by these conservatives who accused them of un-American behavior. Lutherans from every denomination represented this point of view. A member of the generally moderate Lutheran Church in America (LCA) blasted the antiwar demonstrations because they had been inspired by unscrupulous faculty members at colleges and universities and "representatives of foreign governments." These adults "exploit the enthusiasm and inquiring mind of a student in a subversive manner" when they urge them to censure the U.S. government. A pastor in one of the small, very conservative Lutheran denominations, the Church of the Lutheran Brethren, carried this argument further. Asserting that the protestors' "goal is the violent overthrow of government" allowed him to condemn the protestors out of hand, without hearing their argument or attempting to understand the people who participated in the antiwar movement. Still another Lutheran complained about an article that supported the protests when he wondered how the church could "desire a cancer that divides and destroys a body," in this case the church and U.S. government. Throughout the Vietnam War, conservative Lutherans refused to question the government and at the same time suspected anyone who did.[3]

This alleged threat to governmental authority led conservative Lutherans to accuse Communists of fomenting the protests. *Evangelize* of the Lutheran Evangelist Movement, another small, conservative body, claimed to know that "in the last five years Communist infiltration and agitation tactics have been especially successful among college students." But if conservatives disliked students who protested, they disdained clergy who spoke out against the war. Claiming that pastors represented the entire church, not just themselves, they were making false statements about the Lutheran laity. A second argument said that the clergy violated God's will by questioning the government, as in the case of an LCA constituent who stated, "I personally don't like to think that a clergyman of the Lutheran church is parading in his clerical garments giving aid and comfort to a cause that is obviously Communist conceived." Other people more generally claimed that Communists led the protests: "The reason there is violence in America is the fact that Communists are afraid that we will go for victory. So they have their henchmen working in the United States." An ALC member concurred that "it was in the plans of the Communists . . . to have protests in this country win the war for the Communists." In short, faith in an anti-Communist doctrine allowed conservatives to believe that Communists provoked the antiwar protests. As one layman wrote, "I have no doubt in my mind that the vast majority of the antiwar groups are composed of . . . active agents of various Communist front groups."[4]

Conservatives also claimed that student protests promoted "rebelliousness." Indeed, the opposition to antiwar protests took place in the context of a larger debate in America about its youth and their counterculture ideals. Whether discussing the most radical of students who lived in communes and promoted free love or more sedate students who otherwise looked like "traditional" students but who criticized the Vietnam War and old-world university structures, conservatives often lumped them all together as endangering the future of America. In the context of the Vietnam War, they insisted that the youth once again manifested a dangerous disregard for authority. A Lutheran Church–Missouri Synod (LCMS) member stated that the demonstrations "were led by stimulators of violence" and "lawlessness." An LCA constituent voiced a similar point of view, complaining that "it seems when bricks and stones are thrown, windows broken and property destroyed and the rights of others hindered, its [*sic*] alright, because its [*sic*] proper dissent!!" Conservatives tended to focus on the most extreme examples when making their points. If a protest turned violent or destroyed property, it became the representative protest in conservative minds, disregarding the fact that most protests were peaceful demonstrations. Conservatives leaned on media portrayals of angry students clashing with law enforcement officials but almost never commented on the many antiwar rallies that took place quietly and respectfully on Lutheran college campuses across the nation. And laypeople were not alone in making these claims. LCMS President J. A. O. Preus called the demonstrators "rebels on campuses." These complaints stemmed from a two-pronged dread. First, the older generation feared young people who questioned the government's actions with loud and occasionally violent protests and, second, combined this anxiety with their persistent horror of communism infiltrating the homefront. Because they sincerely believed that Communists undermined U.S. democracy, they concluded that student unrest resulted from Communist agitation. Thus, they vehemently denounced the student protests. After the Kent State University shootings, an LCA layman proclaimed that "four students were shot at one college and I shed no tears; they had no business being there. But it is a good excuse for the hippies to start another riot and break windows."[5]

Conservative Lutherans believed that to solve this tension *all* Americans had to trust the government. This related again to their interpretation of Lutheran two kingdoms theology. They argued that Martin Luther ordered peasants to stop revolting and obey German authorities during his life and therefore concluded that they could make the same demand of protestors during their lifetimes. The 1967 Wisconsin Evangelical Lutheran Synod (WELS) convention showcased this position when it resolved that the church "urge upon all its members full respect for governmental authority and the obedience to the laws of the State which Scripture requires." Indeed, the WELS fully backed the government regarding Vietnam and made forceful statements against anyone who questioned it. Other Lutherans more bluntly called the demonstrations "well-nigh treason," insisted that Americans must use peaceful political means to achieve their goals, and felt that protests weakened democracy and catered to Communists. They further argued that peace could not "come by having people arouse and divide the nation in a way that gives the enemy the impression that they can gain their objectives simply by delay and unyielding response." Once again, conservative Lutherans combined their fear of the protests with their unease about Communist aims. They demanded that students respect the government's wishes and cease antiwar advocacy.[6]

In contrast to conservative opinions, antiwar Lutherans insisted that people had a Christian responsibility to demonstrate against an unnecessary war. The Lutheran Theological Seminary Student Association wrote President Nixon that its members "support all non-violent protest against your policy in Southeast Asia." They therefore suspended classes on 7 and 8 May 1970 at Gettysburg Seminary to protest the continued fighting in Southeast Asia. This collective action by younger seminary students had backing from individual Lutherans. Without commenting on the Lutheran two kingdoms theology, an LCA laywoman questioned Lutherans who thought that good Christians must always obey the law. She compared the demonstrators to Jesus and stated that "Christ was arrested . . . and taken into custody by the Romans on the night of his agony in the garden after his betrayal by Judas Iscariot. That arrest has not embarrassed subsequent Christianity." She saw the protestors as responsible citizens who acted out their Christian convictions much like Christ had. An LCA pastor furthered this argument and insisted that "every Christian has the awesome responsibility to study the issues in depth, to reason them out in light of Christian conscience, to speak and act in accordance with his conclusions."[7]

The belief that Christian responsibility demanded protest led antiwar Lutherans to try to convince their denominations to renounce the war. A small group formed the Lutheran Action Committee (LAC), which attacked "Lutheran quietism in social, economic, and political matters." It further asserted that "sound theological and common intelligence call for an end to the silence." Though small in number, this organization represented an attempt by some laypeople to voice their opinion and move the church to action. Importantly, it also demonstrates how more moderate Americans participated in the antiwar movement. Though they took a stand against the government, they did so through the traditional means of gathering together to write protest letters and attempt to influence elections. The Kent State University shootings prompted antiwar Lutherans to speak out, as had their conservative colleagues. An LCA laywoman maintained that "if dissent in this country is going to be oppressed by guns then it is time for the church to take a stand." An LCMS congregation voiced similar opinions to J. A. O. Preus when it asserted that "in our Christian role of peace maker and reconciler, we felt you could serve well with a statement to our people calling for cool heads and non-violence on both sides of the gun barrel."[8]

Antiwar Lutherans defended the student protestors. A group of Lutheran campus ministers stated that "we affirm the right of the students and faculty as citizens of the United States to peacefully dissent, assemble and express their protest to what seems to many of them a decision of our president to expand and escalate our military involvement in Indo-China." Rather than fear the students, these pastors had first-hand experience with the younger generation and appreciated their genuine concern for the United States. They also pointed out the American right of dissent and wondered why conservatives wanted this fundamental entitlement revoked. Additionally, as with the conservative point of view, the overall political or theological conservatism of a denomination did not necessarily determine how each person within that entity would respond to the protestors. An LCMS pastor wondered, "Why are we fighting in Vietnam if we do not respect at home the right of youth to refuse to bear arms for conscience sake?" He then complained to an LCMS official that "I resent the implication that young people are not expressing responsible citizenship when they write, assemble, and otherwise peacefully bring their grievances and views before the church, and the nation. I resent it when you do it as much as I resent it when the President of the United States does it." Antiwar Lutherans also supported dissenters because they did not fear the younger generation's rebellion and claimed that "one difficulty that contributes to the generation gap is that many older people simply will not recognize the attraction of young people to an involvement in social and political issues as an example of their heightened ethical feelings." In other words, antiwar Lutherans concluded that the protestors posed no danger to democracy's future while their conservative counterparts feared that Communists brainwashed youthful protestors.[9]

To this end, these Lutherans maintained that student protestors were not radicals. Once again, seminary students best articulated this viewpoint. A group of seminary students defended their generation in a letter to President Nixon: "As we deem dissent to be the right of a free people, we also deplore your disparagement of those who engage in such dissent, as well as the unjustifiable violence of the murder of four innocent students. We are neither 'bums' nor 'radicals,' but we affirm our right to be heard in protest against your expansion of this immoral and destructive war." They asserted that protestors were responsible citizens, not young fanatics trying to foment revolution. A *Lutheran Witness* (LCMS) letter to the editor made a similar point. It asserted, "I am no fiery eyed radical" but "just think our country is wrong about Vietnam and confused in its priorities." The laywoman concluded that this "means that my family and I sometimes march and sometimes wear the symbol of peace. We are not 'commie dupes.'" Importantly, even antiwar Lutherans condemned the protestors if their actions became violent. Lutheran antiwar advocates generally held moderate points of view, especially in regard to what they saw as permissible dissent, insisting that demonstrations remain peaceful and asking all participants to obey law enforcement officials. LCA President Robert J. Marshall declared, "I have been deeply concerned about recent developments pertaining to the destruction of draft board records. I have the conviction our pastors should not be involved in such practices." Thus, antiwar Lutherans agreed with the protestors and defended their *peaceful* demonstrations, but they also cautioned that destructive behavior or violence hindered the peace movement's cause.[10]

The LCA's *Lutheran* magazine provides an excellent example of the protest movement debate. George C. Reese, a professor at Thiel College, defended the protestors in a 1965 article. Describing how a prowar citizen beat a protestor while a police officer looked the other way, Reese emphasized that the student did not retaliate. He found this demonstrator's courage to be "the courage of thousands more in the present student generation. It is courage that will not be defeated. Nor will it be daunted by waving the flag against them, by calling them cowards, and labeling them unpatriotic." This composition prompted numerous responses. Some people defended the author, such as a laywoman who stated that "it is reassuring to find someone who is willing to be objective and not so quick to condemn student demonstrators." Another reader asserted that "if democracy is to function it is not only our right but our duty to agitate, to demonstrate, to protest actions which we think unwise on the part of our government." But other LCA readers vehemently disagreed and linked the protestors and their defenders to communism. A laywoman asked that "God forgive you for helping the Communist cause" by defending the demonstrations. Another reader stated that the war was "against open aggression and for a free and independent Vietnam." Furthermore, he maintained that "the American people are involved in a struggle against an adversary who oppresses religion, liberty, and the respect for human dignity."[11]

A 1967 article generated the same debate. O. Robert Oberkehr, pastor at Epiphany Lutheran Church in Camden, New Jersey, wrote about his participation in a protest while wearing his clerical collar because he wanted to "say by my presence that more was involved than just another outraged conscience." Rather, he "felt as though I were being called on to disavow the present administration on the basis of deep and abiding American principles." It was not mere politics that prompted his activism: he felt a religious responsibility to do so. A fellow protestor wrote, "Pastor Oberkehr and I love America. We see America destroying herself. We say: let us stop and reconsider." Their stance is another example of the antiwar platform's counterpatriotism; they stressed their loyalty to the United States and protested to protect its future, not to undermine it as charged by the conservatives. While antiwar Lutherans called for peace, prowar Lutherans linked the pastor and his colleagues to communism. A layman complained, "I don't like to think that a clergyman of the Lutheran church is parading in his clerical garments giving aid and comfort to a cause that is obviously Communist-conceived and dominated." Once again, the protests split pro- and antiwar Lutherans into factions based on either their fearful view of communism or their more complex understanding of variances within this ideology.[12]

Cold War philosophies indeed affected opinions about the antiwar protests. Prowar Lutherans despised the demonstrations because they feared that dissent aided the worldwide Communist conspiracy and believed that Communist agents in the United States sparked the protests. They also worried that student discord undermined the government and dishonored U.S. soldiers. In contrast, antiwar Lutherans almost never mentioned communism when they addressed the protests, separating the Cold War against the Soviet Union and China from the Vietnam War and disliking anti-Communist witchhunts. Their conscience demanded an end to the fighting; they publicly proclaimed their position or defended the protests even if they did not directly participate. Antiwar Lutherans displayed a different understanding when they proclaimed that protestors were patriotic Americans dismayed about their country's foreign policy, not radical revolutionaries trying to dismantle democracy.

LUTHERANS, THE DRAFT, AND RETURNING VETERANS

The Cold War debate also factored into Lutheran opinions about the draft and returning Vietnam War veterans. Congress had kept in place the Selective Service Act after World War II because of Cold War tensions. The act required all young men to register for the draft; when the Vietnam hostilities began, the government therefore had the means to draft men into the army when not enough volunteered. Naturally, the Vietnam War's controversy led to arguments about the draft; those who advocated the fighting saw the draft as necessary to battle communism while antiwar citizens protested that it committed people to combating a questionable war. This also prompted a discussion over how to view returning veterans. Some Lutherans saw them as war heroes; others thought that they were war casualties who would suffer forever because of flawed Cold War policies.[13]

Conservative Lutherans derided those who refused to enter the military as "draft dodgers." They advocated the draft because they thought that the United States had to win the Vietnam War. Their stance on the Selective Service System related to their continued faith in containment: neo-conservatives saw it as part of the duty of a strong state in protecting its citizens. An LCA layman, stating that "I detest draft dodgers and those who assist them spiritually, mentally, or physically," denounced young men who avoided the draft and condemned the church for counseling against military service if a young person's conscience opposed the war. This individual never mentioned theology in his argument, despite the fact that his point of view contradicted the Lutheran belief that an individual is to follow his or her conscience, regardless of whether or not it squares with majority opinion. But some church bodies made the same point: the Wisconsin Evangelical Lutheran Synod's *Northwestern Lutheran* applauded the WELS for disallowing men to join the seminary in order to avoid the draft simply because the law exempted clergy from service. It proclaimed that "we have not abused that privilege; our seminary is not a haven for draft dodgers."[14]

Conservative Lutherans then related these feelings directly to their fear of communism. An LCMS member criticized *Lutheran Witness* editor Martin W. Mueller for defending those who avoided the draft. He asserted that "it is obvious that you are willing to betray your country and the men fighting to protect *your* religious freedoms and give the communist world great pleasure in knowing that one of our supposed strong churches in America have consented to give voice to preaching their 'god' [communism]." In short, he accused Mueller of undermining the religious battle against communism. Another constituent stated that "communism is cruel and satanic" and therefore necessitated the war. She concluded that "those poor people over there are fighting for their very existence, and some of our youth today want to turn their backs on them." Another reader eluded to the religious implications of the Cold War by arguing that "the draft offers an opportunity for a man to serve his beloved America and to fight evil." An American Lutheran Church (ALC) layman mirrored these sentiments; he was disgusted after the ALC advocated allowing men to do alternative service if they refused to fight. He claimed that this policy "will leave us with inadequate means to readily defend our shores" from a Communist invasion. These Lutherans based much of their draft defense on continued fears of communism, clinging to anticommunism and assuming that every stand against communism defended U.S. freedom.[15]

Conservative Lutherans also constructed a theological justification for this position by returning once again to Lutheran two kingdoms theology. They asserted that the Bible and Luther taught Christians to obey the government unless it clearly ordered a person to betray Christianity, asserting that even if a young man opposed the Vietnam War, God commanded him to serve. Small, politically and theologically conservative Lutheran bodies especially made this claim. The Evangelical Lutheran Synod's *Lutheran Sentinel* declared that "there is one simple test I, as a Christian, have to make. It is to ask: does this law, this order, clearly compel me to violate the Word of God? If not, I must obey." Since prowar Lutherans viewed the war as a conflict against evil, they concluded that it did not go against God's law. The Church of the Lutheran Confession's *Lutheran Spokesman* concurred that "until the government's position is changed by congressional action or at the ballot box the individual must conform his conduct to the present position of the government." This sentiment persisted when the journal discussed returning veterans: "We must speak highly of our returning servicemen, for they did that which God expects every Christian citizen to do, namely, they obeyed the government, though it meant going to war." Conservative Lutherans proclaimed that God expected young men to follow the government because it fought for "God's Will" against Communist forces.[16]

Conservative Lutherans also insisted that a man performed his Christian duty to society by consenting to the draft. This argument often had the backing of denominations or at least constituencies within them, thus demonstrating its popularity for many Lutherans. The Lutheran Church–Missouri Synod Committee on Social Action maintained that "a Christian should be willing to accept man's common burden" and serve in the military if called upon. It therefore rejected requests for the LCMS to join Protestant efforts to combat the draft. This statement was specifically made in response to other church bodies that organized efforts to assist young men who opposed the war in their effort to avoid military service, including both the American Lutheran Church and the Lutheran Church in America. In other words, the LCMS draft stance represented another way that it differentiated itself from the other two large Lutheran denominations. Lutherans within the armed forces often voiced similar opinions. An army chaplain claimed that "the Church's declared concern for all people in our society is negated by its failure to defend vigorously the majority of young Americans while it spends much of its energies in debate about the rights of a small minority, largely college youths, who feel conscience bound to protest the war in Vietnam and the draft." He wanted Lutheran churches to stop helping men who refused to fight and instead urged them to advocate that Christians conform to societal standards; in this case, that meant joining the army. This chaplain also wrote about his son: "Mike feels our [his parents'] love for him and recognizes we would never relish having him in Vietnam, for no parent truly wants that. But to merely avoid the war in Vietnam or military service as such is no service to us and is an affront to him as a maturing Christian. For that would merely bring what I prefer to call 'the big I' front and center in his life." Rather, he thought that drafted men must serve because others also had to fight. Rightist Lutherans exhorted Christians to recognize their civic duty, even if it called for combat detail.[17]

Furthermore, conservative Lutherans asserted that draft critics psychologically injured returning veterans and claimed that these soldiers would abandon the church if it denounced the U.S. military. The LCMS's *Advance* stated that "the veteran who, while overseas, read that clergymen at home were describing him as the dupe of a war-mad government and were disrupting draft and enlistment procedures may perhaps be pardoned if he remains skeptical about professions of pastoral concern when he returns." *In Step*, published by the Lutheran Council, U.S.A., which generally opposed the war effort, also published an article that reproved anti-draft rallies and statements. The article declared that veterans, many of them addicted to drugs, "return home to an often cold, unsympathetic public." These Lutherans challenged those who wanted the church to denounce the draft because they feared that it alienated Vietnam veterans.[18]

Conservative opinions about the draft and returning veterans mirrored exactly their position on other Cold War issues. They advocated any efforts to combat communism and expanded this into a defense of the draft. They insisted that the U.S. young men fought in Southeast Asia to preserve democracy and therefore thought that if the army failed to recruit enough people then Selective Service had to force men to serve. Indeed, their rhetoric further demonstrated an intense fear of communism. Once again, however, they faced opposition from their antiwar colleagues.

Quite simply, antiwar Lutheran denunciations questioned the use of a draft to force men into military service. Believing that they had a good claim against an unjust war, they thought it wrong for the government to force people to fight in it against their will. As with other topics, the typical political or theological tone of a denomination did not necessarily reflect entirely the opinion of all of its members. While most LCMS members and some of its committees supported the draft, one LCMS pastor lamented that "I cannot in good conscience keep feeding them [draft age men] the line that they must make their own decision (how can 17- to 19-year-olds make such a grave decision?). Nor can I say that they should follow the dictates of the government unreservedly." He therefore declared his dislike for the draft. Another Lutheran leader asserted that "coercion is a weak substitute for the moral authority that is a democratic government's only legitimate source of power." He concluded that "it is past time to return to the Congress and to the political process the decisions about where and for what American boys should kill and be killed." As a commentator in the LCMS's *Lutheran Witness* explained, "The prospect of military obligation intimidates many, makes uncertain their futures, and sets them adrift on a sea of doubts."[19]

The fact that antiwar Lutherans called the Vietnam War immoral naturally affected their opinions on the draft. A Lutheran School of Theology professor complained that the draft "impinges upon a man's freedom to decide what is the will of God for him, and how he will respond to the particular situation at hand." This especially troubled him because so many young men disagreed with the Vietnam War and saw it as a fight against innocent people. In contrast to conservatives who ignored the Lutheran edict for an individual to follow his or her conscience, the theologian took that seriously and worried that forced military service imperiled this biblical mandate. A seminarian concurred that the war went against his religious sensibilities, believing that "the draft, as it operates, smashes and corrupts lives with a subtle violence." For Lutherans who opposed the war, the draft violated their sense of democracy. They disliked it because the government took any men it wanted and forced them into combat, even if it meant they had to betray their conscience. Thus, like their conservative colleagues, their anti-draft stance was a religious issue because it forced men to serve, which violated the Lutheran ethic of obeying one's conscience if he disagreed with the war.[20]

Antiwar Lutherans also exposed discrepancies in the Selective Service System. From its inception prior to World War II until the end of the Vietnam War, the Selective Service System operated an arbitrary procedure for selecting men. Leaving decisions about such things as conscientious objector status, war-industry deferments, and the need to provide for a family to local draft boards meant that enforcement differed from region to region, and even within cities; draft boards often made decisions about a man's draft status based on their own prejudices, not on the guidelines handed down from Washington. Additionally, the head of the Selective Service System, Lewis B. Hershey, and other officials had little power to overturn all of the inequities committed by a system that had little standardization. Antiwar Lutherans often recognized this reality, such as an ALC pastor who maintained that anti-draft propaganda "properly focuses on alleged inequities in the draft—unfair to the poor and uneducated, drawing older men before younger, keeping men in unnecessary suspense for too many years, permitting too many variances as rules are interpreted by local draft boards." Anti-draft Lutherans insisted that the government needed to discontinue the draft because of its unfair implementation. An ALC member declared that the draft for years "has been an inefficient, unfair way to provide for national defense." These Lutherans also blasted selective service boards that refused to grant conscientious objector status to Lutherans. According to Lutheran theology, a person had the individual responsibility to decide upon this matter, and thus none of the churches took a formal stance. But some local boards only granted conscientious objector status to traditional pacifist denominations. This prompted ALC President Frederik A. Schiotz to retort that "if local draft boards are going to interpret the law that only Quakers and Jehovah's Witnesses have the protection of the law, then the American Lutheran Church may have to take this matter up with the proper authorities in Washington, D.C."[21]

Additionally, while conservative Lutherans defended the draft in part because they thought this stance honored the soldiers, antiwar Lutherans used returning veterans to prove that the draft damaged innocent people. Many antiwar Lutherans lamented that "the socioeconomic class of many of the men who were in the military, the experience of fighting such a war, and the reaction of the American public to that war all work together to spell trouble for the Vietnam-era veteran." Rather than proclaiming them national heroes, left-leaning Lutherans saw a difficult reality faced by these men. An article by Charles P. Lutz, the director of Lutheran Selective Service Information, an inter-Lutheran organization called to provide draft counseling to Lutherans, quoted a veteran who stated that "we feel like we're sneaking back into American society, just as we were sneaked [*sic*] into Vietnam." This alienation intensified opinions against the draft among Lutherans who insisted that many returning veterans felt betrayed and unwanted.[22]

The draft became another battleground for Lutherans regarding the Vietnam War. Conservatives supported all efforts to subdue Communist expansion, and so they championed the draft, further insisting that a pro-draft stance validated returning veterans' service in the war. Rightist Lutherans lived in a world of anticommunism that led them to believe that young men had to serve in the military to preserve democracy; they thought that their patriotic attitude would shelter returning veterans from abuse and depression. In contrast, their antiwar counterparts displayed a different understanding of the situation. They asserted that the Vietnam War did not threaten U.S. security and instead viewed it as an imperialistic war. They disliked forcing young men to fight it and outlined a difficult life that veterans faced upon returning to a divided nation.

CONSCIENTIOUS OBJECTION

If Lutherans differed over how to view the draft, they positively feuded over conscientious objection. Lutheran theology did little to assist in this matter because it was individually based and subject to interpretation. It allowed for a broad spectrum of opinions, and each side insisted that it had the one true answer. Much of this confusion stemmed from the conflicting messages of Luther's admonition to obey the government yet simultaneous instruction not to disobey one's conscience. Lutherans disagreed about pacifism in general, but they contentiously fought one another over whether an American could conscientiously object to one war (Vietnam) without always being a pacifist in principle. Once again, this dilemma was not unique to the Lutheran churches; a number of denominations struggled with this same problem, especially because many local draft boards insisted that, unless a church body adopted a pacifist stance, its members could not claim conscientious objector status. Thus, this secular Vietnam issue collided with the churches because according to the government they had the religious authority to decide this issue. The conservative Lutheran position once again related to the fear of communism, accusing conscientious objectors (outside of the traditional peace churches) of communism and demanding that men who refused to fight go to jail. Antiwar Lutherans defended pacifism because they agreed with why so many young people hated the Vietnam conflict. Cold War opinions affected even the seemingly separate issue of how Lutherans felt about conscientious objection to the Vietnam War.

Right-leaning Lutherans accused conscientious objectors of aiding communism. Their entrenched anticommunism led them to believe that anyone who thwarted U.S. efforts to contain it undermined democracy and thereby aided an atheist ideology. After an LCA publication explained why Lutherans could conscientiously object, a laywoman responded that "Communists, throughout the world rejoice with your reasoning." In other words, for many conservatives, people either agreed with their position or became enemies of the United States. But if authors in Lutheran journals angered conservatives, then a 1968 LCA Convention resolution positively enraged them. LCA delegates voted to support conscientious objectors within their church, prompting a layman to retort that it gave "the Communist World a great Moral Victory." Another constituent requested, "Don't turn us over any further to communism than you already have done by your decision on Conscientious Objection." A World War II veteran further asserted that "I for one *do not* back the C. O.s, or the hippies, or the yippies, or the draft dodgers, or the draftcard burners, or any of the other unwashed punks hiding behind some ideological or religious front." Because the LCA was a mainline Protestant denomination with a moderately liberal leadership and moderate to conservative laity, it opened itself up to such attacks more frequently than did its sister bodies because conservatives belonged to the church, too. In other words, it had a very mixed political and theological population, so actions by the delegates had more of a chance of coming under attack than did moves taken in the more conservative denominations, which had a less diverse membership.[23]

Conservative Lutherans also argued, as they had regarding antiwar protests, that Christians had to maintain law and order. Conscientious objection presumably undermined this because it defied the government. As opposed to the LCA convention that backed conscientious objection, the more conservative delegates to the 1967 LCMS convention resolved that "we discourage selective conscientious objection" because it "tends to promote chaos and anarchy." Conservatives within the LCA who disliked the 1968 resolution voiced similar opinions, one layman complaining that it "is a repudiation of responsible American citizenship and church membership." An LCA pastor argued that "if once you say that a man is to be excused from obeying a draft law to which he has moral objection, then you must be consistent and say that every man is entitled to be excused from obedience to *any* law to which he has moral objection." In addition to criticizing Vietnam War pacifists, this demonstrated how Americans in the 1960s feared disorder. Even some Lutherans who accepted conscientious objection criticized it when it became selective. Fifty-six LCA members wrote that "the conscientious objector of a particular war challenges the decisions made by the duly constituted authority of the United States, rather than the moral issues of war in general, and is in fact questioning the integrity of national leaders." Conservative Lutherans labeled conscientious objectors unlawful citizens and called for them to obey the government. Furthermore, their law and order attitude never recognized that young people had no voting power at that time, and thus had no voice in who passed the laws that forced them into combat. Conservatives also had the U.S. Supreme Court on their side. A number of challenges to the draft laws finally led the Supreme Court to hear a case about selective conscientious objection to a particular war. The court ruled against this, thereby buttressing in conservative eyes the idea that such a stance undermined authority in America.[24]

Prowar Lutherans also claimed that selective conscientious objection promoted individualism. An army chaplain complained that it was "only used as an individual's cloak for devising his own mode of life." Conservatives felt that this allowed people to avoid military service without a valid excuse and assumed that young men used selective conscientious objection to justify their fear of combat. An LCA member stated that "I think 90% of these so called C.O.s are really 'yellow bellied cowards.'" Rightist Lutherans also applauded the U.S. Supreme Court when it disallowed selective objection. One person wrote that "I, for one, (and how many more?) was relieved and pleased to have the U.S. Supreme Court knock into a cocked hat the half-backed thinking that selective service in the military could be put on a personal selective basis. Such thinking is quite immature, unworthy of leaders, unpatriotic, destructive of the image of those holding it; and last but not least, I question how Christian." Conservatives believed that the government had the right to command anyone to serve if U.S. leaders deemed it necessary and shunned the notion of individual choice.[25]

Conservative Lutherans also thought that selective conscientious objection catered to the younger generation's unrest. Many people feared that the United States was spiraling into chaos as law and order slipped away. In the context of the 1960s race riots, numerous antiwar protests, and student revolts on campuses, conservatives across the nation feared that a general unrest threatened the nation. Anything that catered to this in their eyes therefore had to be challenged. To solve the problem, they concluded that the government could stem this tide, in part, by forcing selective conscientious objectors to serve time in jail; they thought that allowing them to avoid military service created disobedience, while imprisonment would force young people to stand up for their convictions. The conservative clergy of the LCMS often made this point. Even LCMS President Oliver R. Harms, who in other venues opposed the Vietnam War, stated that "the church . . . says that if a man's conscience thus gets him into difficulty, he must be ready to take the consequences." Another LCMS pastor articulated that "a person who believes that a war is unjust must work for a change through legislation and peaceful protest, but he either must serve if called upon or be willing for conscience sake to suffer the consequences of the law." Indeed, much of their fight against selective objection demonstrates how conservatives feared lawlessness during the Vietnam era. Although they wanted young men to fight if called upon, they allowed for the possibility that someone's conscience could lead them to oppose the war. But rather than let these people go free, conservatives insisted that they should uphold their beliefs by going to prison.[26]

While conservatives fought selective conscientious objection because it "promoted anarchy," antiwar Lutherans defended it as a patriotic ideal. Once again, many of these arguments came from the moderate Lutheran Church in America. Its magazine for women, *Lutheran Women*, explained that "persons are more loyal and more productive citizens if they may act freely according to conscience." Indeed, LCA antiwar protestors declared that conscientious objection to the Vietnam War upheld an American tradition of dissent from tyranny. In fact, they stated that these "true Americans" helped reduce U.S. involvement in the war. An LCA layman asserted, "Thank God for the conscientious objectors! Had it not been for them, we may still be contemplating higher escalation of the V.N. war." In contrast to their right-leaning colleagues, antiwar Lutherans did not fear unrest from the selective conscientious objectors. Rather, they viewed them as responsible Americans dismayed by U.S. foreign policy. Their support for selective CO status buttressed their construction of a counter-patriotism that allowed for questioning the government without undermining a person's loyalty.[27]

Antiwar Lutherans further explained that Lutheran theology allowed for selective conscientious objection. They therefore asserted that it violated the separation of church and state to disallow this contingency and were dismayed when the Supreme Court ruled against them. To this end, the LCA's Social Ministry Board commanded pastors to "extend a supportive ministry to all in their care who are conscientious objectors." They based this on the fact that "the individual who, for reasons of conscience, objects to participation in a particular war is acting in harmony with Lutheran teaching." *Dialog*, a leftist theological journal, also delineated this position, stating that Lutheran theology demanded that if a man opposed a war, whether or not that individual was right, he must not serve because it violated his conscience. They concluded that "our present laws, however, compel such a man either to fight in violation of his conscience, or to break the law. The present laws are, therefore, discriminatory against the Lutheran 'religion'—over against churches that direct their members to refuse service in any war, and churches that do not at all raise the possibility of refusing." An LCMS pastor furthered this reasoning: "A conscience may be in error or inadequately instructed, but it is neither safe nor right to act against conscience."[28]

Antiwar Lutherans also supported conscientious objectors because they focused on the individual. Similar to their Vietnam War opposition, they examined the human element involved. They assessed each case separately and, by examining the young men who took this position, found compassion for their plight. Letters from young men in turmoil often shaped this position, such as one from an LCMS constituent who stated, "I am not gonna shoot anybody." He eventually refused to fight in Vietnam because his conscience would not allow it. Many of the Lutheran leaders who counseled these young men and saw their agony were led to support selective conscientious objection because of it. The LCMS's *Lutheran Witness* attempted to explain this when it wrote that "the young Lutheran who has decided he can't go off to fight in Vietnam probably is a lonely figure, scorned by many fellow Lutherans, neglected by others. He is looked upon as a maverick, if not a coward." LCA leaders, too, made this argument and wanted national recognition for that denomination's support of selective conscientious objection. They felt it would "provide other young men of our church with a position which would be respected to the same degree as the pacifist position is given." In other words, they fought the religious prejudice against Lutheran allowances for selective objection. Personal examples also fueled their cause. A pastor advocated this stance after a draft board denied his brother-in-law's claim; a young LCMS man felt that "the Church has abandoned me, and thousands like me, to [the] anti-Christian, military organization"; an ALC constituent claimed that "a church, named after a man who laid the foundations for it by an act of conscientious objection (Luther), which cannot in its turn condemn war and institutions thereof (which Jesus was wholly against) or even actively support an individual who has taken such a stand, is not in my opinion worthy of bearing the name 'Christian.'" Individual cases prompted Lutheran support for conscientious objection from each of the three largest denominations because a person's emotional well-being guided this stance. Furthermore, this position squared with their theological emphasis on a Lutheran's responsibility not to go against their conscience, which in this case told them that the Vietnam War was immoral.[29]

Importantly, the pro-conscientious objection stance also stressed the need for obeying the law, an example of how moderate Americans opposed the war and various aspects of it without advocating radical demonstrations or denunciations of the American system of government. When the 1968 American Lutheran Church convention defended the conscientious objector it also stated that "as he does so he knows that he must be willing to accept the consequences, both spiritual and civic." ALC President Frederik A. Schiotz echoed these sentiments. He reminded students that "if there is real conscientious objection and it gets them into trouble with the law, they must be ready to accept the consequences." An ALC pastor concurred; he wrote that "a person who believes that war is unjust must work for a change through legislation and peaceful protest, but he either must serve if called upon or be willing for conscience sake to suffer the consequences of the law." LCA members agreed. A congregation declared that "we respect the young man who refuses to fight on moral grounds and either takes an alternative course of positive action or is willing to be jailed for what he believes." But they distrusted those who averted service without repercussions. To that end, they wanted alternative service for those opposed to the war because they thought sending them to jail for following their religious convictions was also unfair. One ALC layman proposed that "some of the damage done by warfare in South Vietnam can be repaired if the idealistic youth who object to fighting there will volunteer their services in rehabilitation work." This statement reflects the desire to allow for conscientious objection but only if those who invoked it did not entirely avoid civic responsibility. Others more logically called for requiring community work within the United States or service abroad in the Peace Corps. Thus, Lutheran support for conscientious objection insisted that resistors did so respectfully, by obeying the law and suffering the consequences of their actions, yet another example of how antiwar Lutherans defended themselves from conservative accusations of being un-American. They wanted conscientious objectors to promote their cause *within* legal parameters that did not undermine traditional authority.[30]

Lutheran Peace Fellowship (LPF), the only Lutheran pacifist organization, especially championed conscientious objection and lamented that the three largest Lutheran bodies did little to aid this cause, despite the LCA and ALC convention resolutions. LPF explained that the LCMS offered little support for conscientious objection, that the ALC recognized this position, and that the LCA pledged to uphold such a stance; but it continued that even the best of these channels failed to assist COs legally. In contrast, LPF helped these men gain legal counsel and apprised them of their rights. Letters to LPF prompted this position, as from a man who wrote that "since the time of my enlistment into the navy, I have come to the realization that war and fighting is wrong, and that God does not want me in this organization." An undergraduate asserted that "when I declared myself a conscientious objector, I found myself in a very lonely position—I know none other in my church (in any congregation), my pastor was hostile, and I had to go it alone." Individual stories of such anguish led LPF members to respond because they understood that these young men truly objected to the Vietnam War. To that end, they asked Lutherans to "support and counsel these young members" as "a charge upon our conscience." They appealed to "pastor-counselors particularly, to help the growing number of our young Lutherans who are searching their consciences in these war-sick days." Although LPF had a small membership and meager finances, it explained why many Lutherans supported conscientious objection. LPF questioned the need for U.S. involvement in Southeast Asia and therefore agreed with young men who refused to fight in Vietnam. Through their counseling, their advice on where to get help, and their call for other Lutherans to listen, LPF constituents protected as many young men as possible.[31]

The debate over conscientious objection demonstrates the difference between those who supported and opposed the Vietnam War. The issue concerned U.S. domestic policy and military recruitment, but Cold War politics lay beneath the surface. Conservative to moderate Lutherans feared Communist expansion and supported all U.S. efforts to thwart this perceived threat. They felt that the situation warranted forced military service and insisted that conscientious objection catered to the Communists, weakened the United States, and threatened global security. This stance stemmed from their fear of communism. Antiwar Lutherans countered this argument by isolating conscientious objection to its truest element: the people involved. Where rightists saw traitors, they saw young men in emotional turmoil who agreed with the antiwar Lutherans that the government was wrong. They asserted that conscientious objectors refused to fight because their moral rectitude instructed them against it.

DRAFT EVADERS IN CANADA

Such bitter wrangling persisted when the two sides discussed the young men who avoided the draft by fleeing to Canada. Throughout the Vietnam War, a stream of men fled to Canada because U.S. officials could not prosecute them there and the Canadian government would not extradite them. Short of going to war against their conscience or going to jail in the United States, young men had only the painful option of leaving their country, most likely to never return again. Lutherans started to debate the fate of these men in the late 1960s, and the argument intensified toward the mid-1970s. Not surprisingly, conservatives despised the "draft-dodgers," calling them traitors and wanting to banish them from the United States forever. Antiwar Lutherans countered this ire with compassion. As they had with the COs, they examined each case individually and thought that the country needed to forgive those who refused to fight the Vietnam War.[32]

Consistent with their anticommunism, conservative Lutherans declared that the boys who fled to Canada aided the Communists. And, once again, the leadership of the LCA that took a position in support of these young men came under attack. One LCA member insisted that a *Lutheran* article favoring amnesty was "the type of publishing material that the Communist, and our enemies, love to see and read. They feel and want us to be a divided people. So in that respect, it [the article] is poisonous and dangerous in scope." This person thought that eternal banishment united Americans against Communist aggression while clemency promoted it. Another layman asserted that North Vietnam and China commit "crimes against humanity," and so the United States had to protect innocent people in Vietnam. "Blanket amnesty for the draft evader" hindered this effort. Typically, conservatives first couched their dislike for something by painting its proponents as Communist.[33]

Conservatives also declared that draft resisters and their supporters betrayed and undermined the U.S. government. When LCA President Robert J. Marshall announced a program to minister to Americans in Canada, a constituent lamented that this devoted "time and money to traitors." Another layman reminded Marshall that "when Christian freedom is exercised against the authority of the state, it should be recognized as carrying with it those legal and social reprisals implicit in contrary behavior." In short, he wanted young men to either serve or go to jail. The Lutheran Council U.S.A.'s Lutheran Selective Service Information also received such condemnations. In addition to counseling the men in Canada, LSSI called for an amnesty that would allow the men to return to the United States without penalty because they had followed their conscience. This lenient position rankled conservatives. A pastor asked, "Do you really believe that the United States would benefit from letting all those [draft evaders] come back and continue to raise hell and try to undermine our government with their continued disregard for the law?" He later proclaimed that "no society could long endure if the violators of the laws established for the well being of all members of that society would be welcomed back as heroes instead of the law-breakers they were." And a laywoman pondered, "Where but in America would these characters be allowed to refuse service to their country and then be granted a *lenient* amnesty?" Conservatives worried throughout the Vietnam era that the younger generation lacked respect for U.S. law and order and therefore rejected amnesty for those in Canada.[34]

Right-leaning Lutherans used language to describe draft evaders that demonstrated their fear and hatred. A *Lutheran* letter to the editor labeled them "spineless," and an LCA member called them "cowardly traitorous mini-gangster drug fiends." One layman more softly called them a negative force when he asked why the Lutheran Church in America ministered to those in Canada and not the many "good" people who served in the military. Conservatives rejected the defense that conscience drove these men to Canada and instead thought that "the conscientious objection in this war was preceded by a 'yellow streak.'" In short, rightists declared that these men had "chicken[ed] out." In fact, they seldom addressed amnesty without including derogatory statements about those who avoided the draft. This exposed a hatred for anything that contradicted their opinions. They exiled the men with hateful words and maintained that they betrayed the United States. Once again, the implication of abetting communism lay underneath the surface; conservatives declared that these hated "cowards" were disloyal to the United States and thereby assisted communism.[35]

Rightist Lutherans finally stated that those who fled to Canada abdicated their right to freedom. An LCA laywoman proclaimed that "the deserters and traitors in Canada" had "a lack of commitment and responsibility to those principals [*sic*] which have throughout history been necessary for the preservation of freedom and liberty. These men, whose character resembles the movements of an eel in a slop bucket, can not be depended upon to uphold these principals [*sic*] in any relationship with God or country." Another member asked, "What makes these young men think they have the right to live in a luxury of a free society that was bought with the blood of countless millions of men? To entertain the thought of granting amnesty to those who willfully deserted their country and their obligations is to forget our honored dead and let weeds grow on their graves." Or, as one man proclaimed in a sign that derided liberalism and insisted that those who avoided the draft forfeited their freedom, "Why grant amnesty to draft dodgers and abolish the death penalty for murder . . . but o.k. innocent men to be killed in wars for them?" Conservatives insisted that the United States had to draft men in order to confront communism before it spread. They therefore thought that anyone who refused to fight in Southeast Asia forfeited their right to live in the United States.[36]

Unlike most discussions about Lutherans and the Cold and Vietnam Wars, the issue of amnesty contained a "gray area." Some liberal to moderate Lutherans agreed with conservatives to the extent that they wanted to punish those who fled to Canada. But unlike rightists who wanted them eternally banished, these Lutherans advocated allowing them to return if it involved retribution. As one LCA pastor explained, "I don't like the war in Viet Nam, and my heart aches for the young men who struggle with their conscience as they reach draft age. And, I do have compassion for these young men in Canada. I believe they have made a sad mistake." But he concluded that "they had other alternatives within the framework of the law." Even *Lutheran* editor and LCA pastor Albert P. Stauderman, who opposed the Vietnam War and supported selective conscientious objection, adhered to this viewpoint. He asserted that "to say that draft evaders are right is to imply that the millions of young men who have served their country are wrong. I can't buy that." He later continued that "I do not consider it realistic to expect that a government which must defend its authority can accept the idea that people who have broken the law should be forgiven unconditionally." An LCA family best summarized this position: "We feel that it is in the best interests of the nation as well as being Christian, to extend amnesty with the qualification that these young men be required to serve a stated period of alternative service of a humanitarian nature."[37]

Despite this qualification, most antiwar Lutherans approached amnesty as they did other domestic Vietnam concerns: they viewed the men as individuals in need of assistance. A Lutheran official explained, they "want to come back. They insist they have not deserted America but have, for the sake of America, refused to be agents of its deadly perversion in Vietnam." Personal stories also led to pro-amnesty stances. A minister described "a moral and very intelligent young man. Married. The Pain. Mine to see the best young men forced to leave this country that not too many years ago welcomed draft resisters." Another pastor asserted that "morally these young men, far from being 'misguided and fearful', include the most intelligent, the best educated, the most morally sensitive of their generation." ALC President David W. Preus, a staunch protestor against the war, wanted to assist "those who for conscience sake took an alternative course. Many of these young men have a deep love for their country." Rather than exile everyone who fled to Canada, these Lutherans saw anguished individuals whose conscience forced them to leave; and they further asserted their patriotism by explaining that they wanted these men who obeyed their conscience to return to help morally strengthen the United States.[38]

Antiwar Lutherans also used their position on the Vietnam War to champion amnesty when they insisted that draft evaders refused to fight an immoral war. Charles P. Lutz, director of Lutheran Selective Service Information, explained to a detractor that "the problem with the Vietnam War was precisely that many who would have served in a conflict like World War II

. . . could not find it in their souls to support *this* war." He had earlier stated that the draft evaders "are saying with an almost unanimous voice, 'It is not we who need to be forgiven, since we refused to participate in the crime of fighting an unjust war. It is our country which made the mistake and should be asking forgiveness from us for giving us no moral option but to go into exile.'" This topic also caused dissension among people who usually agreed because of their opposition to the war. An LCA member criticized *Lutheran* editor Stauderman for favoring punishment rather than amnesty because "he implies that those who have refused involvement in the immoral war in Indo-China are in need of forgiveness. Yet these are the men and women who have refused to participate in an immoral act!"[39]

The ALC and LCA presidents and periodicals also argued theologically in favor of amnesty. In a letter to pastors, Robert J. Marshall reminded them that "many conscientious objectors have already paid a price—separation from family, defamation, ostracism by friends and neighbors, deferment of vocation, and for some, imprisonment." He concluded that "the church's contribution in the present situation can be this call to seek God's grace" through amnesty because "all of us need God's forgiveness—those who supported the war and those who opposed it." By the mid-1970s, a full blown debate about amnesty had swept the nation and prompted President Gerald Ford to construct a plan for conditional amnesty. Ford's clemency program allowed resisters to return if they swore an allegiance oath to the United States and did two years of alternative public service. However, the plan did not include anyone discharged from the military dishonorably or anyone with a criminal record, and ultimately few took advantage of it. While some cheered this move, others questioned its limited nature. ALC President David W. Preus "affirmed" Ford's move toward conditional amnesty but urged him toward unconditional amnesty because it "is analogous to the grace which marks God's dealing with us as people"; "it is a gift." The letter also compared amnesty to Ford's pardon of President Nixon regarding the Watergate scandal: "I am confident that in granting a pardon for Richard Nixon you were expressing your genuine concern for the national good and the welfare of Mr. Nixon and his family. Surely amnesty for those still suffering legal disabilities because of their opposition to the Viet Nam War would serve a similar function for this country, for those directly involved and for their families." These Lutheran leaders used their theological education to ask for forgiveness and grace; their position as church officials thus contributed a religious authority and voice of compassion to the contentious amnesty debate.[40]

Antiwar Lutherans also asserted that even draft evaders deserved religious counseling. They had to make this argument because many conservatives wanted the men in Canada completely banished and exiled. LCA President

Robert J. Marshall explained that Christians must "be obedient to Christ's commands to show our love for all persons by providing pastoral care and physical relief." Where conservatives sought retribution, Marshall called for reconciliation. He even told a constituent that "I am somewhat dismayed that you feel they should not receive any pastoral ministry from the church" because everyone deserved such care. An ALC official similarly detailed how the church wanted to "center in on the issue of ministry to all men and . . . our moral responsibility to be involved in meeting this great human need and brokenness." *Lutheran* editor Albert P. Stauderman more sarcastically stated that the church provided "ministry to them in accordance with the biblical mandate that we serve all men—the sick, the bereaved, prisoners, and even draft evaders." While the LCA actively counseled the men in Canada, other churches failed to act; ALC officials privately promoted amnesty and counseling while LCMS leaders did nothing. This disturbed laypeople, such as one who declared that "I am distressed that the Church's [ALC] ministry to those in exile has not been discussed." He worried about "the spiritual needs of these ex-patriots." Antiwar Lutherans focused on the individual's needs regarding amnesty and saw young people in need who had conscientiously fled the country and wanted the church to assist them in any way possible.[41]

Amnesty for draft resistors paralleled other Lutheran discussions regarding Vietnam War domestic concerns. A deep fear of communism plagued conservatives who insisted that the United States fight every form of communism; when young men refused military service, it therefore seemed treasonous. They advocated the draft because they feared that the Vietnam War imperiled democracy. Thus, those who declined to fight inherently aided communism and abdicated their right to freedom. Antiwar Lutherans viewed amnesty differently. Each person made a personal choice based on religious convictions regarding the war. These Lutherans therefore called for amnesty because it honored conscientious objection against the war. Because Vietnam's communism did not frighten them, they analyzed the situation on an individual basis and focused on healing the nation's divisions, not on retribution.

STATUS QUO ANTE AND RECONCILIATION

Historians often assert that Americans became numb to the Vietnam War by the mid-1970s, that they grasped for an impossible *status quo ante* by ignoring the fact that the war occurred. Yet, this depiction ignores the difficulty Americans had with the post-Vietnam War world. The Lutheran reaction in this regard provides a good example of how U.S. society coped with the conflict's aftermath. Lutherans desperately sought to resolve their disagreements over the Vietnam conflict and looked to the theological concept of reconciliation for guidance. Reconciliation allowed them to overlook their discord about the Vietnam War. They concluded that the United States needed to heal and that the church had to lead in this effort. Rather than focus on differences, they agreed to reunite people through reconciliation; in other words, as Christians they understood the propensity to sin (in this case, fight over the Vietnam War) but mandated that Lutherans overcome this argument and focus on God's will for peace and harmony. Their rhetoric after 1970 moved closer and closer toward reconciliation and farther from derisive debates. By 1975, Lutherans by and large forgot that they had fought contentiously over the Vietnam War. Reconciliation, however, masked significant problems. Although they stopped publicly feuding, they still disagreed about how to prosecute the Cold War; thus, this debate took place privately and therefore failed to take the lessons of Vietnam and apply them to average Americans' foreign policy opinions. Indeed, reconciliation over the Vietnam War accented their hatred of the Communist giants because they both despised the Soviet Union and the People's Republic of China. Rather than learning from the Vietnam War's failure, Lutherans ignored their disagreements in favor of a nebulous reconciliation.

Lutherans first moved toward reconciliation when they sought to accept both sides' viewpoint. Already in 1970, American Lutheran Church delegates resolved that "we express our concerns and prayers for the two groups of young Americans, both often forgotten, our men imprisoned in North Vietnam and our men exiled in Canada and other countries who have made different choices, but who both need to know that we pray for that day soon when they may be reunited with their families." In 1972, the Lutheran Council U.S.A. declared that "the concern of the churches must be for understanding, acceptance and reconciliation among Americans who disagree about the war." The pain caused by the Vietnam War led to this desire for harmony. The ALC's journal for women, *Scope*, printed an article that told the story of a "mother whom I met at a conference convention who told me how torn she was between love for her only son who was in Canada, and her husband who rejected him for not fighting and would neither speak of him nor write to him." Unfortunately for Americans, such stories were not unique. This fact, combined with the weariness over the continued public debate, led Lutherans to seek reconciliation.[42]

American Lutheran Church President David W. Preus epitomized Lutheran attempts to use reconciliation to heal Vietnam wounds by advocating amnesty for the men in Canada. Until the mid-1970s, this topic induced an argument between Lutherans; Preus and other leaders, however, changed this debate by couching their pro-amnesty rhetoric in terms of reconciliation. Preus wrote to

President Ford that "amnesty is an act of reconciling mercy." He asserted that amnesty did not require a victor, it merely necessitated mercy and understanding, principles that especially appealed to Christians. After the ALC passed a pro-amnesty resolution, Preus explained to its critics that "many favoring this resolution did so out of concern for putting the divisiveness of the Vietnam War behind us." He reemphasized that the church never took a firm position either in favor of the conservative, moderate, or liberal viewpoint: "We were not trying to deal with the matter on the basis of justice but on the basis of Reconciliation and healing." He also asserted that the resolution urged Americans to understand "the need for healing and reconciliation with our separated sons and daughters." Amnesty still represented a contentious issue between the various Lutheran factions but became more palatable when presented in terms of reconciliation.[43]

The resettlement of Vietnamese refugees also moved Lutherans toward reconciliation. In 1975, Communist forces seized control of Saigon and ended the Vietnamese civil war with a Communist victory. This created a flood of Vietnamese refugees who had supported the United States and South Vietnam and who had to flee for their lives. With no personal possessions, money, or place to go, these people relied upon good will for survival, and the churches stepped in to help them. Indeed, this topic united both conservative and liberal opinions. Conservatives thought that it allowed the church to assist Christians misplaced by communism, while liberal/moderates focused on the chance to help humans torn apart by an unnecessary war. Regardless of which position an individual Lutheran took, they were united in aiding the refugees and thereby soothed some of the Vietnam War friction. One proponent of assisting the refugees declared that "the Vietnamese refugees offer our church body an opportunity to unite in helping to provide a Christian solution to a serious national problem. Perhaps in the process, we as a church might find our own soul again." And upon the resettlement of the one hundred thousandth refugee, the Lutheran Council U.S.A. issued a press release proclaiming the "oneness of humanity" that such acts of kindness celebrated. Although Lutherans still disagreed about the Vietnam War, they put aside such disagreements when they focused on the refugees and thereby united their divided opinions.[44]

After a decade of sparring over the Vietnam War, Lutherans desperately sought reconciliation by the mid-1970s. They insisted that the church lead efforts to heal the nation and move beyond Vietnam. Through calmer debates about amnesty, the resettlement of refugees, and a lack of discussions about Vietnam, Lutherans succeeded in this endeavor. Despite the seemingly positive effects of ending their bitter debate, reconciliation had a negative side. Lutherans from every part of the political spectrum simply stopped debating theories of containment and Communist expansionism, both terminating their public disagreements and hindering their ability to learn from the United States' failure in the Vietnam War. Conservatives still feared communism and advocated strong measures to stop it, while others wondered how to fight the Soviet Union and China but ceased discussing domino theory topics publicly.

CONCLUSION

Lutherans also debated about the United States' stand on communism when they addressed Vietnam War domestic issues. They took positions regarding the antiwar protest movement, the draft, returning veterans, conscientious objection, and amnesty that squared with their Cold War philosophy. Conservatives championed all efforts to fight the war and so despised domestic efforts to hinder it. They accused protestors and anti-draft advocates of communism and thought that the potential for communism to spread around the globe warranted military conscription. They also wanted to punish draft resisters because they feared that such an attitude imperiled U.S. democracy. Liberal/moderate Lutherans once again fought these notions and focused on the individual human element of each topic. Their position in favor of the protests, against the draft, and for amnesty stemmed from their conviction that the Vietnam War was unnecessary. They also knew that the young men who opposed the war did so out of a conscientious decision to resist U.S. involvement in an imperialistic war. In short, Lutheran opinions regarding domestic Vietnam War issues depended upon whether or not a person thought that communism still endangered U.S. society.

Although Lutherans fought about the Vietnam War, by 1975 few manifestations of this debate appeared. Americans had become numb to the fighting, wanted to move beyond the Vietnam War, and tried to forget about the damage it caused. Christians often couched this hope for tranquility in the Christian need for reconciliation. Reconciliation avoided the need for one side or the other to win the argument while allowing Lutherans to coexist peacefully, regardless of political persuasion.

NOTES

1. Charles DeBenedetti and Charles Chatfield's *An American Ordeal: The Antiwar Movement of the Vietnam Era* (Syracuse, NY: Syracuse University Press, 1990) remains the seminal work on the protest movement. Other quality studies include Terry H. Anderson's *The Movement and the Sixties: Protest in America from Greensboro to Wounded Knee* (New York: Oxford University Press, 1995); Kenneth J. Heineman's *Campus Wars: The Peace Movement at American State*

Universities in the Vietnam Era (New York: New York University Press, 1993); and Tom Wells's *The War Within: America's Battle over Vietnam* (Berkeley: University of California Press, 1994). Solid studies of the Christian protest movement include Mitchell K. Hall's *Because of Their Faith: CALCAV and Religious Opposition to the Vietnam War* (New York: Columbia University Press, 1990) and Michael Brooks Friedland's *Lift Up Your Voice Like a Trumpet: White Clergy and the Civil Rights and Antiwar Movements, 1954–1973* (Chapel Hill: University of North Carolina Press, 1998). Adam Garfinkle's *Telltale Hearts: The Origins and Impact of the Vietnam Antiwar Movement* (New York: St. Martin's Press, 1995).

2. J. D. Boland, "Reporter Finds Most Peace Marchers Duped and Misinformed," *Christian News* 5 (18 May 1967): 3; "Thou Shall Not Kill," *Lutherans Alert* 6 (January 1971): 22–23.

3. Clarence M. Turley to G. Elson Ruff, 26 January 1966, Evangelical Lutheran Church in America Archives, Chicago, Illinois (hereafter ELCA), G. Elson Ruff Papers, box 15, "Tr"; Robert Overgaard, "Student Unrest," *Faith and Fellowship* 37 (5 June 1970): 2–3; Lee Christensen to Mr. Solheim, 19 February 1973, ELCA, LCUSA 2/1, General Secretary, Administrative Files, box 14, "Lutz, Lutheran Selective Service Information, 1971–74."

4. Theodore B. Hax, "Signs of the Times," *Evangelize* 21 (May 1965): 12–13; Morris E. Johnson to G. Elson Ruff, 30 November 1967, ELCA, G. Elson Ruff Papers, box 8, "Joc"; Mrs. Harry J. Coulter to Robert J. Marshall, 18 May 1970, ELCA, Robert J. Marshall Papers, box 117, "War in Vietnam and Cambodia"; Andrew H. Henrich to Frederik A. Schiotz, 27 June 1970, ELCA, Frederik A. Schiotz Papers, box 63, "Cambodia/LWF Location"; R. M. Gholston to Albert P. Stauderman, 23 January 1973, ELCA, Albert P. Stauderman Papers, box 91, "G 1973." Peace movement studies regarding Communist charges against it are DeBenedetti, *An American*; and Anderson, *Movement*. Regarding presidential opinions, see Small, *Johnson, Nixon and the Doves* (New Brunswick: Rutgers University Press, 1988); Robert Dallek, *Flawed Giant: Lyndon Johnson and His Times, 1961–1973* (New York: Oxford University Press, 1998); and Jeffrey Kimball, *Nixon's Vietnam War* (Lawrence: University Press of Kansas, 1998).

5. Gerhard F. Neils to J. A. O. Preus, 24 May 1970, Concordia Historical Institute, St. Louis, Missouri (hereafter CHI), Executive Office, UPN box 79, "United States Government Offices, 1969–1971"; Earl C. Cashman to Robert J. Marshall, 29 May 1970, ELCA, Robert J. Marshall Papers, box 117, "War in Vietnam and Cambodia"; J. A. O. Preus to Carl H. Plumhoff, 5 June 1970, CHI, Executive Office, UPN box 79, "United States Government, 1969–1971"; Robert E. Valgren to G. Elson Ruff, 5 January 1971, ELCA, G. Elson Ruff Papers, box 22, "1970–1972 Last Letters."

6. Wisconsin Evangelical Lutheran Synod, 1967 Convention Minutes, 292, Wisconsin Evangelical Lutheran Synod Archives, Mequon, Wisconsin (hereafter WELS); Kermitt C. Grundahl to Frederik A. Schiotz, 14 September 1967, ELCA, Frederik A. Schiotz Papers, box 151, "Grundahl, Kermitt C."; Donald G. Raup to Robert J. Marshall, 24 May 1970, ELCA, Robert J. Marshall Papers, box 117, "War in Vietnam and Cambodia."

7. Lutheran Theological Seminary Student Association to Richard M. Nixon, 7 May 1970, ELCA, Robert J. Marshall Papers, box 106, "?"; Gertrude K. Sevin to Albert P. Stauderman, 19 January 1973, ELCA, Albert P. Stauderman Papers, box 92, "Sa-Si 1973"; Francis R. Bell to Albert P. Stauderman, 25 April 1973, ELCA, Albert P. Stauderman Papers, box 91, "B 1973."

8. "Lutheran Action Committee," 6 September 1967, ELCA, Lutheran Council U.S.A., Office of Communication and Interpretation, News Bureau, General Topical Files, box 26, "War and Peace"; Brooke Stanford to Robert J. Marshall, 4 May 1970, ELCA, Robert J. Marshall Papers, box 117, "War in Vietnam and Cambodia"; John E. Puelle to J. A. O. Preus, 6 May 1970, CHI, Executive Office, No box, "Vietnam: Peace, 1972–1973."

9. Lutheran Campus Ministry Staff in Wisconsin, Illinois, and Indiana to Lutheran Church Presses, District and Synod Presidents, 4–5 May 1970, ELCA, Lutheran Council U.S.A. 12/1/4,

Division of Education Services, Administrative Files, box 1, "Campus Strife"; Dean C. Kell to George W. Price, 4 January 1970, CHI, Executive Office, "Conscientious Objection, 1970–1971"; John C. Cooper, "Religious Ferment on the Campus," *Lutheran Teacher* 46 (December 1971): 12–14.

10. 26 Students to Richard M. Nixon, 7 May 1970, ELCA, Lutheran Council U.S.A. 12/1/4, Division of Educational Services, Administrative Files, box 1, "Campus Strife"; Carolyn Lorenz Utech, "Letter of the Month," *Lutheran Witness* 89 (September 1970): 20; Robert J. Marshall to Donald F. Hetzler, 11 October 1968, ELCA, National Lutheran Campus Ministry, No box, "Draft Counseling."

11. George C. Reese, "We Reserve the Right to Disagree with Anybody," *Lutheran* 3 (8 December 1965): 11–13; J. Karen Flint, "Protesting about Vietnam," *Lutheran* 4 (5 January 1966): 49; Arnold Carlson, "War in Vietnam," *Lutheran* 4 (19 January 1966): 49; Mrs. E. Fantini, "The Right to Disagree," *Lutheran* 3 (22 December 1965): 49; Juris Lecis, "Protesting about Vietnam," *Lutheran* 4 (5 January 1966): 49.

12. O. Robert Oberkehr, "Confessions of a Peace Marcher: A Patriotic Christian Agonizes over the Vietnam Protests," *Lutheran* 5 (6 December 1967): 10–11; Stephan H. Hornberger, "Marching for Peace," *Lutheran* 6 (3 January 1968): 49; L. O. Thompson, "Marching for Peace," *Lutheran* 6 (3 January 1968): 49.

13. For a synopsis of the draft during this period see George Q. Flynn, *The Draft, 1940–1973* (Lawrence: University Press of Kansas, 1993), 166–282.

14. C. O Kienbusch to Robert J. Marshall, 2 February 1971, ELCA, Robert J. Marshall Papers, box 117, "War in Vietnam and Cambodia"; Carleton Toppe, "No Wisconsin Synod Draft Haven," *Northwestern Lutheran* 58 (9 May 1971): 151.

15. Ralph L. Sundin to Martin W. Mueller, 28 December 1967, CHI, Lutheran Witness Letters, box 3, "Se-Su" (emphasis in original); Joanna Dobson, "Fight for Christianity," *Lutheran Witness* 90 (April 1971): 21; Paul B. Johnson to Martin W. Mueller, 8 March 1971, CHI, Lutheran Witness Letters, box 2, "J"; Dan Saunders to Kent S. Knutson, 27 March 1972, ELCA, Kent S. Knutson Papers, box 2, "S."

16. Hugo Handberg, "A Christian and the Draft," *Lutheran Sentinel* 51 (9 May 1968): 159–60; W. Schaller, Jr., "Selective Conscientious Objection," *Lutheran Spokesman* 11 (August 1968): 7–8; Egbert Albrecht, "The War Is Over," *Lutheran Spokesman* 15 (March 1973): 5–6.

17. Arthur M. Ahlschwede to All College and Seminary Presidents, 23 November 1966, CHI, Executive Office, UPN box 69, "Social Action, Committee On"; Thomas W. Klewin, "A Chaplain Views the Churches and the Draft," *Lutheran Forum* 2 (June 1968): 11–12; Thomas W. Klewin, "Our Son and the Draft," *This Day* 20 (October 1968): 8–9.

18. James Harvey, "Vietnam: Serving Returning Servicemen," *Advance* 16 (April 1969): 10–14; Tammy Tanaka, "The Vietnam Veteran: Coming Home a Drug Addict," *In Step* 3 (May/June 1972): 2–3.

19. Jerry D. Ehrlich to Oliver R. Harms, 24 May 1966, CHI, Executive Office, box 12, "Conscientious Objection, 1963–1969"; Richard John Neuhaus, "On Serving America," *Lutheran Forum* 3 (October 1969): 23; Keith Gerberding, "The Draft: 'What's a Kid Supposed to Do?'" *Lutheran Witness* 90 (March 1971): 5–9, 23.

20. Otto Liljenstolpe to G. Elson Ruff, 23 February 1967, ELCA, G. Elson Ruff Papers, box 9, "Le"; John F. Backe to Frederik A. Schiotz, 29 May 1969, ELCA, Frederik A. Schiotz Papers, box 143, "CO"; Edward M. Kennedy, "Let's Change the Draft," *Event* 9 (June 1969): 6.

21. Flynn's *The Draft*; and Christian G. Appy, *Working-Class War: American Combat Soldiers and Vietnam* (Chapel Hill: University of North Carolina Press, 1993) best expose the inequities of the draft. Carl F. Reuss, "Voices from 'Back Home' Needed in Reaching Decisions on Draft," *Commentator* 7 (May 1967): 6; Mrs. E. W. Anacker, "The C.O. and the Draft,"

Lutheran Standard 9 (9 December 1969): 18; Frederik A. Schiotz to Jerry Thompson, 30 October 1969, ELCA, Frederik A. Schiotz Papers, box 143, "CO."

22. Richard Killmer, "No Victory Parades," *Circle* (May 1972): 1; Charles P. Lutz, "Victims of Duty," *Lutheran Women* 11 (March 1973): 19–21, 27.

23. Mrs. Philip N. Reed to Robert J. Marshall, 31 July 1968, ELCA, Robert J. Marshall Papers, box 117, "Statement on C.O."; Humphrey May, Jr., to Robert J. Marshall, 5 August 1968, ELCA, Robert J. Marshall Papers, box 117, "Statement on C.O." (emphasis in original); Thomas G. Barkley to Robert J. Marshall, 15 August 1968, ELCA, Robert J. Marshall Papers, box 117, "Statement on C.O."; Raymond B. Mericle to Robert J. Marshall, 29 October 1968, ELCA, Robert J. Marshall Papers, box 117, "Statement on C.O." (emphasis in original).

24. Lutheran Church–Missouri Synod, 1967 Convention Minutes, 96–97, CHI; William A. Rohrbach to Robert J. Marshall, 6 July 1968, ELCA, Robert J. Marshall Papers, box 117, "Statement on C.O."; Thomas Basisch, "Anarchy and the Lutheran Church in America," *The Advent Lutheran* 13 (12 July 1968): 1 (emphasis in original); 56 LCA Members to the Board of Social Ministry, n.d., ELCA, Robert J. Marshall Papers, box 117, "Statement on C.O." For a complete explanation on selective conscientious objection and the Supreme Court ruling, see Flynn, *The Draft*; Anderson, *Movement*; Peter N. Carroll, *It Seemed Like Nothing Happened: America in the 1970s* (New Brunswick, NJ: Rutgers University Press, 1982).

25. Theodore Koepke to Arthur Piepkorn, 31 October 1969, ELCA, Arthur Piepkorn Papers, box 108, "Pacifism and Conscientious Objection"; John F. Brillhart to G. Elson Ruff, 30 July 1968, ELCA, G. Elson Ruff Papers, box 17, "Bo-Bz"; John Edward Wilson to Herb W. David, 13 March 1971, ELCA, Lutheran Council U.S.A. 16/2, Office of Communication and Interpretation, Administrative Files, box 4, "Public Affairs: Testimonies Conscientious Objection, 1970–71."

26. Oliver R. Harms to Richard Ankle, 14 November 1967, CHI, Executive Office, box 12, "Conscientious Objection, 1963–1969"; Donald Docken to J. A. O. Preus, 18 August 1969, CHI, J. A. O. Preus Papers, box 26, "Selective Service System: Conscientious Objection."

27. LaVonne Althouse, "Military Draft and Objections of Conscience," *Lutheran Women* 8 (February 1970): 7–11; Paul F. Shagnot to Albert P. Stauderman, 25 April 1971, ELCA, Albert P. Stauderman Papers, box 88, "Sa-Si."

28. Lutheran Church in America, 1964 Convention Minutes, 145, ELCA; Lutheran Church in America, 1968 Convention Minutes, 635–36, ELCA; "God and Caesar," *Dialog* 7 (Spring 1968): 84; Arthur Piepkorn to Theodore V. Koepke, 17 November 1969, ELCA, Arthur Piepkorn Papers, box 108, "Pacifism and Conscientious Objection."

29. Mike Waycaster to Peter Fishle, 24 August 1972, ELCA, Lutheran Council U.S.A. 2/1, General Secretary, Administrative Files, box 14, "Lutz, Lutheran Selective Service Information, 1971–74"; R. J., "War and Conscience," *Lutheran Witness* 87 (November 1968): 7–9; Stewart W. Herman to Robert J. Marshall, 16 July 1969, ELCA, Robert J. Marshall Papers, box 117, "Statement on C.O."; Karl A. Schneider to Robert J. Marshall, 5 September 1969, ELCA, Robert J. Marshall Papers, box 117, "Statement on C.O."; James R. Anderson to J. A. O. Preus, 19 March 1970, CHI, Executive Office, box 12, "Conscientious Objection 1970–71"; Mark Rorem to Kent S. Knutson, 5 December 1971, ELCA, Kent S. Knutson Papers, box 2, "Ro."

30. American Lutheran Church, 1968 Convention Minutes, 484–88, ELCA; Frederik A. Schiotz to Daryl M. Hanson, 17 September 1968, ELCA, Frederik A. Schiotz Papers, box 47, "WCC Reactions to 1968 Assembly I"; Donald Docken to Frederik A. Schiotz, n.d., ELCA, Frederik A. Schiotz Papers, box 149, "Docken, L. D."; Robert Forkner to Robert J. Marshall, 17 December 1969, ELCA, Robert J. Marshall Papers, box 117, "War in Vietnam and Cambodia"; "Rehabilitation Work in Vietnam Called Challenge to U.S. Youth," 26 December 1968, ELCA, Lutheran Council U.S.A. 16/6/6, Office of Communication and Interpretation, News Bureau, Country Files, "Vietnam."

31. Vincent L. Hawkinson to Doug Manning, 21 October 1968, Swarthmore College Peace Collection, Swarthmore, Pennsylvania (hereafter SCPC), Lutheran Peace Fellowship, DG 171, box 1, "1968"; J. Philip Stark to Vincent L. Hawkinson, 28 March 1966, SCPC, Lutheran Peace Fellowship, DG 171, box 1, "1966"; James LeRoy Johnson to Vincent L. Hawkinson, n.d., SCPC, Lutheran Peace Fellowship, DG 171, box 1, "1966"; Robert F. Weiskotten and Vincent L. Hawkinson to "Fellow-Lutherans," n.d., SCPC, Lutheran Peace Fellowship, DG 171, box 1, "1968."

32. For a good history of the young men who fled to Canada, see John Hagan, *Northern Passage: American Vietnam War Resisters in Canada* (Cambridge, MA: Harvard University Press, 2001).

33. Ben O. Olson to G. Elson Ruff, 25 February 1971, ELCA, Albert P. Stauderman Papers, box 87, "N-O"; Harry H. Weaver, II, to Albert P. Stauderman, 1 April 1972, ELCA, Albert P. Stauderman Papers, box 90, "W, X, Y, Z, 1972."

34. Harry E. Butts to Robert J. Marshall, 10 December 1969, ELCA, Robert J. Marshall Papers, box 117, "War in Vietnam and Cambodia"; Richard O. Scherch to Robert J. Marshall, 10 December 1969, ELCA, Robert J. Marshall Papers, box 117, "War in Vietnam and Cambodia"; Ben G. Hoffman to Charles P. Lutz, 10 April 1973, ELCA, Lutheran Council U.S.A. 2/1, General Secretary, Administrative Files, box 14, "Lutz, Lutheran Selective Service Information, 1971–74"; Ben G. Hoffmann to Charles P. Lutz, 5 May 1973, ELCA, Lutheran Council U.S.A. 2/1, General Secretary, Administrative Files, box 14, "Lutz, Lutheran Selective Service Information, 1971–74"; Alice Dierks to David W. Preus, 15 October 1974, ELCA, David W. Preus Papers, box 13, "Draft Counseling" (emphasis in original).

35. Derwood Dudley, "Forgiving Draft Resisters," *Lutheran* 11 (18 April 1973): 48; Ralph W. Cowden to Albert P. Stauderman, 19 February 1971, ELCA, Albert P. Stauderman Papers, box 86, "C"; James R. Corgee to G. Elson Ruff, 22 February 1971, ELCA, Albert P. Stauderman Papers, box 86, "C"; Charles S. Ballentine to Albert P. Stauderman, 2 April 1973, ELCA, Albert P. Stauderman Papers, box 91, "B 1973"; Mrs. Frank White to David W. Preus, 20 October 1974, ELCA, David W. Preus Papers, box 13, "Draft Counseling."

36. Raymond Mires to G. Elson Ruff, 3 April 1971, ELCA, Albert P. Stauderman Papers, box 87, "M"; Mike E. Key to Albert P. Stauderman, 14 June 1972, ELCA, Albert P. Stauderman Papers, box 89, "K, 1972"; Carl Braaten, "Religion as Patriotism or Protest," *Event* 12 (November 1972): 5.

37. William J. Moschell to Robert J. Marshall, 22 February 1971, ELCA, Robert J. Marshall Papers, box 117, "War in Vietnam and Cambodia"; Albert P. Stauderman to Richard Niebanck, 4 February 1972, ELCA, Albert P. Stauderman Papers, box 90, "N-O, 1972"; Albert P. Stauderman to Paul Kuenning, 4 April 1972, ELCA, Albert P. Stauderman Papers, box 89, "K, 1972"; Leinung Family to Robert J. Marshall, 27 March 1973, ELCA, Lutheran Council U.S.A. 2/1, General Secretary, Administrative Files, box 14, "Lutz, Lutheran Selective Service Information, 1971–74."

38. Richard John Neuhaus, "The Deserters: Room for Them in America," *Lutheran Forum* 2 (December 1968): 17; Wayne W. Landgrebe to Frederik A. Schiotz, 31 March 1970, ELCA, Frederik A. Schiotz Papers, box 143, "C.O."; Paul Kuenning to Albert P. Stauderman, 17 February 1972, ELCA, Albert P. Stauderman Papers, box 89, "K 1972"; David W. Preus to Mrs. F. White, 19 November 1974, ELCA, David W. Preus Papers, box 13, "Draft Counseling."

39. Charles P. Lutz to Ben G. Hoffman, 23 April 1973, ELCA, Lutheran Council U.S.A. 2/1, General Secretary, Administrative Files, box 14, "Lutz, Lutheran Selective Service Information, 1971–74" (emphasis in original); Charles P. Lutz to Albert P. Stauderman, 3 February 1972, ELCA, Albert P. Stauderman Papers, box 89, "L, 1972"; Martin Bergbusch to Albert P. Stauderman, 1 February 1972, ELCA, Albert P. Stauderman Papers, box 88, "B, 1972."

40. Robert J. Marshall, "Letter to Pastors," *Ministers Information Service* (1 March 1973): 1–3; David W. Preus to Gerald R. Ford, 10 September 1974, ELCA, David W. Preus Papers, box 13, "Draft Counseling."

41. Robert J. Marshall to Paul L. Conrad, 29 December 1969, ELCA, Robert J. Marshall Papers, box 117, "War in Vietnam and Cambodia"; Robert J. Marshall to C. O. Kienbach, 12 February 1971, ELCA, Robert J. Marshall Papers, box 117, "War in Vietnam and Cambodia"; James A. Siefkes to Frederik A. Schiotz, 12 May 1970, ELCA, Frederik A. Schiotz Papers, box 143, "C.O."; Albert P. Stauderman to Robert J. Burlingame, 10 March 1971, ELCA, Albert P. Stauderman Papers, box 86, "B"; J. Donaldson Edwards to David W. Preus, 23 November 1976, ELCA, David W. Preus Papers, box 13, "Draft Counseling."

42. American Lutheran Church, 1970 Convention Minutes, 64, ELCA; "Toward Reconciliation," Lutheran Council U.S.A. Annual Meeting Minutes, 28–29 February 1972, ELCA, Lutheran Council U.S.A. 2/1, General Secretary, Administrative Files, box 18, "?"; Marge Wold, "Directly to You," *Scope* 13 (November 1973): 31–33.

43. David W. Preus to the President, 10 September 1974, ELCA, David W. Preus Papers, box 13, "Draft Counseling"; David W. Preus to Henry A. Johnson, 10 December 1976, ELCA, David W. Preus Papers, box 13, "Draft Counseling"; David W. Preus to J. Donald Edwards, 10 December 1976, ELCA, David W. Preus Papers, box 13, "Draft Counseling."

44. Louis J. Reith to Frank D. Starr, 5 May 1975, CHI, Lutheran Witness Letters, box 3, "R"; "Vietnam," 19 September 1975, ELCA, Lutheran Council U.S.A. 16/6/6, Office of Communication and Interpretation, News Bureau, Country Files, box 16, "Vietnam."

Chapter Seven

The Lutheran Cold and Vietnam Wars' Legacy

Lutherans from all political and theological spectrums had a lot to say about foreign and domestic policy during a very contentious decade. Prowar Lutherans agreed with the U.S. government when it defended its participation in Vietnam because the fight against communism necessitated the combat. Yet not all Lutherans agreed; opposition to the Vietnam War countered this argument and challenged both the Johnson and Nixon administration policies in Southeast Asia. Indeed, the Southeast Asian conflict produced a debate within U.S. society that Lutherans vigorously participated in about how to resist global communism. Lutherans by and large agreed upon a need to confront the Union of Soviet Socialist Republics (USSR) and the People's Republic of China (PRC), especially because of their atheist agenda and proof that the Communist giants oppressed their citizens and in particular religious believers. But some Lutherans clung to the domino theory and a staunch anticommunism while others castigated it as an outmoded methodology when they discussed the Vietnam War. Understanding that a split took place between Lutherans, a predominately moderate sampling of people unlikely to take extreme measures about their positions one way or another, furthers historical awareness of the Vietnam War era. Lutheranism reveals a broad array of opinions, from a total disdain for the war to advocacy of using nuclear weapons in Southeast Asia, and everything between. Lutheran history also demonstrates that fear of communism survived for many U.S. citizens well beyond 1950s McCarthyism. And most Lutherans still advocated some type of confrontation with the USSR and the PRC. But they disagreed about other aspects of communism by the mid-1960s, primarily because the entire nation began debating traditional Cold War policies in the midst of the Vietnam War and based on the quarrel about McCarthyism. Some continued to think that Communists tried to infiltrate U.S. society while others shunned this notion.

This investigation has also examined how Lutherans approached these secular, foreign policy and domestic matters in relationship to their theology, or how they often failed to do so. This includes their conversations about both the just war theory and religious faith in general. To their credit, very few used the charged language of a religious crusade in describing the Cold or Vietnam Wars. Yet this did not stop conservatives from arguing that the war was justified; despite few attempts to outline the seven just war tenets and apply them to the war, many Lutherans insisted that God was on their side and opposed to communism everywhere. Perhaps more remarkably, given that the laity, clergy, and leadership of almost every Lutheran denomination articulated views about Vietnam and the Cold War in their religious journals, conventions, and letters to one another, very few people couched their argument in terms of their theology or faith. Instead, most came to the debate with firm opinions regarding the Cold War, internal Communist threats, and the Vietnam War and mentioned their theology as it fit these political opinions or, more often, assumed that the connection was obvious despite now being ambiguous. Lutheran decisions regarding the justness of Vietnam often seem to have lacked careful exegesis or religious meditation. Religious rhetoric played a major role in how Lutherans couched their various positions about the debates of the 1960s and 1970s but did not appear to induce either side to rethink their stance.

In deliberating about foreign policy issues in their church bodies and periodicals between 1964 and 1975, American Lutherans agreed that the Soviet Union and China threatened U.S. security and that communism's attack on worldwide Christianity especially demanded their attention. Yet they disagreed about domestic Communist dangers and the need for U.S. participation in the Vietnam War. Prowar Lutherans feared any form of communism, thought that it sought to infiltrate U.S. institutions, including the churches, and advocated the Vietnam War as an important battle against Communist expansionism. In contrast, their antiwar counterparts dismissed their fears, explained that no internal Communist threat imperiled the United States or its church bodies, and wanted a U.S. withdrawal from Vietnam because they viewed the conflict there as a civil war, separate from the fight against Soviet and Chinese communism. According to nearly all Lutherans, the United States needed to fight communism as if it were a dangerous tiger that imperiled all of humanity. Prior to Vietnam they had largely agreed upon how to hunt this "atheist enemy." But the Vietnam War shattered this agreement and forced some people to reconsider their "tiger hunting" tactics.

Regarding the Soviet Union and the People's Republic of China, Lutherans by and large presented a unified voice of condemnation. The Soviet Union persecuted its own citizens, outlawed religion, and unnerved Americans with its global power. Proof that the USSR hindered religious practices solidified these opinions. Formerly thriving Lutheran churches in Estonia, Latvia, and Lithuania faced near-extinction and required aid from Lutherans around the world. The situation regarding Red China paralleled that of the Soviet Union. Lutherans condemned Mao Zedong's government for prohibiting religious faith and questioned its dictatorial powers. Refugees in Hong Kong buttressed these claims. Lutheran missionaries relayed stories about how Christians suffered because of their faith and needed protection and economic assistance. The USSR and PRC remained global threats throughout this period in Lutheran minds, and they asked that Christians around the globe combat these Communist giants because of religious persecution within their borders.

Nonetheless, issues about internal Communist threats to the United States diminished Lutheran unity. Far-right and conservative Lutherans persisted with their suspicion of communism and believed that it intended to encircle the globe; this included the notion that spies infiltrated the United States in order to convert people to communism and eventually assist in taking over the U.S. government. They even warned that their Lutheran church bodies had succumbed to at least advocating Communist programs in the United States. Other Lutherans countered this fear. Moderates and liberals asserted that no immediate menace existed within the United States and instead claimed that when people pursued this policy it harmed innocent victims. When conservative Lutherans accused the World Council of Churches and National Council of Churches of Christ of harboring Communists, these Lutherans explained that no Communists secretly used these Christian organizations to undermine religion. This disagreement also manifested itself when the two sides discussed the civil rights movement and the ministry of Richard Wurmbrand. Where one side saw chaos and a reasoned warning, the other saw harmful and closed-minded thinking.

Conservative Lutherans further maintained their fear of communism when they addressed the Vietnam War. They firmly believed that Soviet and Chinese Communists directed a worldwide conspiracy to control the entire earth and rid it of Christianity. Losing another country to communism therefore threatened the existence of democracy and Christianity and imperiled U.S. security. To that end, they depicted North Vietnam as a Soviet and Chinese puppet that tyrannically oppressed its citizens. They also maintained that patriotic Americans supported their government when it waged war because U.S. officials knew more than most citizens about international affairs and how to preserve U.S. interests. As the war progressed, they translated these beliefs into reasons for supporting U.S. soldiers. They warned that North Vietnam refused to release prisoners of war and that only a show of U.S. strength could free them. They saw the Vietnam War as a crucial battle in the struggle against atheistic communism because they feared that a monolithic "demon" threatened to encircle the globe. The conflict was a political battle against communism *and* a religious struggle against atheistic forces.

Antiwar Lutherans contested this argument about the Vietnam War. They explained that the United States had involved itself in a civil war on the side of a corrupt regime in South Vietnam. Although they emphasized their continued disdain for communism, they also asserted that the United States had no right to demand that the Vietnamese resist communism if the people of that nation wanted it. To this end, they repeatedly asserted that the Vietnam War negated the domino theory. They explained that the war injured innocent people, that the Vietnamese merely sought self-determination, and that the United States needed to withdraw from the war before North Vietnam would free the prisoners of war. According to them, the Vietnam War represented a tragedy of immense proportions, and the longer the fighting persisted the worse it became. They, too, supported their position with religious ideals: the war was not only ill-fated and politically questionable, but it was also unjust and immoral. Because antiwar Lutherans did not fear a global disaster if Vietnam "fell" to communism, they focused on the damage that the war did to the Vietnamese people and the United States' stability when they campaigned to get U.S. forces out of Vietnam.

This debate also caused Lutheran disunity about domestic issues that involved the Vietnam War. Conservative Lutherans criticized anything that questioned the U.S. government or the need for fighting in Southeast Asia. Moderate Lutherans disagreed and supported dissension to the war. One side couched its rhetoric in terms of fighting a monolithic Communist demon, while the other lamented the turmoil that the war caused on the U.S. domestic scene. The two factions squared off in debates about the antiwar protest movement, the draft, conscientious objection, and amnesty for draft evaders. Despite these feuds, the end of the war found Lutherans reconciled with one another when they stopped arguing about the domino theory and its relationship to Vietnam War issues. Rather, they focused on healing the United States' wounds by forgetting about the discord and moving forward.

Lutherans in America therefore left a conflicted legacy regarding the Vietnam War. Much of this mixed message, of course, stems from the very diversity of American Lutherans, who represent a broad spectrum of theological and political points of view, despite their overall moderate to conservative temperament. But, in addition, the legacy was affected by a relatively universal Lutheran desire for reconciliation by the mid-1970s. They had argued about Cold War policies and especially the Vietnam War for over a decade and wanted to move beyond the contention. They could not do so, however, by crafting an agreement about their views and so instead turned to the notion of reconciliation. It is important to note that this desire to move beyond Vietnam came at a contentious point in Lutheran history regarding other issues. The Lutheran Church–Missouri Synod made a sharp turn toward conservatism early in the decade that splintered the denomination, led to the expulsion of seminary faculty, and the founding of the Association of Evangelical Lutheran Churches by the ousted moderates. The Lutheran Church in America and American Lutheran Church internally fought over the ordination of women despite the fact that both denominations began ordaining women in 1970. Other tension within Lutheranism included debates about biblical inerrancy, unionism and ecumenism, and denominational mergers. It was too much for a historic group of Americans who disliked such friction. The discussion about the Vietnam War became a convenient way to move away from some of this tension because it was a secular issue to which few tied deeply held religious convictions. If the religious issues would not go away, at least they could attain reconciliation regarding war and foreign policy. One can hardly blame them for wanting this peace, and the ability to forgive one another lived out their Christian conviction. Yet, on the other hand, they left unresolved how to deal with conflict over U.S. foreign policy and wartime issues.

Lutherans provide a glimpse about how at least one group of "average" Americans viewed foreign policy concerns during this decade. Evidence suggests that these Americans from 1964 to 1975 still believed that communism threatened their security, especially as manifested in the Soviet Union and People's Republic of China. But they disagreed about whether or not spies lurked in the United States and about the Vietnam War. Some Lutherans learned from the Vietnam War that the domino theory represented U.S. imperialism more than it did a noble effort to defend the world from tyranny. But many other citizens, blinded by years of fear, never changed their conservative anti-Communist opinions, even after the United States pulled out of Vietnam. Throughout this era, they warned about Communist expansionism. Furthermore, even the people who castigated the Vietnam War persisted with Cold War rhetoric against the Soviet Union and Red China. Thus, they questioned containment but never stopped fighting the Cold War. In short, the Lutheran perspective suggests that the United States was still a conservative nation. In the midst of the civil rights movement, women's liberation, antiwar protests, the sexual revolution, the dawn of the gay and lesbian movement, American Indian activism, and many other cries for liberation and equality, the United States clung to its conservative roots. This is evident in the election of Richard M. Nixon, the sharp turn to the right in the 1970s, and the eventual election of Ronald W. Reagan. As historians delve into more and more sources that reveal the opinions of "average" Americans during this period, this conservatism will become more obvious. A close look at Lutheranism revealed it all too well.

Lutherans despised the Soviet Union and Red China, debated about the presence of internal Communists and about the Vietnam War, but together sought to reunite the nation after U.S. troops pulled out of Saigon. This hardly presents the picture of a radically changing society.

American Lutherans learned some lessons from the Vietnam War and allowed other problems to go unnoticed. In short, they debated about what strategy to use in hunting the Communist tiger but still feared its presence. And they quickly turned away from the matter after the United States withdrew from Southeast Asia in 1973, reaching a tentative accord by the fall of Saigon in 1975 that refocused energy on resettling refugees and reconciliation. Unfortunately, this left little legacy for future Lutherans to follow when dealing with secular, foreign policy matters, especially as they relate to war. Today, the United States once again finds itself embroiled in international conflicts and at war in a foreign country. The largest Lutheran denominations, the Evangelical Lutheran Church in America (ELCA), the Lutheran Church–Missouri Synod (LCMS), and the Wisconsin Evangelical Lutheran Synod (WELS) fit the pattern of response modeled during the 1960s and 1970s. ELCA presiding Bishop Mark S. Hanson has followed his LCA and ALC predecessors in consistently questioning the war and advocating for peace, as have other ELCA leaders and publications. But the ELCA as a whole, despite social statements that champion global efforts toward peace and a more active social justice program than ever before witnessed in America Lutheran history, has either avoided comment about the Iraqi War or carefully crafted statements to allow for a variety of opinions so as not to offend ELCA prowar advocates. The LCMS and WELS, too, have stepped around comment on the war but otherwise tacitly accepted it. If the lesson from the Vietnam War era is to promote reconciliation, avoid divisive debates, and couch statements to appeal to the largest number of people, perhaps it is time to rethink this legacy.

Selected Bibliography

RELIGIOUS PERIODICALS AND NEWSPAPERS

Note: Unless otherwise mentioned, each periodical was already publishing in 1964 and was still publishing in 1975. ALC (American Lutheran Church), LCA (Lutheran Church in America), LCMS (Lutheran Church–Missouri Synod), and LCUSA (Lutheran Council in the USA) denote official publications of these bodies. The word "affiliated" following these initials indicates that the periodical was published by members of that church without official sanction. All other organizations are spelled out completely after their periodical's title.

Advance (LCMS)
Affirm (LCMS affiliated; began in 1971)
American Lutheran (LCMS affiliated; became *Lutheran Forum* in 1967)
Arena (LCMS; merged with *One* to become *Arena One* in 1967)
Arena One (ALC/LCMS; formed in January 1967 with the merger of *Arena* and *One*, after October 1967 became *Edge*)
Christian Century (Independent Protestant)
Christian Monthly (Apostolic Lutheran Church of America)
Christian News (LCMS affiliated; began in 1968, formerly *Lutheran News*)
Christianity Today (Independent Protestant)
Commentator (ALC)
Dialog (Independent Lutheran)
Edge (ALC/LCMS; previously *Arena One*, last published in October 1968)
Evangelize (Lutheran Evangelistic Movement)
Event (ALC; began in 1969, previously *Greater Works*, stopped publication in 1974)
Faith and Fellowship (Church of the Lutheran Brethren)
Faith-Life (Protestant Conference [Conservative Lutheran])
Focus (LCUSA; began in 1967)
Forum Letter (Independent Lutheran; began in 1972)
Greater Works (ALC; became *Event* in 1969)
In Step (LCUSA; began in 1970, formerly *A Mighty Fortress*)
Interchange (LCUSA; began in 1967)

185

Jesus to the Communist World (Jesus to the Communist World Incorporated, independent Lutheran; began in 1967)

Learning With (ALC; began in 1973, previously *Lutheran Teacher*)

Lutheran (LCA)

Lutheran Ambassador (Association of Lutheran Congregations)

Lutheran Beacon (Synod of Evangelical Lutheran Churches; absorbed into *Lutheran Witness* in 1970)

Lutheran Brotherhood Bond (Lutheran Brotherhood)

Lutheran Chaplain (LCMS; ceased publication in 1970)

Lutheran Digest (Independent Lutheran)

Lutheran Forum (Independent Lutheran; began in 1967, previously *American Lutheran*)

Lutheran Laymen (Lutheran Laymen's League, primarily LCMS)

Lutheran News (LCMS affiliated; became *Christian News* in 1968)

Lutheran Quarterly (ALC/LCA, Council of Lutheran Theological Seminaries)

Lutheran Scholar (LCMS, Lutheran Academy for Scholarship)

Lutheran Sentinel (Evangelical Lutheran Synod)

Lutheran Service Commission News (National Lutheran Council and LCMS, ceased publication in 1966)

Lutheran Social Concern (LCUSA; began in 1972, previously *Lutheran Social Welfare*; stopped publication in 1974)

Lutheran Social Welfare (LCUSA; began in 1968, previously *Lutheran Social Welfare Quarterly*; became *Lutheran Social Concern* in 1972)

Lutheran Social Welfare Quarterly (LCA; became *Lutheran Social Welfare* in 1968)

Lutheran Spokesman (Church of the Lutheran Confession)

Lutheran Standard (ALC)

Lutheran Teacher (ALC; became *Learning With* in 1973)

Lutheran Witness (LCMS)

Lutheran Witness Reporter (LCMS; began in May 1965)

Lutheran Woman's Quarterly (LCMS)

Lutheran Women (LCA)

Lutheran World (Lutheran World Federation)

Lutherans Alert National (ALC affiliated; began in 1966)

Metanoia (Independent Lutheran; began in 1969)

A Mighty Fortress (National Lutheran Council/LCUSA; became *In Step* in 1970)

Minister's Information Service (LCA)

Missouri in Perspective (Evangelical Lutherans in Mission; began in 1973)

National Lutheran (National Lutheran Council; ceased publication in 1966)

News Bureau (LCUSA; began in 1967)

Newsletter for Lutheran Chaplains (National Lutheran Council; absorbed by *Lutheran Chaplain* in 1967)

Northwestern Lutheran (Wisconsin Evangelical Lutheran Synod)

One (ALC; merged with *Arena* to become *Arena One* in 1967)

Religion in Communist Dominated Areas (National Council of Churches of Christ)

Scope (ALC)

Shepherd (Evangelical Lutheran Church of Canada)

Sola Scriptura (Federation of Authentic Lutheranism; began in 1970)

Teen Ways (ALC; ceased publication in 1969)

This Day (LCMS; ceased publication in 1971)

Through to Victory (LCMS affiliated; ceased publication in 1974)
World Encounter (LCA)

ARCHIVES

Billy Graham Center, Wheaton College, Wheaton, IL. Evangelical Archives and Repository.
Concordia Lutheran Seminary, St. Louis, MO. Library.
Evangelical Lutheran Church in America Headquarters, Chicago, IL. Department of Denominational Archives.
Lutheran Church–Missouri Synod, Concordia Historical Institute, St. Louis, MO. Department of Archives.
Lutheran Laymen's League, St. Louis, MO. Department of Archives.
Swarthmore College Peace Collection, Swarthmore, PA. Archives of the Lutheran Peace Fellowship.
Trinity Lutheran Seminary, Columbus, OH. Library.
Wisconsin Evangelical Lutheran Synod, Wisconsin Lutheran Seminary, Mequon, WI. Department of Archives.
Wisconsin Lutheran Seminary, Mequon, WI. Library.

ARTICLES, BOOKS, AND DISSERTATIONS

Abrams, Elliott, ed. *The Influence of Faith: Religious Groups and U.S. Foreign Policy.* Lanham, MD: Rowman and Littlefield Publishers, 2001.
Adler, Les K. *The Red Image: American Attitudes toward Communism in the Cold War Era.* New York: Garland Publishing, Inc., 1991.
Ahlstrom, Sydney E. *A Religious History of the American People.* New Haven, CT: Yale University Press, 1972.
Aitken, Jonathan. *Nixon: A Life.* Washington, DC: Regnery Publishing, 1993.
Allin, Dana H. *Cold War Illusions: America, Europe and Soviet Power, 1969–1989.* New York: St. Martin's Press, 1994.
Allitt, Patrick. *Religion in America since 1945: A History.* New York: Columbia University Press, 2003.
Alonso, Harriet Hyman. *Peace as a Women's Issue: A History of the U.S. Movement for World Peace and Women's Rights.* Syracuse, NY: Syracuse University Press, 1993.
Alperovitz, Gar. *Atomic Diplomacy: Hiroshima and Potsdam.* Boulder, CO: Pluto Press, 1994.
Ambrose, Stephen E. *Nixon*, vol. 1, *The Education of a Politician, 1913–1962.* New York: Touchstone Books, 1987.
———. *Nixon*, vol. 3, *Ruin and Recovery, 1973–1990.* New York: Touchstone Books, 1991.
Anderson, David L. *Trapped by Success: The Eisenhower Administration and Vietnam, 1953–1961.* New York: Columbia University Press, 1991.
Anderson, Terry H. *The Movement and the Sixties: Protest in America from Greensboro to Wounded Knee.* New York: Oxford University Press, 1995.
Andrew, John A. III. *The Other Side of the Sixties: Young Americans for Freedom and the Rise of Conservative Politics.* New Brunswick, NJ: Rutgers University Press, 1997.

Appleby, Joyce, Lynn Hunt, and Margaret Jacob. *Telling the Truth about History.* New York: W. W. Norton and Company, 1994.

Appy, Christian G., ed. *Cold War Constructions: The Political Culture of United States Imperialism, 1945–1966.* Amherst: University of Massachusetts Press, 2000.

——. *Working-Class War: American Combat Soldiers and Vietnam.* Chapel Hill: University of North Carolina Press, 1993.

Asselin, Pierre. *A Bitter Peace: Washington, Hanoi, and the Making of the Paris Peace Agreement.* Chapel Hill: University of North Carolina Press, 2002.

Au, William A. *The Cross, the Flag, and the Bomb: American Catholics Debate War and Peace, 1960–1983.* Westport, CT: Greenwood Press, 1985.

Augustine, Saint. *Concerning the City of God against the Pagans.* Translated by John O'Meara. New York: Penguin Books, 1984.

Austin, Randall Dean. "Caution Christian Soldiers: The Mainline Protestant Churches and the Cold War." Ph.D. diss., University of Arkansas, 1997.

Avery, William O. *Empowered Laity: The Story of the Lutheran Laity Movement.* Minneapolis: Augsburg Fortress Press, 1997.

Avorn, Jerry L. *Up against the Ivy Wall: A History of the Columbia Crisis.* New York: Atheneum, 1970.

Bachman, John W. *Together in Hope: 50 Years of Lutheran World Relief.* Minneapolis: Kirk House Publishers, 1995.

Bachmann, E. Theodore. *The United Lutheran Church in America, 1918–1962.* Minneapolis: Fortress Press, 1997.

Bailey, Beth. *Sex in the Heartland.* Cambridge, MA: Harvard University Press, 1999.

Baritz, Loren. *Backfire: A History of How American Culture Led Us into Vietnam and Made Us Fight the Way We Did.* New York: William Morrow and Company, 1985.

Becker, Jasper. *Hungry Ghosts: Mao's Secret Famine.* New York: Free Press, 1996.

Bennett, David H. *The Party of Fear: The American Far Right from Nativism to the Militia Movement.* New York: Vintage Books, 1988.

Bentley, Eric, ed. *Thirty Years of Treason: Excerpts from Hearings before the House Committee on Un-American Activities, 1938–1968.* New York: Thunder's Mouth Press, 2002.

Bernstein, Carl, and Bob Woodward. *All the President's Men.* New York: Warner Books, 1974.

Beschloss, Michael R., ed. *Reaching for Glory: Lyndon Johnson's Secret White House Tapes, 1964–1965.* New York: Simon and Schuster, 2001.

——. *Taking Charge: The Johnson White House Tapes, 1963–1964.* New York: Simon and Schuster, 1997.

Bill, James A. *George Ball: Behind the Scenes in U.S. Foreign Policy.* New Haven, CT: Yale University Press, 1997.

Billingsley, Kenneth Lloyd. *Hollywood Party: How Communism Seduced the American Film Industry in the 1930s and 1940s.* Rocklin, CA: Forum Publishing, 1998.

Billingsley, William J. *Communists on Campus: Race, Politics, and the Public University in Sixties North Carolina.* Athens: University of Georgia Press, 1999.

Blumhofer, Edith L., ed. *Religion, Politics, and the American Experience: Reflections on Religion and American Public Life.* Tuscaloosa: University of Alabama Press, 2002.

Bodroghkozy, Aniko. *Groove Tube: Sixties Television and the Youth Rebellion.* Durham, NC: Duke University Press, 2001.

Borstelmann, Thomas. *Apartheid's Reluctant Uncle: The United States and Southern Africa in the Early Cold War.* New York: Oxford University Press, 1993.

Bowman, John S., ed. *The World Almanac of the Vietnam War.* New York: World Almanac, 1985.

Boyer, Paul. *By the Bomb's Early Light: American Thought and Culture at the Dawn of the Atomic Age.* Chapel Hill: University of North Carolina Press, 1985.

———. *Fallout: A Historian Reflects on America's Half-Century Encounter with Nuclear Weapons.* Columbus: Ohio State University Press, 1998.

———. *When Time Shall Be No More: Prophecy Belief in Modern American Culture.* Cambridge, MA: Harvard University Press, 1992.

Bradley, Mark Philip. *Imagining Vietnam and America: The Making of Postcolonial Vietnam, 1919–1950.* Chapel Hill: University of North Carolina Press, 2000.

Brands, H. W. *The Devil We Knew: Americans and the Cold War.* New York: Oxford University Press, 1993.

Brauer, Janice Kerper, ed. *One Cup of Water: Five True Stories of Missionary Women in China.* St. Louis: International Lutheran Women's Missionary League, 1997.

Braun, Mark E. *A Tale of Two Synods: Events That Led to the Split between Wisconsin and Missouri.* Milwaukee: Northwestern Publishing House, 2003.

Brennan, Mary C. *Turning Right in the Sixties: The Conservative Capture of the GOP.* Chapel Hill: University of North Carolina Press, 1995.

Brett, Edward T. *The U.S. Catholic Press on Central America: From Cold War Anticommunism to Social Justice.* Notre Dame: University of Notre Dame Press, 2003.

Brigham, Robert K. *Guerilla Diplomacy: The NLF's Foreign Relations and the Viet Nam War.* Ithaca, NY: Cornell University Press, 1999.

Broadwater, Jeff. *Eisenhower and the Anti-Communist Crusade.* Chapel Hill: University of North Carolina Press, 1992.

Brown, Judith M., and Rosemary Foot, eds. *Hong Kong's Transitions, 1842–1997.* New York: St. Martin's Press, 1997.

Buckingham, Peter H. *America Sees Red: Anticommunism in America, 1870s to 1980s.* Claremont, CA: Regina Books, 1988.

Bundy, William. *A Tangled Web: The Making of Foreign Policy in the Nixon Presidency.* New York: Hill and Wang, 1998.

Burgess, Andrew S., ed. *Lutheran Churches in the Third World.* Minneapolis: Augsburg Publishing House, 1970.

Burgess, John P. *The East German Church and the End of Communism.* New York: Oxford University Press, 1997.

Burns, Stewart. *Social Movements of the 1960s: Searching for Democracy.* New York: Twayne Publishers, 1990.

Buzzanco, Robert. *Masters of War: Military Dissent and Politics in the Vietnam Era.* Cambridge: Cambridge University Press, 1996.

———. *Vietnam and the Transformation of American Life.* Malden, MA: Blackwell Publishers, 1999.

Cahill, Lisa Sowle. *Love Your Enemies: Discipleship, Pacifism, and Just War Theory.* Minneapolis: Fortress Press, 1994.

Caplow, Theodore, Howard M. Bahr, John Modell, and Bruce A. Chadwick. *Recent Social Trends in the United States, 1960–1990.* Montreal: McGill-Queen's University Press, 1991.

Capps, Walter H. *The Unfinished War: Vietnam and the American Conscience.* Boston: Beacon Press, 1982.

Carlock, Chuck. *Firebirds: The Best First-Person Account of Helicopter Combat in Vietnam Ever Written.* Arlington, TX: The Summit Publishing Group, 1995.

Caro, Robert A. *The Years of Lyndon Johnson: The Path to Power.* New York: Alfred A. Knopf, 1982.

Carpenter, Joel A. *Revive Us Again: The Reawakening of American Fundamentalism*. New York: Oxford University Press, 1997.

Carroll, Peter N. *It Seemed Like Nothing Happened: America in the 1970s*. New Brunswick, NJ: Rutgers University Press, 1982.

Carter, Dan T. *The Politics of Rage: George Wallace, the Origins of the New Conservativism, and the Transformation of American Politics*. Baton Rouge: Louisiana State University Press, 2000.

Castile, George Pierre. *To Show Heart: Native American Self-Determination and Federal Indian Policy, 1960–1975*. Tucson: University of Arizonia Press, 1998.

Chadwick, Owen. *The Christian Church in the Cold War*. New York: Penguin Books, 1992.

Chalmers, David. *And the Crooked Places Made Straight: The Struggle for Social Change in the 1960s*. Baltimore: Johns Hopkins University Press, 1991.

Chambers, Whittaker. *Witness*. Washington, DC: Regenery Publishing, 1952.

Chang, Gordon H. *Friends and Enemies: The United States, China, and the Soviet Union, 1948–1972*. Stanford: Stanford University Press, 1990.

Chong, Denise. *The Girl in the Picture: The Story of Kim Phuc, the Photograph, and the Vietnam War*. New York: Viking Press, 1999.

Cimino, Richard, ed. *Lutherans Today: American Lutheran Identity in the 21st Century*. Grand Rapids, MI: William B. Eerdmans, 2003.

Cobb, William W., Jr. *The American Foundation Myth in Vietnam: Reigning Paradigms and Raining Bombs*. Lanham, MD: University Press of America, 1998.

Cone, James H. *Martin and Malcolm and America: A Dream or a Nightmare?* Maryknoll, NY: Orbis Books, 1991.

Corber, Robert J. *Homosexuality in Cold War America: Resistance and the Crisis of Masculinity*. Durham, NC: Duke University Press, 1997.

——. *In the Name of National Security: Hitchcock, Homophobia, and the Political Construction of Gender in Postwar America*. Durham, NC: Duke University Press, 1993.

Courtois, Stephane, et al. *The Black Book of Communism: Crimes, Terror, Repression*. Cambridge, MA: Harvard University Press, 1999.

Crowley, Monica. *Nixon in Winter: His Final Revelations about Diplomacy, Watergate, and Life out of the Arena*. New York: Random House, 1998.

Crozier, Brian. *The Rise and Fall of the Soviet Empire*. Rocklin, CA: Forum Publishing, 1999.

Cuibe, Leons. *The Lutheran Church of Latvia in Chains*. Stockholm: Vastmanlands Folkblads Tryckeri, 1963.

Curtin, Michael. *Redeeming the Wasteland: Television Documentary and Cold War Politics*. New Brunswick, NJ: Rutgers University Press, 1995.

D'Emilio, John. *Lost Prophet: The Life and Times of Bayard Rustin*. Chicago: University of Chicago Press, 2003.

——. *Sexual Politics, Sexual Communities: The Making of a Homosexual Minority in the United States, 1940–1970*. Chicago: University of Chicago Press, 1998.

Dallek, Robert. *Flawed Giant: Lyndon Johnson and His Times, 1961–1973*. New York: Oxford University Press, 1998.

——. *Lone Star Rising: Lyndon Johnson and His Times, 1908–1960*. New York: Oxford University Press, 1991.

Davidson, Phillip B. *Vietnam at War: The History, 1946–1975*. New York: Oxford University Press, 1988.

Davis, Nathaniel. *A Long Walk to Church: A Comtemporary History of Russian Orthodoxy*. Boulder, CO: Westview Press, 1995.

Dean, John W., III. *Blind Ambition: The White House Years*. New York: Simon and Schuster, 1976.

Dean, Robert. *Imperial Brotherhood: Gender and the Making of Cold War Foreign Policy.* Amherst: University of Massachusetts Press, 2001.

DeBenedetti, Charles, and Charles Chatfield. *An American Ordeal: The Antiwar Movement of the Vietnam Era.* Syracuse, NY: Syracuse University Press, 1990.

Deletant, Dennis. *Communist Terror in Romania: Gheorghiu-Dej and the Police State, 1948–1965.* New York: St. Martin's Press, 1999.

Di Leo, David L. *George Ball, Vietnam, and the Rethinking of Containment.* Chapel Hill: University of North Carolina Press, 1991.

Disno, Richard W. "American Lutheran Historiography: A Regional Approach." In The Lutheran Historical Conference, vol. 13 (1988), *American Lutheranism: Crisis in Historical Consciousness?* Minneapolis: Augsburg Publishing House, 1990.

Divine, Robert A. *The Sputnik Challenge: Eisenhower's Response to the Soviet Satellite.* New York: Oxford University Press, 1993.

Dower, John W. *War without Mercy: Race and Power in the Pacific War.* New York: Pantheon Books, 1986.

Drinnon, Richard. *Facing West: The Metaphysics of Indian-Hating and Empire-Building.* Norman: University of Oklahoma Press, 1997.

Dudziak, Mary L. *Cold War Civil Rights: Race and the Image of American Democracy.* Princeton, NJ: Princeton University Press, 2000.

Duiker, William J. *The Communist Road to Power in Vietnam.* 2nd Edition. Boulder, CO: Westview Press, 1996.

——. *Ho Chi Minh: A Life.* New York: Hyperion, 2000.

——. *Sacred War: Nationalism and Revolution in a Divided Vietnam.* New York: McGraw Hill, 1995.

——. *Vietnam: Revolution in Transition.* 2nd Edition. Boulder, CO: Westview Press, 1995.

Duin, Edgar C. *Lutheranism under the Tsars and the Soviets.* 2 vols. Ann Arbor, MI: Xerox University Microfilms, 1975.

Dyson, Michael Eric. *I May Not Get There with You: The True Martin Luther King, Jr.* New York: Simon and Schuster, 2000.

Ehrhart, W. D. *Passing Time: Memoir of a Vietnam Veteran against the War.* Jefferson, NC: McFarland, 1986.

Ehrlichman, John. *Witness to Power: The Nixon Years.* New York: Simon and Schuster, 1982.

Ellwood, Robert S. *The Sixties Spiritual Awakening: American Religion Moving from Modern to Postmodern.* New Brunswick, NJ: Rutgers University Press, 1994.

Elshtain, Jean Bethke, ed. *Just War Theory.* New York: New York University Press, 1992.

Emerson, Gloria. *Winners and Losers: Battles, Retreats, Gains, Losses and Ruins from the Vietnam War.* New York: Harcourt Brace Jovanovich, 1976.

Emery, Fred. *Watergate: The Corruption of American Politics and the Fall of Richard Nixon.* New York: Times Books, 1994.

Engelhardt, Tom. *The End of Victory Culture: Cold War America and the Disillusioning of a Generation.* New York: Basic Books, 1995.

Enloe, Cynthia. *Bananas, Beaches, and Bases: Making Feminist Sense of International Politics.* Berkeley: University of California Press, 1990.

Fadiman, Anne. *The Spirit Catches You and You Fall Down: A Hmong Child, Her American Doctors, and the Collision of Two Cultures.* New York: Farrar, Straus, and Giroux, 1997.

Fairbank, John K., and Edwin O. Reischauer. *China: Tradition and Transformation.* Revised ed. Boston: Houghton Mifflin, 1989.

Fariello, Griffin. *Red Scare: Memories of the American Inquisition.* New York: Avon Books, 1995.

Fernlund, Kevin J., ed. *The Cold War American West, 1945–1989*. Albuquerque: University of New Mexico Press, 1998.

Field, Hermann, and Kate Field. *Trapped in the Cold War: The Ordeal of an American Family*. Stanford: Stanford University Press, 1999.

Findlay, James F., Jr. *Church People in the Struggle: The National Council of Churches and the Black Freedom Movement, 1950–1970*. New York: Oxford University Press, 1993.

Finke, Roger, and Rodney Starks. *The Churching of America, 1776–1990: Winners and Losers in Our Religious Economy*. New Brunswick, NJ: Rutgers University Press, 1992.

Fitzgerald, Frances. *Fire in the Lake: The Vietnamese and the Americans in Vietnam*. New York: Vintage Books, 1972.

Flynn, George Q. *The Draft, 1940–1973*. Lawrence: University Press of Kansas, 1993.

Fogelsong, David S. *America's Secret War against Bolshevism: U.S. Intervention in the Russian Civil War, 1917–1920*. Chapel Hill: University of North Carolina Press, 1995.

Foley, Michael S. *Confronting the War Machine: Draft Resistance during the Vietnam War*. Chapel Hill: University of North Carolina Press, 2003.

Fousek, John. *To Lead the Free World: American Nationalism and the Cultural Roots of the Cold War*. Chapel Hill: University of North Carolina Press, 2000.

Fowler, Robert Booth. *A New Engagement: Evangelical Political Thought, 1966–1976*. Grand Rapids, MI: William B. Eerdmans, 1982.

Fox, Richard W. *Jesus in America: Personal Savior, Cultural Hero, National Obsession*. San Francisco: HarperCollins Publishers, 2005.

Franklin, H. Bruce. *M.I.A. or Mythmaking in America: How and Why Belief in Live POWs Has Possessed a Nation*. New York: Lawrence Hill Books, 1992.

Freedman, Lawrence. *Kennedy's Wars: Berlin, Cuba, Laos, and Vietnam*. New York: Oxford University Press, 2000.

Fried, Richard M. *The Russians Are Coming! The Russians Are Coming! Pageantry and Patriotism in Cold-War America*. New York: Oxford University Press, 1998.

Friedland, Michael Brooks. *Lift Up Your Voice Like a Trumpet: White Clergy and the Civil Rights and Antiwar Movements, 1954–1973*. Chapel Hill: University of North Carolina Press, 1998.

Fursenko, Aleksandr, and Timothy Naftali. *One Hell of a Gamble: Krushchev, Castro, Kennedy and the Cuban Missile Crisis, 1958–1964*. London: Pimlico, 1999.

Gaddis, John Lewis. "The Emerging Post-Revisionist Synthesis on the Origins of the Cold War." *Diplomatic History* 7 (Summer 1983): 171–204.

———. *Strategies of Containment: A Critical Appraisal of Postwar American National Security Policy*. New York: Oxford University Press, 1982.

Gaiduk, Ilya. *The Soviet Union and the Vietnam War*. Chicago: Ivan R. Dee, 1996.

Galchutt, Kathryn M. *The Career of Andrew Schulze, 1924–1968: Lutherans and Race in the Civil Rights Era*. Macon, GA: Mercer University Press, 2005.

Garber, Majorie, and Rebecca L. Walkowitz, eds. *Secret Agents: The Rosenberg Case, McCarthyism, and Fifties America*. New York: Routledge, 1995.

Gardner, Lloyd C. *Pay Any Price: Lyndon Johnson and the Wars for Vietnam*. Chicago: Ivan R. Dee, 1995.

Garfinkle, Adam. *Telltale Hearts: The Origins and Impact of the Vietnam Antiwar Movement*. New York: St. Martins Press, 1995.

Garrow, David J. *The FBI and Martin Luther King, Jr.: From Solo to Memphis*. New York: W. W. Norton, 1981.

Gibson, James William. *The Perfect War: The War We Couldn't Lose and How We Did*. New York: Vintage Books, 1986.

――. *Warrior Dreams: Violence and Manhood in Post-Vietnam America*. New York: Hill and Wang, 1994.

Gilbert, James. *Another Chance: Postwar America, 1945–1985*. Belmont, CA: Wadsworth Publishing Company, 1981.

――. *Redeeming Culture: American Religion in an Age of Science*. Chicago: University of Chicago Press, 1997.

Gilbert, W. Kent. *Commitment to Unity: A History of the Lutheran Church in America*. Philadelphia: Fortress Press, 1988.

Gill, Jill Kristine. "'Peace Is Not the Absence of War but the Presence of Justice': The National Council of Churches' Reaction and Response to the Vietnam War, 1965–1972." Ph.D. diss., University of Pennsylvania, 1996.

Gitlin, Todd. *The Sixties: Years of Hope, Days of Rage*. New York: Bantam Books, 1987.

Glendon, Mary Ann. *A World Made New: Eleanor Roosevelt and the Universal Declaration of Human Rights*. New York: Random House, 2001.

Gordon, William A. *The Fourth of May: Killings and Coverups at Kent State*. Buffalo, NY: Prometheus Books, 1990.

Gottlieb, Annie. *Do You Believe in Magic: The Second Coming of the 60's Generation*. New York: Time Books, 1987.

Graebner, Alan. *Uncertain Saints: The Laity in the Lutheran Church–Missouri Synod, 1900–1970*. Westport, CT: Greenwood Press, 1975.

Greenberg, David. *Nixon's Shadow: The History of an Image*. New York: W. W. Norton and Company, 2003.

Greene, Graham. *The Quiet American*. New York: Penguin Books, 1973.

Griffith, Robert. *The Politics of Fear: Joseph R. McCarthy and the Senate*. Amherst: University of Massachusetts Press, 1970.

Gritsch, Eric W. *Fortress Introduction to Lutheranism*. Minneapolis: Fortress Press, 1994.

Gritsch, Eric W., and Robert W. Jenson. *Lutheranism: The Theological Movement and Its Confessional Writings*. Philadelphia: Fortress Press, 1976.

Guth, James L., John C. Green, Corwin E. Smidt, Lyman A. Kellstedt, and Margaret M. Poloma. *The Bully Pulpit: The Politics of Protestant Clergy*. Lawrence: University Press of Kansas, 1997.

Hagan, John. *Northern Passage: American Vietnam War Resisters in Canada*. Cambridge, MA: Harvard University Press, 2001.

Hahn, Peter L., and Mary Ann Heiss, eds. *Empire and Revolution: The United States and the Third World since 1945*. Columbus: Ohio State University Press, 2001.

Halberstam, David. *Ho*. New York: Vintage Books, 1971.

Haldeman, H. R. *The Haldeman Diaries: Inside the Nixon White House*. New York: G. P. Putnam's Sons, 1994.

Hall, Mitchell K. *Because of Their Faith: CALCAV and Religious Opposition to the Vietnam War*. New York: Columbia University Press, 1990.

――. *Crossroads: American Popular Culture and the Vietnam Generation*. Lanham, MD: Rowman and Littlefield Publishers, 2005.

Hallin, Daniel C. *The "Uncensored War": The Media and Vietnam*. Berkeley: University of California Press, 1986.

Hamilton, Michael P. *The Vietnam War: Christian Perspectives*. Grand Rapids, MI: William B. Eerdmans, 1967.

Hammond, William M. *Public Affairs: The Military and the Media*. Washington, DC: Center of Military History, United States Army, 1988.

――. *Reporting Vietnam: Media and Military at War*. Lawrence: University of Kansas Press, 1998.

Hart, D. G. *That Old-Time Religion in Modern America: Evangelical Protestantism in the Twentieth Century*. Chicago: Ivan R. Dee, 2002.

Heale, M. J. *American Anticommunism: Combating the Enemy Within, 1830–1970*. Baltimore: Johns Hopkins University Press, 1990.

Heineman, Kenneth J. *Campus Wars: The Peace Movement at American State Universities in the Vietnam Era*. New York: New York University Press, 1993.

Heiss, Mary Ann. *Empire and Nationhood: The United States, Great Britain, and Iranian Oil, 1950–1954*. New York: Columbia University Press, 1997.

Henriksen, Margot A. *Dr. Strangelove's America: Society and Culture in the Atomic Age*. Berkeley: University of California Press, 1997.

Herman, Arthur. *Joseph McCarthy: Reexamining the Life and Legacy of America's Most Hated Senator*. New York: Free Press, 2000.

Herr, Michael. *Dispatches*. New York: Vintage Books, 1968.

Herring, George C. *America's Longest War: The United States and Vietnam, 1950–1975*. New York: Wiley, 1979.

Hess, Gary R. "The Unending Debate: Historians and the Vietnam War." In Michael J. Hogan, ed., *America in the World: The Historiography of American Foreign Relations since 1941*. Cambridge: Cambridge University Press, 1995.

Hixson, Walter L. *Parting the Curtain: Propaganda, Culture, and the Cold War, 1945–1961*. New York: St. Martin's Press, 1998.

Hoffman, Oswald C. J., and Ronald J. Schlegel. *What More Is There to Say but Amen: The Autobiography of Dr. Oswald C. J. Hoffmann*. St. Louis: Concordia Publishing House, 1996.

Holm, Tom. *Strong Hearts, Wounded Souls: Native American Veterans of the Vietnam War*. Austin: University of Texas Press, 1996.

Holy Bible. Revised Standard Version. New York: American Bible Society, 1971.

Horne, Gerald. *Black Liberation/Red Scare: Ben Davis and the Communist Party*. Newark: University of Delaware Press, 1994.

———. *Class Struggle in Hollywood, 1930–1950: Moguls, Mobsters, Stars, Reds, and Trade Unionists*. Austin: University of Texas Press, 2001.

———. *Fire This Time: The Watts Uprising and the 1960s*. Charlottesville: University Press of Virginia, 1995.

Howard, Gerald, ed. *The Sixties: The Art, Attitudes, Politics, and Media of Our Most Explosive Decade*. New York: Marlowe and Company, 1995.

Huchthausen, Peter. *K-19: The Widowmaker: The Secret Story of the Soviet Nuclear Submarine*. Washington, DC: National Geographic Society, 2002.

Hudnut-Beumler, James. *Looking for God in the Suburbs: The Religion of the American Dream and Its Critics, 1945–1965*. New Brunswick, NJ: Rutgers University Press, 1994.

Hulsether, Mark David. *Building a Protestant Left: Christianity and Crisis Magazine, 1941–1993*. Knoxville: University of Tennessee Press, 1999.

———. "Liberals, Radicals, and the Contested Social Thought of Postwar Protestantism: 'Christianity and Crisis' Magazine, 1941–1976." Ph.D. diss., University of Minnesota, 1992.

Hunt, Andrew E. *The Turning: A History of Vietnam Veterans against the War*. New York: New York University Press, 1999.

Hunt, Michael H. *Crises in U.S. Foreign Policy: An International History Reader*. New Haven, CT: Yale University Press, 1996.

———. *Ideology and U.S. Foreign Policy*. New Haven, CT: Yale University Press, 1987.

———. *Lyndon Johnson's War: America's Cold War Crusade in Vietnam, 1945–1968*. New York: Hill and Wang, 1996.

Hunt, Richard A. *Pacification: The American Struggle for Vietnam's Hearts and Minds*. Boulder, CO: Westview Press, 1995.

Hunter, James Davison. *American Evangelicalism: Conservative Religion and the Quandary of Modernity*. New Brunswick, NJ: Rutgers University Press, 1983.

Hunter, Jane. *The Gospel of Gentility: American Women Missionaries in Turn-of-the-Century China*. New Haven, CT: Yale University Press, 1984.

Hutchinson, Earl Ofari. *Blacks and Reds: Race and Class in Conflict, 1919–1990*. East Lansing: Michigan State University Press, 1995.

Hutchison, William R., ed. *Between the Times: The Travail of the Protestant Establishment in America, 1900–1960*. Cambridge: Cambridge University Press, 1989.

———. *Errand to the World: American Protestant Thought and Foreign Missions*. Chicago: University of Chicago Press, 1987.

Inglis, Fred. *The Cruel Peace: Everyday Life and the Cold War*. New York: Basic Books, 1991.

Iriye, Akira. "Western Perceptions and Asian Realities." *The Harmon Memorial Lectures in Military History*. United States Air Force Academy, 1981, 1–15.

Isaacs, Arnold R. *Vietnam Shadows: The War, Its Ghosts, and Its Legacy*. Baltimore: Johns Hopkins University Press, 1997.

Jacobs, Seth. "'Our System Demands the Supreme Being': The U.S. Religious Revival and the 'Diem Experiment,' 1954–55." *Diplomatic History* 25 (Fall 2001): 589–624.

Jeffords, Susan. *The Remasculinization of America: Gender and the Vietnam War*. Bloomington: Indiana University Press, 1989.

Jeffreys-Jones, Rhodri. *Changing Differences: Women and the Shaping of American Foreign Policy, 1917–1994*. New Brunswick, NJ: Rutgers University Press, 1995.

———. *Peace Now! American Society and the Ending of the Vietnam War*. New Haven, CT: Yale University Press, 1999.

Jenkins, Philip. *Cold War at Home: The Red Scare in Pennsylvania, 1945–1960*. Chapel Hill: University of North Carolina Press, 1999.

Jespersen, T. Christopher. *American Images of China, 1931–1949*. Stanford: Stanford University Press, 1996.

Jian, Chen. *Mao's China and the Cold War*. Chapel Hill: University of North Carolina Press, 2001.

Johnson, James Turner. *The Holy War Idea in Western and Islamic Traditions*. University Park: Pennsylvania State University Press, 1997.

Johnson, Jeff G. *Black Christians: The Untold Lutheran Story*. St. Louis: Concordia Publishing House, 1991.

Jones, Howard. *Death of a Generation: How the Assassinations of Diem and JFK Prolonged the Vietnam War*. New York: Oxford University Press, 2003.

Jones, Howard, and Randall B. Woods. "The Origins of the Cold War: A Symposium." *Diplomatic History* 17 (Spring 1993): 251–310.

Kaplan, Amy, and Donald E. Pease, eds. *Cultures of United States Imperialism*. Durham, NC: Duke University Press, 1993.

Kent, Stephen A. *From Slogans to Mantras: Social Protest and Religious Conversion in the Late Vietnam War Era*. Syracuse, NY: Syracuse University Press, 2001.

Kersten, Lawrence L. *The Lutheran Ethic: The Impact of Religion on Laymen and Clergy*. Detroit: Wayne State University Press, 1970.

Kessler, Lawrence D. *The Jiangyin Mission Station: An American Missionary Community in China, 1895–1951*. Chapel Hill: University of North Carolina Press, 1996.

Kimball, Jeffrey. *Nixon's Vietnam War*. Lawrence: University Press of Kansas, 1998.

Kirby Dianne, ed. *Religion and the Cold War*. New York: Palgrave Macmillan, 2003.

Kissinger, Henry. *White House Years*. Boston: Little, Brown and Company, 1979.

——. *Years of Upheaval*. Boston: Little, Brown and Company, 1982.

Kittelson, James M. *Luther the Reformer: The Story of the Man and His Career*. Minneapolis: Augsburg Publishing House, 1986.

Klehr, Harvey, and John Earl Haynes. *Venona: Decoding Soviet Espionage in America*. New Haven, CT: Yale University Press, 1999.

Klehr, Harvey, John Earl Haynes, and Kyrill M. Anderson. *The Soviet World of American Communism*. New Haven, CT: Yale University Press, 1998.

Klehr, Harvey, John Earl Haynes, and Fridrikh Igorevich Firsov. *The Secret World of American Communism*. New Haven, CT: Yale University Press, 1995.

Klein, Christa R. *Politics and Policy: The Genesis and Theology of Social Statements in the Lutheran Church in America*. Minneapolis: Fortress Press, 1989.

Kotlowski, Dean J. *Nixon's Civil Rights: Politics, Principle, and Policy*. Cambridge, MA: Harvard University Press, 2001.

Kovel, Joel. *Red Hunting in the Promised Land: Anticommunism and the Making of America*. New York: Basic Books, 1994.

Krenn, Michael L. *Black Diplomacy: African Americans and the State Department, 1945–1969*. London: M. E. Sharpe, 1999.

Kuisel, Richard F. *Seducing the French: The Dilemma of Americanization*. Berkeley: University of California Press, 1993.

Kutler, Stanley I., ed. *Abuse of Power: The New Nixon Tapes*. New York: Touchstone Books, 1997.

——. *The Wars of Watergate: The Last Crisis of Richard Nixon*. New York: Alfred A. Knopf, 1990.

Kuznick, Peter J., and James Gilbert, eds. *Rethinking Cold War Culture*. Washington, DC: Smithsonian Institution Press, 2001.

LaFeber, Walter. *America, Russia, and the Cold War, 1945–1966*. New York: Wiley, 1967.

Lagerquist, L. DeAne. *From Our Mothers' Arms: A History of Women in the American Lutheran Church*. Minneapolis: Augsburg Publishing House, 1987.

——. *The Lutherans*. Westport, CT: Greenwood Press, 1999.

Landers, James. *The Weekly War: Newsmagazines and Vietnam*. Columbia: University of Missouri Press, 2004.

Larson, Deborah Welch. *Anatomy of Mistrust: U.S.-Soviet Relations during the Cold War*. Ithaca, NY: Cornell University Press, 1997.

Lasch, Christopher. *The Culture of Narcissism: American Life in an Age of Diminishing Expectations*. New York: W. W. Norton and Company, 1979.

Layton, Azza Salama. *International Politics and Civil Rights Policies in the United States, 1941–1960*. Cambridge: Cambridge University Press, 2000.

Leab, Daniel J. *I Was a Communist for the FBI: The Unhappy Life and Times of Matt Cvetic*. University Park: Pennsylvania State University Press, 2000.

Lederer, William J., and Eugene Burdick. *The Ugly American*. New York: W. W. Norton and Company, 1965.

Lee, J. Edward, and Toby Haynsworth, eds. *White Christmas in April: The Collapse of South Vietnam, 1975*. New York: Peter Lang, 1999.

Leffler, Melvyn P. "The Cold War: What Do 'We Now Know'?" *American Historical Review* 104 (April 1999): 501–24.

——. *A Preponderance of Power: National Security, the Truman Administration, and the Cold War*. Stanford: Stanford University Press, 1992.

Levang, Joseph H. *The Church of the Lutheran Brethren, 1900–1975: A Believers' Fellowship— A Lutheran Alternative.* Fergus Falls, MN: Lutheran Brethren Publishing Company, 1980.

Levine, Daniel. *Bayard Rustin and the Civil Rights Movement.* New Brunswick, NJ: Rutgers University Press, 2000.

Levy, David W. *The Debate over Vietnam.* Baltimore: Johns Hopkins University Press, 1991.

Lewis, Lionel S. *Cold War on Campus: A Study of the Politics of Organizational Control.* New Brunswick, NJ: Transaction Publishers, 1988.

Lieberman, Robbie. *The Strangest Dream: Communism, Anticommunism, and the U.S. Peace Movement, 1945–1963.* Syracuse, NY: Syracuse University Press, 2000.

Lockhart, Greg. *Nation in Arms: The Origins of the People's Army of Vietnam.* Wellington, New Zealand: Allen and Unwin, 1989.

Lodwick, Kathleen L. *Crusaders against Opium: Protestant Missionaries in China, 1874–1917.* Lexington: University Press of Kentucky, 1996.

Logevall, Fredrik. *Choosing War: The Lost Chance for Peace and the Escalation of War in Vietnam.* Berkeley: University of California Press, 1999.

Lorence, James J. *The Suppression of Salt of the Earth: How Hollywood, Big Labor, and Politicians Blacklisted a Movie in Cold War America.* Albuquerque: University of New Mexico Press, 1999.

Lowe, Peter, ed. *The Vietnam War.* New York: St. Martin's Press, 1998.

Lucas, Scott. *Freedom's War: The American Crusade against the Soviet Union.* New York: New York University Press, 1999.

Lutherans and Catholics in Dialogue: Eucharist and Ministry. IV. New York: U.S.A. National Committee of the Lutheran World Federation and the Bishops' Committee for Ecumenical and Interreligious Affairs, 1970.

Lutz, Catherine A., and Jane L. Collins. *Reading National Geographic.* Chicago: University of Chicago Press, 1993.

Lutz, Charles P., ed. *Church Roots: Stories of Nine Immigrant Groups that Became the American Lutheran Church.* Minneapolis: Augsburg Publishing House, 1985.

———. *Loving Neighbors Far and Near: U.S. Lutherans Respond to a Hungry World.* Minneapolis: Augsburg Fortress Press, 1994.

MacPherson, Myra. *Long Time Passing: Vietnam and the Haunted Generation.* New York: Anchor Books, 1984.

Mann, Robert. *A Grand Delusion: America's Descent into Vietnam.* New York: Basic Books, 2001.

Maraniss, David. *They Marched into Sunlight: War and Peace, Vietnam and America, October 1967.* New York: Simon and Schuster, 2003.

Marsden, George M. *Fundamentalism and American Culture: The Shaping of Twentieth-Century Evangelicalism, 1870–1925.* New York: Oxford University Press, 1980.

———. *Religion and American Culture.* New York: Harcourt Brace College Publishers, 1990.

Marty, Martin E. *Modern American Religion*, vol. 3, *Under God, Indivisible, 1941–1960.* Chicago: University of Chicago Press, 1996.

———. *Pilgrims in Their Own Land: 500 Years of Religion in America.* New York: Penguin Books, 1984.

Mason, Katrina R. *Children of Los Alamos: An Oral History of the Town Where the Atomic Age Began.* New York: Twayne Publishers, 1995.

Mastny, Vojtech. *The Cold War and Soviet Insecurity: The Stalin Years.* New York: Oxford University Press, 1996.

Matusow, Allen J. *Nixon's Economy: Booms, Busts, Dollars, and Votes.* Lawrence: University Press of Kansas, 1998.

————. *The Unraveling of America: A History of Liberalism in the 1960s*. New York: Harper and Row, 1984.

May, Elaine Tyler. *Homeward Bound: American Families in the Cold War Era*. New York: Basic Books, 1988.

McCormick, Thomas J. *America's Half-Century: United States Foreign Policy in the Cold War*. Baltimore: Johns Hopkins University Press, 1989.

McEnaney, Laura. *Civil Defense Begins at Home: Militarization Meets Everyday Life in the Fifties*. Princeton, NJ: Princeton University Press, 2000.

McGirr, Lisa. *Suburban Warriors: The Origins of the New American Right*. Princeton, NJ: Princeton University Press, 2001.

McKnight, Gerald D. *The Last Crusade: Martin Luther King, Jr., the FBI, and the Poor People's Campaign*. Boulder, CO: Westview Press, 1998.

McMahon, Robert J. *The Limits of Empire: The United States and Southeast Asia since World War II*. New York: Columbia University Press, 1999.

McManners, John, ed. *The Oxford History of Christianity*. New York: Oxford University Press, 1993.

McMaster, H. R. *Dereliction of Duty: Lyndon Johnson, Robert McNamara, the Joint Chiefs of Staff, and the Lies that Led to Vietnam*. New York: HarperPerennial, 1997.

McNamara, Robert S. *In Retrospect: The Tragedy and Lessons of Vietnam*. New York: Random House Books, 1995.

McNamara, Robert S., James G. Blight, and Robert K. Brigham. *Argument without End: In Search of Answers to the Vietnam Tragedy*. New York: PublicAffairs, 1999.

McNeal, Patricia. *Harder Than War: Catholic Peacemaking in Twentieth-Century America*. New Brunswick, NJ: Rutgers University Press, 1992.

Mead, Frank S., revised by Samuel S. Hill. "Lutheran." *Handbook of Denominations in the United States*. Nashville, TN: Abingdon Press, 1995.

Meyerowitz, Joanne, ed. *Not June Cleaver: Women and Gender in Postwar America, 1945–1960*. Philadelphia: Temple University Press, 1994.

Michener, James A. *Kent State: What Happened and Why*. New York: Random House, 1971.

Mieczkowski, Yanek. *Gerald Ford and the Challenges of the 1970s*. Lexington: University Press of Kentucky, 2005.

Miller, Douglas T. *On Our Own: Americans in the Sixties*. Lexington, MA: D. C. Heath and Company, 1996.

Miller, Richard B. *Interpretations of Conflict: Ethics, Pacifism, and the Just-War Tradition*. Chicago: University of Chicago Press, 1991.

Miller, Timothy. *The 60s Commune: Hippies and Beyond*. Syracuse, NY: Syracuse University Press, 1999.

Mishler, Paul C. *Raising Reds: The Young Pioneers, Radical Summer Camps, and Communist Political Culture in the United States*. New York: Columbia University Press, 1999.

Mitchell, Greg. *Tricky Dick and the Pink Lady: Richard Nixon vs. Helen Gahagan Douglas— Sexual Politics and the Red Scare, 1950*. New York: Random House, 1998.

Moise, Edwin E. *Tonkin Gulf and the Escalation of the Vietnam War*. Chapel Hill: University of North Carolina Press, 1996.

Mooney, James W., and Thomas R. West, eds. *Vietnam: A History and Anthology*. St. James, NY: Brandywine Press, 1994.

Moore, Barrington, Jr. *Moral Purity and Persecution in History*. Princeton, NJ: Princeton University Press, 2000.

Morgan, Joseph G. *The Vietnam Lobby: The American Friends of Vietnam, 1955–1975*. Chapel Hill: University of North Carolina Press, 1997.

Moser, Richard. *The New Winter Soldiers: GI and Veteran Dissent during the Vietnam Era*. New Brunswick, NJ: Rutgers University Press, 1996.

Nadel, Alan. *Containment Culture: American Narratives, Postmodernism, and the Atomic Age*. Durham, NC: Duke University Press, 1995.

Nash, Philip. *The Other Missiles of October: Eisenhower, Kennedy, and the Jupiters, 1955–1963*. Chapel Hill: University of North Carolina Press, 1997.

Nelson, E. Clifford, ed. *The Lutherans in North America*. Philadelphia: Fortress Press, 1975.

Nelson, Keith L. *The Making of Détente: Soviet-American Relations in the Shadow of Vietnam*. Baltimore: Johns Hopkins University Press, 1995.

Neu, Charles E., ed. *After Vietnam: Legacies of a Lost War*. Baltimore: Johns Hopkins University Press, 2000.

Nhu Tang, Truong. *A Viet Cong Memoir*. New York: Vintage Books, 1985.

Nicosia, Gerald. *Home to War: A History of the Vietnam Veterans' Movement*. New York: Crown Publishing, 2001.

Ninkovich, Frank. *Modernity and Power: A History of the Domino Theory in the Twentieth Century*. Chicago: University of Chicago Press, 1994.

Noell, Chuck, and Gary Wood. *We Are All POWs*. Philadelphia: Fortress Press, 1975.

Noll, Mark A. *A History of Christianity in the United States and Canada*. Grand Rapids, MI: William B. Eerdmans, 1992.

O'Neill, Dan. *The Firecracker Boys*. New York: St. Martin's Press, 1994.

O'Neill, William L. *Coming Apart: An Informal History of America in the 1960s*. New York: Random House, 1971.

O'Reilly, Kenneth. *"Racial Matters": The FBI's Secret File on Black America, 1960–1972*. New York: Free Press, 1989.

Oakes, Guy. *The Imaginary War: Civil Defense and American Cold War Culture*. New York: Oxford University Press, 1994.

Olson, Gregory A. *Mansfield and Vietnam: A Study of Rhetorical Adaptation*. East Lansing: Michigan State University Press, 1995.

Oppenheimer, Mark. *Knocking on Heaven's Door: American Religion in the Age of the Counterculture*. New Haven, CT: Yale University Press, 2003.

Oshinsky, David M. *A Conspiracy So Immense: The World of Joe McCarthy*. New York: Free Press, 1983.

Oudes, Bruce, ed. *From The President: Richard Nixon's Secret Files*. New York: Harper and Row, 1989.

Pahl, Jon. *Hopes and Dreams of All: The International Walther League and Lutheran Youth in American Culture, 1893–1993*. Chicago: Wheat Ridge Ministries, 1993.

———. *Youth Ministry in Modern America: 1930 to the Present*. Peabody, MA: Hendrickson Publishers, 2000.

Pankow, Fred, and Edith Pankow. *75 Years of Blessings and the Best Is Yet to Come! A History of the International Lutheran Laymen's League*. St. Louis: International Lutheran Laymen's League, 1992.

Partner, Peter. *God of Battles: Holy Wars of Christianity and Islam*. Princeton, NJ: Princeton University Press, 1997.

Paterson, Thomas G. *Meeting the Communist Threat: Truman to Reagan*. New York: Oxford University Press, 1988.

Pells, Richard H. *The Liberal Mind in a Conservative Age: American Intellectuals in the 1940s and 1950s*. New York: Harper and Row, 1985.

Perlstein, Rick. *Before the Storm: Barry Goldwater and the Unmaking of the American Consensus*. New York: Hill and Wang, 2001.

Pierard, Richard. "Billy Graham and Vietnam: From Cold Warrior to Peacemaker." *Christian Scholars Review* 10 (1980): 37–51.

Pinn, Anne H., and Anthony B. Pinn. *Fortress Introduction to Black Church History*. Minneapolis: Fortress Press, 2002.

Plummer, Brenda Gayle. *Rising Wind: Black Americans and U.S. Foreign Affairs, 1935–1960*. Chapel Hill: University of North Carolina Press, 1996.

Porterfield, Amanda. *The Transformation of American Religion: The Story of a Late-Twentieth-Century Awakening*. New York: Oxford University Press, 2001.

Pospielovsky, Dimitry. *The Russian Church under the Soviet Regime, 1917–1982*. 2 vols. Crestwood, NY: St. Vladimir's Seminary Press, 1984.

Powers, Richard Gid. *Not without Honor: The History of American Anticommunism*. New York: Free Press, 1995.

Preston, William, Jr. *Aliens and Dissenters: Federal Suppression of Radicals, 1903–1933*. Urbana: University of Illinois Press, 1963.

Rabe, Stephen G. *The Most Dangerous Area of the World: John F. Kennedy Confronts Communist Revolution in Latin America*. Chapel Hill: University of North Carolina Press, 1999.

Ramirez, Juan. *A Patriot after All: The Story of a Chicano Vietnam Vet*. Albuquerque: University of New Mexico Press, 1999.

Redal, Rueben H., and Paul G. Vigness. *The Rape of a Confessional Church: The Story of the Excommunication of Central Lutheran Church, Tacoma, Washington by the American Lutheran Church*. Tacoma, WA: Elmer F. Groshong and Associates, 1981.

Reeves, Richard. *President Kennedy: Profile of Power*. New York: Simon and Schuster, 1993.

——. *President Nixon: Alone in the White House*. New York: Simon and Schuster, 2001.

Reinitz, Richard. *Irony and Consciousness: American Historiography and Reinhold Niebuhr's Vision*. Lewisburg: Bucknell University Press, 1980.

Rhodes, Richard. *Dark Sun: The Making of the Hydrogen Bomb*. New York: Simon and Schuster Publishers, 1995.

——. *The Making of the Atomic Bomb*. New York: Touchstone Books, 1986.

Robert, Dana L. "From Missions to Mission to Beyond Missions: The Historiography of American Protestant Foreign Missions since World War II." In Harry S. Stout and D. G. Hart, eds., *New Directions in American Religious History*. New York: Oxford University Press, 1997.

Robin, Ron. *The Making of the Cold War Enemy: Culture and Politics in the Military-Intellectual Complex*. Princeton, NJ: Princeton University Press, 2001.

Rochester, Stuart I., and Frederick Kiley. *Honor Bound: American Prisoners of War in Southeast Asia, 1961–1973*. Annapolis: Naval Institute Press, 1999.

Roof, Wade Clark, and William McKinney. *American Mainline Religion: Its Changing Shape and Future*. New Brunswick, NJ: Rutgers University Press, 1987.

Rorabaugh, W. J. *Berkeley at War: The 1960s*. New York: Oxford University Press, 1989.

Rose, Kenneth D. *One Nation Underground: The Fallout Shelter in American Culture*. New York: New York University Press, 2001.

Rose, Lisle A. *The Cold War Comes to Main Street: America in 1950*. Lawrence: University Press of Kansas, 1999.

Rotter, Andrew J. "Christians, Muslims, and Hindus: Religion and U.S.-South Asian Relations, 1947–1954." *Diplomatic History* 24 (Fall 2000): 593–640 (with commentary by Robert Dean, Robert Buzzanco, and Patricia R. Hill).

——. *Comrades at Odds: The United States and India, 1947–1964*. Ithaca, NY: Cornell University Press, 2000.

——. *The Path to Vietnam: Origins of the American Commitment to Southeast Asia*. Ithaca, NY: Cornell University Press, 1987.

Rowe, John Carlos, and Rick Berg, eds. *The Vietnam War and American Culture*. New York: Columbia University Press, 1991.

Said, Edward W. *Culture and Imperialism*. New York: Vintage Books, 1994.

———. *Orientalism*. New York: Vintage Books, 1978.

Sarotte, M. E. *Dealing with the Devil: East Germany, Détente, and Ostpolitik, 1969–1973*. Chapel Hill: University of North Carolina Press, 2001.

Saunders, Frances Stonor. *The Cultural Cold War: The CIA and the World of Arts and Letters*. New York: New Press, 1999.

Schmidt, Jean Miller. *Souls or the Social Order: The Two-Party System in American Protestantism*. New York: Carlson Publishing, Inc., 1991.

Schmitz, David F. *Thank God They're on Our Side: The United States and Right-Wing Dictatorships, 1921–1965*. Chapel Hill: University of North Carolina Press, 1999.

Schoenwald, Jonathan M. *A Time for Choosing: The Rise of Modern American Conservatism*. New York: Oxford University Press, 2001.

Schrecker, Ellen. *Many Are the Crimes: McCarthyism in America*. Boston: Little, Brown and Company, 1998.

Schroeder, Steven. *A Community and a Perspective: Lutheran Peace Fellowship and the Edge of the Church, 1941–1991*. Lanham, MD: University Press of America, 1993.

Schulman, Bruce J. *Lyndon B. Johnson and American Liberalism: A Brief Biography with Documents*. New York: St. Martin's Press, 1995.

Schultz, Richard H., Jr. *The Secret War against Hanoi: Kennedy's and Johnson's Use of Spies, Saboteurs, and Covert Warriors in North Vietnam*. New York: HarperCollins Publishers, 1999.

Schultze, Quentin J. *Christianity and the Mass Media in America: Toward a Democratic Accomodation*. East Lansing: Michigan State University Press, 2003.

Schulzinger, Robert D. *A Time for War: The United States and Vietnam, 1941–1975*. New York: Oxford University Press, 1997.

Scott, Joan Wallach. *Gender and the Politics of History*. New York: Columbia University Press, 1988.

Settje, David E. "Has the Tiger Changed Its Stripes? Lutheran Responeses to the Cold War, Fears of Internal Communist Threats, and the Vietnam War, 1964–1975." Ph.D. diss., Kent State University, 2001.

———. "A Historian's View of Current Ethics: Vietnam and Iraq Compared." *Journal of Lutheran Ethics* 4 (August 2004), www.elca.org/scriptlib/dcs/jle/article.asp?aid=338.

———. "Justifiable War or an Offense to the Conscience? Lutheran Responses to the Vietnam War, 1964–1975." *Lutherans in America: A Twentieth Century Retrospective: Lutheran Historical Conference Essays and Reports* 19 (2000): 20–47.

———. "Lutheran Women Warriors: Gender and the Cold and Vietnam Wars, 1964–1975." *Lutheran Historical Conference* 20 (In Press with the Lutheran Historical Conference).

———. "'Sinister' Communists and Vietnam Quarrels: *The Christian Century* and *Christianity Today* Respond to the Cold and Vietnam Wars." *Fides et Historia* 32 (Winter/Spring 2000): 81–97.

Sherry, Michael S. *In the Shadow of War: The United States since the 1930s*. New Haven, CT: Yale University Press, 1995.

Sherwin, Martin J. *A World Destroyed: Hiroshima and the Origins of the Arms Race*. New York: Vintage Books, 1973.

Sirgiovanni, George. *An Undercurrent of Suspicion: Anti-Communism in America during World War II*. New Brunswick, NJ: Transaction Publishers, 1990.

Sittser, Gerald L. *A Cautious Patriotism: The American Churches and the Second World War*. Chapel Hill: University of North Carolina Press, 1997.

Slotkin, Richard. *Gunfighter Nation: The Myth of the Frontier in Twentieth-Century America.* New York: Atheneum Books, 1992.

Small, Melvin. *Antiwarriors: The Vietnam War and the Battle for America's Hearts and Minds.* Lanham, MD: Scholarly Resources, 2003.

——. *Covering Dissent: The Media and the Anti-Vietnam War Movement.* New Brunswick, NJ: Rutgers University Press, 1994.

——. *Democracy and Diplomacy: The Impact of Domestic Politics on U.S. Foreign Policy, 1789–1994.* Baltimore: Johns Hopkins University Press, 1996.

——. *Johnson, Nixon, and the Doves.* New Brunswick, NJ: Rutgers University Press, 1988.

——. *The Presidency of Richard Nixon.* Lawrence: University Press of Kansas, 1999.

Solberg, Richard W. *Lutheran Higher Education in North America.* Minneapolis: Augsburg Publishing House, 1985.

——. *Open Doors: The Story of Lutherans Resettling Refugees.* St. Louis: Concordia Publishing House, 1992.

Sorley, Lewis. *A Better War: The Unexamined Victories and Final Tragedy of America's Last Years in Vietnam.* New York: Harvest Books, 1999.

Staub, Michael E., ed. *The Jewish 1960s: An American Sourcebook.* Waltham, MA: Brandeis University Press, 2004.

Steigerwald, David. *The Sixties and the End of Modern America.* New York: St. Martin's Press, 1995.

Stephanson, Anders. *Kennan and the Art of Foreign Policy.* Cambridge, MA: Harvard University Press, 1989.

Stern, Mark. *Calculating Visions: Kennedy, Johnson, and Civil Rights.* New Brunswick, NJ: Rutgers University Press, 1992.

Stevens, Richard L. *Mission on the Ho Chi Minh Trail: Nature, Myth, and War in Viet Nam.* Norman: University of Oklahoma Press, 1995.

Stormer, John A. *None Dare Call It Treason.* New York: Buccaneer Books, 1964.

Sueflow, August R. *Heritage in Motion: Readings in the History of the Lutheran Church–Missouri Synod, 1962–1995.* St. Louis: Concordia Publishing House, 1998.

Sugrue, Thomas J. *The Origins of the Urban Crisis: Race and Inequality in Postwar Detroit.* Princeton, NJ: Princeton University Press, 1996.

Summers, Anthony. *The Arrogance of Power: The Secret World of Richard Nixon.* New York: Penguin Books, 2000.

Swerdlow, Amy. *Women Strike for Peace: Traditional Motherhood and Radical Politics in the 1960s.* Chicago: University of Chicago Press, 1993.

Taylor, Sandra C. *Vietnamese Women at War: Fighting for Ho Chi Minh and the Revolution.* Lawrence: University Press of Kansas, 1999.

Tipton, Steven M. *Getting Saved from the Sixties: Moral Meaning in Conversion and Cultural Change.* Berkeley: University of California Press, 1982.

Todd, Mary. *Authority Vested: A Story of Identity and Change in the Lutheran Church–Missouri Synod.* Grand Rapids, MI: William B. Eerdmans, 2000.

Tomes, Robert R. *Apocalypse Then: American Intellectuals and the Vietnam War, 1954–1975.* New York: New York University Press, 1998.

Tucker, Nancy Bernkopf. "Taiwan Expendable? Nixon and Kissinger Go to China." *Journal of American History* 92 (June 2005): 109–35.

Ung, Loung. *First They Killed My Father: A Daughter of Cambodia Remembers.* New York: HarperCollins Publishers, 2000.

Unger, Irwin, and Debi Unger. *America in the 1960s.* St. James, NY: Brandywine Press, 1988.

Van DeMark, Brian. *Into the Quagmire: Lyndon Johnson and the Escalation of the Vietnam War.* New York: Oxford University Press, 1995.

Van Devanter, Lynda. *Home before Morning: The Story of an Army Nurse in Vietnam.* Amherst: University of Massachusetts Press, 1983.

Von Rohr, John. *The Shaping of American Congregationalism, 1620–1957.* Cleveland: Pilgrim Press, 1992.

Wagnleitner, Reinhold. *Coca-Colonization and the Cold War: The Cultural Mission of the United States in Austria after the Second World War.* Chapel Hill: University of North Carolina Press, 1994.

Walker, J. Samuel. "Historians and Cold War Origins: The New Consensus." In Gerald K. Haines and J. Samuel Walker, eds., *American Foreign Relations: A Historiographical Review.* Westport, CT: Greenwood Press, 1981.

Walter, Ingrid. "One Year after Arrival: The Adjustment of Indochinese Women in the United States." *International Migration* 19 (1981): 129–52.

Walter, Ingrid, and Cordelia Cox. "Resettlement in the United States of Unattached and Unaccompanied Indochinese Refugee Minors by Lutheran Immigration and Refugee Services." *International Migration* 17 (1979): 139–61.

Walzer, Michael. *Just and Unjust Wars: A Moral Argument with Historical Illustrations.* 2nd Edition. New York: Basic Books, 1977.

Weigand, Kate. *Red Feminism: American Communism and the Making of Women's Liberation.* Baltimore: Johns Hopkins University Press, 2001.

Weigel, George. *The Final Revolution: The Resistance Church and the Collapse of Communism.* New York: Oxford University Press, 1992.

Weisbrot, Robert. *Freedom Bound: A History of America's Civil Rights Movement.* New York: Plume Books, 1990.

Wells, Ronald A. *The Wars of America: Christian Views.* Macon, GA: Mercer University Press, 1991.

Wells, Tom. *The War Within: America's Battle over Vietnam.* New York: Henry Holt and Company, 1994.

———. *Wild Man: The Life and Times of Daniel Ellsberg.* New York: Palgrave Publishers, 2001.

Weseley-Smith, Peter. *Unequal Treaty, 1897–1997: China, Great Britain, and Hong Kong's New Territories.* New York: Oxford University Press, 1983.

Westad, Odd Arne, ed. *Brothers in Arms: The Rise and Fall of the Sino-Soviet Alliance, 1945–1963.* Stanford: Stanford University Press, 1998.

Westheider, James E. *Fighting on Two Fronts: African Americans and the Vietnam War.* New York: New York University Press, 1997.

Whitfield, Stephen J. *The Culture of the Cold War.* Baltimore: Johns Hopkins University Press, 1991.

Wiederaenders, Robert C., ed. *Historical Guide to Lutheran Church Bodies of North America.* 2nd ed. St Louis: Lutheran Historical Conference, 1998.

Williams, Peter W. *America's Religions: Traditions and Cultures.* New York: Macmillan Publishing Company, 1990.

Williams, William Appleman. *The Tragedy of American Diplomacy.* New York: W. W. Norton and Company, 1959; reprint 1988.

Wittner, Lawrence S. "Peace Movements and Foreign Policy: The Challenge to Diplomatic Historians." *Diplomatic History* 11 (Fall 1987): 355–70.

———. *Rebels against War: The American Peace Movement, 1933–1983.* Philadelphia: Temple University Press, 1984.

Woods, Jeff. *Black Struggle, Red Scare: Segregation and Anti-Communism in the South, 1948–1968*. Baton Rouge: Louisiana State University Press, 2004.

Woods, Randall Bennett. *Fulbright: A Biography*. Cambridge: Cambridge University Press, 1995.

——. *J. William Fulbright, Vietnam, and the Search for a Cold War Foreign Policy*. Cambridge: Cambridge University Press, 1998.

Wurmbrand, Richard. *Christ on the Jewish Road*. Bartlesville, OK: Living Sacrifice Book Company, 1970.

——. *From Suffering to Triumph!* Grand Rapids, MI: Kregel Publications, 1993.

——. *In God's Underground*, ed. Charles Foley. Bartlesville, OK: Living Sacrifice Book Company, 1968.

——. *My Correspondence with Jesus*. Eastbourne, England: Monarch Publications, 1990.

——. *Tortured for Christ*. Bartlesville, OK: Living Sacrifice Book Company, 1998.

——. *With God in Solitary Confinement*. Bartlesville, OK: Living Sacrifice Book Company, 1969.

Wuthnow, Robert. *The Restructuring of American Religion: Society and Faith since World War II*. Princeton, NJ: Princeton University Press, 1988.

Wyatt, Clarence R. *Paper Soldiers: The American Press and the Vietnam War*. Chicago: University of Chicago Press, 1993.

Yergin, Daniel. *Shattered Peace: The Origins of the Cold War*. New York: Penguin Books, 1977.

Young, Marilyn B. *The Vietnam Wars, 1945–1990*. New York: HarperPerennial, 1991.

Zamoyski, Adam. *Holy Madness: Romantics, Patriots, and Revolutionaries, 1776–1871*. New York: Viking Press, 1999.

Zaroulis, Nancy, and Gerald Sullivan. *Who Spoke Up? American Protest against the War in Vietnam, 1963–1975*. Garden City, NY: Doubleday and Company, 1984.

Zhai, Qiang. *China and the Vietnam Wars, 1950–1975*. Chapel Hill: University of North Carolina Press, 2000.

Zhufeng, Luo, ed. *Religion under Socialism in China*. Armonk, NY: M. E. Sharpe, 1991.

Index

African American discrimination. *See* black power movement

African Americans: disproportionately went to combat, 137. *See also* black power movement

ALC. *See* American Lutheran Church (ALC)

America, conservatives, 95–97

America, politics: America questioned involvement in "civil war," 4, 180, 182; arms limitation agreements, 21; belief that South Vietnam needed protection from communism, 4, 92–93, 96–97, 100; black power movement, 70; burning of American flag, 72; Cambodian bombings, 123; Christianity, 58; Cold War, 2–3, 14, 19, 21, 154; communism, 2–4, 14, 51–54; conservatives, 95–97; domestic concerns, 147; fear of Communist expansion, 93; Johnson's Great Society programs, 56; King, Martin Luther, Jr., 70; Lutheran diversity representative of Americans, 11–12; opposition to arms race, 4; Red China, 20, 41; Ruff, Elson G., 60; Soviet Union, 30, 31; Vietnam War. *See* Vietnam War

American Christians, 5; antiwar Christians, 120; Cold War, 20; opposed to Communist oppression of Christians, 28; opposed to Communist Red China, 36–37; theological justification against the war, 128–30

American Lutheran Church (ALC), 169–72; accused of Communist ideas, 64; arms race position, 22–23; believed cooperation with Soviet Union protected Christians inside Communist countries, 30; biblical view, 9; civil rights movement, 70; communism, 21, 29, 32; confidence in government decisions about war, 102–3; conscientious objectors, 163; conservative members, 21, 63, 95; détente, 21; feared discussions of war would fracture church, 132; Lutherans-Alert National (LAN), 9, 55; Lutheran World Federation, 32; member demography, 8, 9; moderate political views, 9; National Council of Churches of Christ, 66–69; North Vietnam brutalities, 99–100; opinion on war, 124; opposed to draft, 156; Oslo congregation, Wurmbrand, Richard, 74; Preus, Jacob Aall

Churches, stated communism had infiltrated the church, 64–66, 181. *See also* Prowar Lutherans

Lutheran, general: after Czechoslovakian invasion little differences among Lutherans political views, 33; aid to the religion oppressed Soviet Union, 26; belief that communism directly threatened U.S. society and saw the Vietnam War as civil war, 2, 182; belief in containment theory of communism, 2; belief in domino theory of communism, 2; belief that a monolithic Communist force existed, 2, 95, 124, 129; civil rights movement, 70; clergy and laity disagreed, 149; clergy who spoke out against the war, 149; disagreed only slightly in their views of the Soviet Union between 1964 and 1975, 30–31; distrusted Soviet Union and Red China because of religious persecution of Christians, 20; draft evaders, 166–73; expelled from Red China, 20; fear of communism, 32, 44; founded the Hong Kong International School, 43; internal Communist threats, 58–60; King, Martin Luther, Jr., 72; Lutheran diversity represents Americans, 11–12; members left the church once they found out the ALC and LCA were members of WCC, 64–65; mirrored American hostility towards Soviet Union, 27; National Council of Churches of Christ, 66–69; opposition to the war, 179; paradox, 14; political classification, 12; Red China viewed the same as Soviet Union by Lutherans, 36–37; refugees from South Vietnam, 172; saw contact with communism as protection of Christianity, 22; saw Red China equal to Soviet Union,

39; social welfare programs, communistic, 57; some believed that the US could negotiate with Red China to ease Cold War, 41; Soviet Union satellite nations, 31; stated North Vietnam promoted atheism, 97; theology, basics, 14; uniting the church after the war, 170–73; ways they debated foreign policy, 2. *See also* antiwar Lutherans

Lutheran, liberals, 12–13, 21; after Czechoslovakian invasion little differences among Lutheran political views, 33; aligned with Lutheran conservatives about Communist satellite countries, 36; amnesty for draft resisters, 147; cooperation with Soviet Union might benefit Christians, 27; definition, 13; domestic concerns, 147; feared politics with Communist countries would affect Christianity, 21; fear of Communist expansion, 32; foreign policies view, 7; internal Communist threats, 58–60; National Council of Churches of Christ, 66–69; spoke against Baltic Christian situation, 35; united with moderates, conservatives, ultra-conservatives against Red China, 42; vs. Lutheran conservatives, 27; wanted peaceful solutions that would lead to further mission opportunities, 42. *See also* antiwar Lutherans

Lutheran, moderates, 7; after Czechoslovakian invasion little differences among Lutherans political views, 33; aligned with Lutheran conservatives about Cold War as a religious war, 36; aligned with Lutheran conservatives about Communist satellite countries, 36; definition, 13; domestic concerns, 182; feared politics with Communist countries would affect Christianity,

About the Author

Dr. **David E. Settje** is associate professor of history at Concordia University Chicago and chair of the Department of History, Philosophy, and Political Science.